The Use of the
Library of Congress
Classification

The Use of the Library of Congress Classification

Proceedings of the Institute on the Use of the Library
of Congress Classification
Sponsored by the American Library Association
Resources and Technical Services Division
Cataloging and Classification Section

New York City, July 7–9, 1966

Edited by
Richard H. Schimmelpfeng and C. Donald Cook

American Library Association
Chicago

ISBN 0-8389-3082-4 (1968)
Library of Congress Catalog Card Number 68-27829
Copyright © 1968 by the American Library Association
Fourth printing, September 1975

Manufactured in the United States of America

Preface

For a number of years there has been a growing interest in the preparation of a manual on the use of the Library of Congress classification. With the increase in the use of the LC classification, the desire and need for guidance in applying it have intensified.

In response to countless requests for assistance, the Classification Committee of the Cataloging and Classification Section of the Resources and Technical Services Division of the American Library Association began, several years ago, the plans which have culminated in the papers presented here.

Catalogers outside the Library of Congress could not by themselves deal with the LC schedules in the detail or from the point of view which would be most helpful; the LC staff, regrettably but understandably, found the pressures of current cataloging so great that the time necessary for the preparation of a complete manual was out of the question. But—could some sort of cooperative venture be worked out?

The Classification Committee proposed an institute which would precede an ALA conference; the Cataloging and Classification Section endorsed this proposal, and an Institute Planning Committee was appointed. The outcome was a plan in which the LC staff would present its own classification schedules in much the same fashion as might be done for a new cataloger joining its staff; catalogers from the field would discuss the application of LC classification in other libraries as well as summarize the significant factors to be considered in adopting the LC classification. The American Library Association agreed to subsidize such an institute, and the Librarian of Congress generously authorized the participation of LC officers and staff. It is for the actual registrants, for those who were unable to attend, and for the cataloging profession as a whole that the present volume has been prepared.

The entire Institute was transcribed by a commercial reporting service. The transcript of each speaker's presentation was returned to him for revision. The papers were then edited from an audio-visual presentation into the chapter form of this volume.

In addition to the staff from the Library of Congress and the catalogers who participated as speakers, the Institute drew on the resources of a third group—the Institute registrants themselves. Questions were invited both before and during the Institute. In some cases, these questions and their answers follow the appropriate chapters; in others, the answers have been incorporated in the revised text. Every question was reviewed; by far the larger part were found to be answered by the speakers or to be answerable by extension from the text of the papers and the accompanying examples presented in this volume.

Inevitably some questions remain which are not fully covered in this volume. The Library of Congress plans to give answers to future questions of general interest it receives by publishing pertinent statements in the *Cataloging Service Bulletin* when explanatory notes are required. The Library also intends to publish in *Library of Congress Classification—Additions and Changes* specific shelflist arrangements, appearing only in the LC Shelflist, which cannot be derived from the classification schedules or from the LC system of author numbers.

The present volume is not the long-awaited definitive manual on the use of the Library of Congress classification. It was not intended to be. It is hoped, however, that the vast amount of information contained herein will be helpful to the profession, and that it may contribute usefully to the preparation of a full manual in the not too distant future.

The Cataloging and Classification Section wishes to express its gratitude to the staff of the Library of Congress and to the other participating speakers. Thanks go also to the many libraries which supplied information on which several of the papers are based. The members of the Institute Planning Committee and of the RTSD office at ALA headquarters deserve particular commendation for their planning and execution of the countless technical details involved in the conference. Richard H. Schimmelpfeng, the principal editor of this volume, took the major responsibility for translating proceedings into text—an onerous chore done with skill and competence. Special thanks must be given to Miss Pauline Cianciolo and Miss Marion Dittman of the ALA Publishing Department for their invaluable help in the arduous task of preparing the manuscript for publication.

C. DONALD COOK   ANNETTE H. PHINAZEE
*Cochairmen, Institute on the Use of the Library
of Congress Classification*

Program of the Institute

AMERICAN LIBRARY ASSOCIATION
RESOURCES AND TECHNICAL SERVICES DIVISION
CATALOGING AND CLASSIFICATION SECTION

INSTITUTE ON THE USE OF
THE LIBRARY OF CONGRESS
CLASSIFICATION

NEW YORK CITY
JULY 7–9, 1966

THURSDAY, JULY 7, 1966

8:30–10:00 Registration

10:00–12:00 Opening Session

Introduction
> C. DONALD COOK, Coordinator of Cataloging, Columbia University Libraries; Chairman, Cataloging and Classification Section

Review of the Use of the Library of Congress Classification
> MAURICE F. TAUBER, Melvil Dewey Professor of Library Service, School of Library Service, Columbia University

Introduction of Library of Congress Participants
> RICHARD S. ANGELL, Chief, Subject Cataloging Division, The Library of Congress

The Library of Congress Classification— Development, Characteristics, Structure
> CHARLES C. BEAD, Principal Cataloger, Subject Cataloging Division, The Library of Congress

2:00–5:00 Session II

Special Problems in Social and Political Science (Classes H and J)
> NICHOLAS HEDLESKY, Senior Subject Cataloger—Social Sciences, The Library of Congress

> *Moderator:* PAUL S. DUNKIN, Professor, Graduate School of Library Service, Rutgers—The State University

5:00 Reception

FRIDAY, JULY 8, 1966

9:00–12:00 Session III

Special Problems in Literature (Class P)

> PATRICIA S. HINES, Formerly Senior Subject Cataloger—Languages and Literature, The Library of Congress

Special Problems in Science and Technology
(Classes Q–V)

> EDWARD J. BLUME, Senior Subject Cataloger—Science and Technology, The Library of Congress
>
> *Moderator:* KATHARINE BALL, Assistant Professor, Library School, University of Toronto

2:00–5:00 Session IV

Assignment of Author (Book) Numbers and Other Shelflisting Operations

> ROBERT R. HOLMES, Assistant Chief, Subject Cataloging Division, The Library of Congress
>
> MRS. ELIZABETH B. LOCKWOOD, Assistant Head, Book Control and Preparation Section, The Library of Congress
>
> MRS. MARY CATHERINE ARICK, Supervisor, Classification Record Unit, The Library of Congress
>
> *Moderator:* FRANCES LUBOVITZ, Head, Cataloging Department, Massachusetts Institute of Technology

SATURDAY, JULY 9, 1966

9:00–12:00 Session V

Changing To or Adopting the Library of Congress Classification

Organization of Materials

> CARL R. COX, Associate for Library Systems, State University of New York
>
> MARIAN SANNER, Head, Cataloging Department, Enoch Pratt Free Library

Orientation of Staff and Clientele

> MARY D. HERRICK, Assistant Director for Bibliographic Organization, Boston University Libraries
>
> *Moderator:* CARLYLE J. FRAREY, Assistant to the Dean, School of Library Service, Columbia University

2:00–5:00   Session VI

Cost Estimates and Time Schedules
JENNETTE E. HITCHCOCK, Chief Librarian, Catalog Division, Stanford University Libraries

General Advantages and Disadvantages of Using the Library of Congress System
MRS. PHYLLIS A. RICHMOND, Supervisor of River Campus Science Libraries, University of Rochester

Moderator: MRS. ANNETTE HOAGE PHINAZEE, Professor, School of Library Service, Atlanta University

Questions in writing from Institute participants will be accepted by the speakers and moderators, and answered to the extent possible within the time and scope of the program.

The Cataloging and Classification Section acknowledges with appreciation the assistance received from

Bro-Dart Industries
Columbia University Audio-Visual Aids Office
The Library of Congress
New York Technical Services Librarians

THE INSTITUTE PLANNING COMMITTEE

Pauline Atherton	Marion Kesselring
Joan Cusenza	Elva Krogh
Jennette E. Hitchcock	David Remington
Robert R. Holmes	Marian Sanner

C. Donald Cook, *Co-Chairman*
Annette Hoage Phinazee, *Co-Chairman*

Contents

Chapter 1   Review of the Use of the Library of Congress
Classification   *Maurice F. Tauber*   1

2   The Library of Congress Classification: Development,
Characteristics, and Structure   *Charles C. Bead*   18

3   Special Problems in Social and Political Sciences
(Classes H and J)   *Nicholas Hedlesky*   33

4   Special Problems in Literature (Class P)
       Patricia S. Hines   62

5   Special Problems in Science and Technology
(Classes Q–V)   *Edward J. Blume*   80

6   Assignment of Author Numbers
       Robert R. Holmes   107

7   Subclassification and Book Numbers in Language
and Literature   *Prepared by Elizabeth Lockwood*
Presented by Patricia S. Hines   121

8   Subclassification and Book Numbers of Documents
and Official Publications   *Mary Catherine Arick*   135

9   The Organization of Materials in Academic Libraries
Changing to the Library of Congress Classification
       Carl R. Cox   162

10 The Organization of Materials in Public Libraries Changing
to the Library of Congress Classification
Marian Sanner 176

11 Orientation of Staff and Clientele into the Library of
Congress Classification *Mary Darrah Herrick* 183

12 Cost Estimates and Time Schedules in Reclassification
Jennette E. Hitchcock 192

13 General Advantages and Disadvantages of Using the
Library of Congress Classification
Phyllis A. Richmond 209

Appendix A List of Libraries Using the Library of Congress
Classification Wholly or in Part
Maurice F. Tauber 221

Bibliography on the Library of Congress Classification
Nathalie C. Batts and Maurice F. Tauber 227

Index
Katherine M. Hartley 241

The Use of the
Library of Congress
Classification

Chapter 1

Review of the Use
of the Library of Congress
Classification

Maurice F. Tauber

The comments I make this morning[1] are in relation to the other papers on the program. That is, I am not going to talk about the internal structure of the Library of Congress system, since the representatives from LC will do this. I also will not become involved with some of the details of changing to the LC system, because other participants will handle that particular aspect. Nor will I, except in an oblique way, be concerned with cost estimates and time schedules in reclassification, as these are assigned to another speaker.

However, as I review certain matters which were included in the questionnaire distributed in the spring of 1966 for purposes of this paper, I will discuss why some of the libraries have begun to use the LC classification. These comments are made without any effort to compare LC with other classifications, since this comparison has been presented in detail in the literature.

I should call attention to the recommendation of the Classification Committee of the Cataloging and Classification Section of the Resources and Technical Services Division of the American Library Association, in the Winter (1965) issue of *Library Resources & Technical Services*, to the effect that the LC classification would be the most advantageous one for new academic libraries to introduce.

Reference should also be made to several bibliographical items which are relevant to any survey or review of the LC classification as it is used in libraries. These include Thelma Eaton's article on classification in *College & Research Libraries* in 1955;[2] Irene Doyle's paper in the 1959 conference proceedings sponsored by the Graduate School of Library Science, University of Illinois;[3] Leo La Montagne's book on *American Library Classification*;[4] two articles by Howard McGaw: one listing libraries using the LC system,[5] and the other a review of the literature on reclassification;[6] Hoage's study of the use of the LC system;[7] Holley's review;[8] and various papers I have published.[9]

In my studies of reclassification and recataloging during the period 1939–41, I found that there was a pronounced movement during the 1920's and the 1930's

Footnotes appear at the end of the chapter.

for academic libraries to start using the LC system in part or wholly. Many libraries shifted during the 1930's when it was possible to obtain inexpensive help. In this same period, many large libraries, such as the universities of California, Chicago, and Michigan, as well as the medical and architectural libraries at Columbia, shifted to the use of the LC system. Also, it was apparent that many Catholic colleges and seminary libraries were using the LC schedules since they found them more suitable for their collections than other systems.

In terms of numbers of libraries using the LC system, Hoage in 1961 located 256 libraries using the LC system. She sent her questionnaire to 128. McGaw's list, cited above, was not complete, even though he used the U.S. Office of Education listing for his data. In *Classification Research*, edited by Pauline Atherton, Richard S. Angell indicated that between 800 and 1000 libraries were using the LC system in 1964.[10] He predicted that in the ensuing eight years this growth would double.

The growth is extraordinary, and is related not only to libraries changing from another classification, but also to new libraries developing in the country, departmental libraries of universities (particularly science and technology collections), and mergers. At Columbia, for example, there has been a shift to LC for various collections in recent years, such as science and technology, business and economics, and music. Other collections, such as psychology, fine arts, graphic arts, architecture, and medicine changed some years ago. Columbia had been using schemes that resembled Dewey, but were not really Dewey since so many modifications had been made in the schedules. This is true of so many of the libraries which have gone to LC. The resemblance to Dewey of some of these schedules is not very clear.

Although comments up to this point seem to be concerned with academic libraries, there have been some public libraries, as well as state, historical, and special libraries, interested in the LC schedules. The Boston Public Library, the St. Paul Public Library, the Enoch Pratt Free Library, the California State Library, and the Buffalo and Erie County Library are among those using LC. The State Historical Society of Wisconsin has recently introduced the system. Federal and other governmental libraries use it, as do many special libraries in all fields.

In regard to size of libraries using the LC system, there is evidence in the questionnaires, as well as in the listings by McGaw, that this is not a significant factor. Small as well as large libraries use the classification, and the Doyle study found that the small libraries (under 100,000 volumes) did not find it an improper or inadequate system for organizing their collections. Statistics on this matter are given below.

The previously mentioned questionnaire was prepared and distributed in 1966 to a sampling of the libraries. The remainder of this presentation is related to the returns from this questionnaire. The effort here has been to bring up to date findings on library activity in the use of the LC classification since my earlier studies about twenty-five years ago.

Questionnaires were mailed to 89 libraries which started using the LC classification in recent years, according to information from LC and other sources. Of the total number of libraries, 81 responded. Of these, 15 responses came in some time after we had tabulated the data. A close examination of the later responses revealed that there were no exceptional conditions which altered the percentages in the earlier tabulations concerning the queries which were included. Thus, for the most part, the statements in the following sections, which follow the question-naire, are based on the responses of the first group of 66 libraries. Several additional statements have been made in connection with conditions arising in the other 15 libraries.

The three-page questionnaire was largely check-off, but longer responses were encouraged. Very few questionnaires did not produce some extended comments. The questionnaire was divided into three sections: (I) "Classification and Other Practices," (II) "General Library Matters," and (III) "Reclassification." The first section had fifteen questions, the second six questions, and the third five questions. Some questions had multiple parts.

Characteristics of Respondents

Of the 81 libraries with analyzable responses, 76 (about 94 percent) were academic libraries: 35 college and 41 university. Included in the total were 3 public and 2 state libraries.

Eleven of the 66 libraries had always used LC. Of the 55 libraries which had changed to LC, 28 (53 percent) had done so since 1961; 37 (67 percent) since 1956; 40 (73 percent) since 1947. Among the remaining 15 of the 55, one library had, in its unamalgamated form, changed to LC as early as 1915! The later returns indicated most changes occurred in the last ten years. Apparent for the sample is the concentrated introduction of LC during the last five years (more than 53 percent of all respondents) and during the last decade (more than two thirds of the respondents).

The wide range of sizes among the libraries and library systems which reported suggests that the information represents libraries from all size groups in the country. Size was measured by the number of volumes held by the library when it began to use LC. Although libraries differed in defining "volumes," 45 of the 66 libraries supplied usable size statistics. Academic libraries ranged in size from 20,000 to more than 3 million volumes. The public and state libraries and library systems ranged from 130,000 to more than 1,800,000 volumes. Total holdings reported by the 45 libraries when they began to use LC were close to 12¼ million volumes. Twenty percent of the 45 libraries held 50,000 or less volumes, 38 percent held 100,000 or less, 51 percent held 150,000 or less, 62 percent held 200,000 or less, 69 percent held 250,000 or less. Fourteen of the 45 libraries each held more than 300,000 volumes. Eight of the 45 libraries each held more than 500,000 volumes. One library had more than 1 million volumes.

These size statistics are significant, not only because of their range, but also because comments by officers from these libraries did not vary to any great extent with their size. Thus, most statements on the PZ3 (Fiction) schedule were similar, regardless of the library's size.

General Findings of the Inquiry

In general, this inquiry confirmed the findings of the 1961 doctoral dissertation by Hoage on "The Library of Congress Classification in the United States," a dissertation prepared under this investigator's supervision. Among the findings reported by Hoage were:

> Priority in developing the Classification at LC is given to practicality rather than logic. . . . Major weaknesses were considered the failure to provide for interpretation and the lack of a general index. Most of the schedules were well accepted by a majority of the libraries in this survey and by writers of critiques pertaining to the Classification. . . . The results of this study support the hypothesis that the characteristics of the Classification that facilitate its use outnumber those that hinder its application in the U.S. . . . Catalogers estimated that 90 to 99 percent of the numbers in the schedules and cards were acceptable to them. . . . Public service librarians and patrons used it most often as a location device and were less concerned about its value as a subject approach. . . . 60 percent of the patrons were not instructed in the use of the Classification, but the librarians thought they needed it. The method used by most librarians—individual, informal instruction—does not appear to be adequate to meet this need. . . . A majority of the librarians surveyed use LC for their entire collections. Both librarians and patrons seemed to be satisfied with it. However, unless the schedules are revised constantly, it is in danger of losing its optimal role. LC staff is aware of this and is doing as much revising as time and funds permit.[11]

The foregoing may be compared with the general findings of the present inquiry. A high degree of satisfaction was expressed by libraries using LC, and although some difficulties were described, there was little doubt that the advantages and convenience of LC cataloging, including classification, far outweighed specific problems. In general, LC cataloging, descriptive and subject, was accepted without major change by most libraries.

The problems repeatedly described by libraries of all sizes were the same which have for years been publicized and discussed at professional meetings and in the professional literature. The implication, therefore, is that the library profession has not yet confronted these problems in any effective way. What seems needed is not to uncover problems but to acknowledge their reality and to implement an effective approach to these problems on the part of the library profession working together with the Library of Congress.

This survey showed unanimity of opinion on the following issues: (1) a general index to all the schedules is needed; (2) many parts of the schedules lack adequately detailed instructions; (3) changes in subject headings are not frequent enough, and are not sufficiently publicized; (4) changes in classification are difficult to keep track of in their present format (a loose-leaf or index-card method of publication is preferable; ideally, new revised schedules incorporating the changes should be printed); (5) a new law schedule (K) is badly needed; and (6) author numbers in the literature schedules should be supplied, since most academic libraries do not use PZ3 and PZ4.

Catalogers and classifiers do not necessarily wish to be told every small detail of the classification mechanics as followed by LC. What they do want to be told is the *general* philosophy or overall scheme behind certain LC practices, e.g., change in author numbers, so that libraries can apply these principles to their specific problems without fear of being later contradicted by LC procedures.

The problems over the last six decades seem to have remained much the same. Is it not perhaps time for the libraries, together with LC, to do something about them? The question is worth repeating. Libraries complained of young catalogers untrained in LC. They also complained of the lack of suitable clerical staff to help in cataloging. Should not library schools change their curricula accordingly and provide more training in LC? Training of clericals might also be more systematic.

Detailed Analysis of Responses

Classification and Other Practices

Previous Classification

Of the 55 libraries which had changed to LC, 85 percent had previously used either Dewey or "Modified Dewey." No other classification system had been widely used. "Other" classifications were generally described as "local." Two libraries had used Cutter Expansive.

More than two and one-half times as many libraries reported using Dewey than "Modified Dewey." This may indicate that libraries did not consider any changes they might have made as sufficiently far-reaching to justify labeling the product officially "Modified." This, in turn, may imply that libraries have changed from Dewey because of basic difficulty. Libraries seem to have recognized that a choice must be made between classification systems as such, rather than an attempt made to modify Dewey to a point of prohibitive complication and expense.

Methods Used in Reporting Size of Collections

The methods employed by the 66 libraries in reporting the size of their collections reemphasize the need for definition and standardization of measurement units in library literature. (As indicated, only 45 libraries presented analyzable size statistics.) Many libraries apologized for the "approximate" nature of their statistics.

Thirty-three of the 66 libraries reported holdings in terms of volumes only; 31 in titles *and* volumes (as requested by the questionnaire); 2 of the 66 in titles only. The varying definition of "volumes" was evident. Some libraries included government documents. One library considered phonodiscs as volumes.

No reliable overall ratio of number of volumes to number of titles could be derived. However, for 23 of 31 libraries which reported volumes *and* titles, the ratio ranged from 1.3 to 1.9 volumes per title. The most frequent (modal) ratio among these 31 libraries was 1.4 volumes per title.

Arrearages

Sixty libraries reported on arrearages. Twenty-five (42 percent) answered "None," and 35 (58 percent) indicated they had arrearages. The questionnaire did not distinguish between "arrearages" and what might be considered "normal backlog." A wide range of arrearage figures was reported—from 300 to 80,000 volumes. Most of these widely varying figures were proportionate to the size of the library; some of the strikingly disproportionate figures were explained as representing situations peculiar to the library and not related to cataloging difficulties.

Forty-one libraries indicated if arrearages had decreased since a change to LC. (Libraries which never had a classification system other than LC were not included in this tabulation.) Nineteen (47 percent) of the 41 said arrearages had decreased; 22 (53 percent) that they had not.

Some who answered "No" added significant comments. One stated that classification with LC moved faster, but that arrearages had not decreased because of a staff shortage. Some libraries commented that factors other than LC had to be taken into account, e.g., book budget, change of staff size, staff turnover. At least 2 libraries reported a greatly increased acquisitions program since LC was adopted, and one of these stated that without LC, the arrearages would have been much greater.

Because of the general degree of satisfaction with LC, already noted, and the substantially increased acquisitions of most American libraries, it may be reasonable to infer that without LC, arrearages generally would have been much greater. The important question may, therefore, be, not whether LC has reduced arrearages but whether LC has enabled libraries not to fall too far behind in their processing of a great increase in acquisitions.

Acceptance of Classifications and Subclassifications as Assigned on LC Printed Cards

Overwhelmingly, the libraries indicated that they accepted with very few changes the LC classifications and subclassifications assigned on LC cards. This confirms the earlier findings of Hoage and Tauber.

Sixty-five libraries stated whether they followed the LC classification assignments on printed LC cards. Twenty-six (40 percent) of the 65 answered "Yes," 39 (60 percent) answered "Most of the time," and none answered "No." Thirty-two of the 39 who answered "Most of the time" estimated the percentage of the time they followed the classification. Twenty-seven (85 percent) of the 32 estimates were "90 percent or over"; 19 (15 percent) of the estimates were "95 percent or over." The lowest estimated percentage (70 percent) was from a library with a substantial theological collection for which a special classification was used.

By far the most frequent reason given for not accepting LC classifications without change was that the library did not use the PZ fiction class, but instead classified in the various national literatures. The next most common exception was for series, where a library would choose to distribute titles by subject instead of consolidating them under the one classification of the LC card. Sometimes, the opposite occurred—LC scattered the titles when the library wished to consolidate. Some libraries used special classifications for part of their collections; this was most common in theology. Some libraries did not accept the LC classification for juvenile literature. Other exceptions noted were UN publications and music materials.

A similar near-unanimity was expressed in answer to the question whether the library accepted the LC subclassifications as printed on LC cards. Sixty-five libraries answered, of whom 46 (71 percent) checked "Yes," 18 (28 percent) "Most of the time," and only 1 library "No." (This last library, however, accepted the major classification.) Three of the 18 libraries estimated the percentage of times they "mostly" accepted the subclassification. None of the three estimates was under 90 percent.

Reasons for not accepting subclassifications were similar to those for not accepting major classifications. The most frequent exceptions were for the PZ schedules. Next most frequent exceptions were for serials. Other problem schedules were Bibliography (Z) and Biography (CT). Two libraries said they modified the LC notation for educational materials applicable to elementary and secondary schools.

Author Numbers

Most libraries used the author numbers assigned by LC, either all or most of the time. Of the 65 libraries which answered this question, 38 (58 percent) accepted the author numbers all the time, and 18 (28 percent) "Most of the time." Only 9 (14 percent) did not generally accept the LC author numbers.

Fifty-seven libraries explained whether they shortened LC author numbers. Only 1 library shortened the numbers all the time; 43 (75 percent) did not shorten; and 13 (23 percent) sometimes shortened.

Twenty-eight libraries indicated which system of author numbers they applied when they did not accept the LC numbers. Twelve (43 percent) used the Cutter tables, 11 (40 percent) the LC author table, and 5 (17 percent) their own system.

Very few explanations were given as to why libraries did not always accept the author numbers printed on LC cards, but it is reasonable to infer that most exceptions arose when, as stated above, the library did not use PZ or classed Biography and Bibliography according to subject.

One library's policy was to shorten LC author numbers three or more digits in length. Another library had once shortened LC author numbers, but discontinued this because of inconsistencies and errors.

Acceptance of LC Descriptive Cataloging

All 65 respondents generally accepted LC descriptive cataloging. One library sometimes made changes in author because of a special theological cataloging scheme.

Acceptance of LC Subject Headings

All 65 respondents generally accepted the LC subject headings. Two libraries sometimes used subject headings from a special Catholic list.

This virtually complete acceptance of LC subject headings suggests two comments:

1. The influence of the numerous available special subject headings lists is not apparent in American academic libraries.
2. At a time when our professional literature is much concerned with problems of subject access to library collections, the apparently unquestioning acceptance of LC subject headings may betray an unduly passive attitude of practitioners. Changing the LC subject headings is not advocated, but perhaps a cooperative though critical examination of the subject headings problem is due.

Use of Clerical Staff with LC Classification

Sixty libraries indicated to what extent they employed clerical staff in LC cataloging and classification when printed cards were available. Thirty-one (52 percent) used clerical staff all or most of the time, 14 (23 percent) part of the time, and 15 (25 percent) rarely or never.

Eight libraries commented they hoped to obtain or increase clerical staff for this purpose, but this depended on available personnel and on projected training programs. Four libraries indicated they used clericals for LC printed card cataloging "completely" or "all." Two points are suggested:

1. Failure to use clerical staff for LC cataloging may not be due to conservative librarianship but to personnel shortages. Perhaps the answer to this problem is to raise the salaries of clerical staff so that they may be recruited for these tasks. Even this increase will result in a significant saving for the library.
2. The possibility of establishing training programs for nonprofessionals or subprofessionals for certain library functions is worth considering.

General Library Matters

Open versus Closed Stack Access to Books

Open access to stacks seems accepted policy among academic libraries of all sizes. Of 64 respondents, 56 (88 percent) had open-stack access, and only 8 (12 percent) a closed-stack policy.

Of the 8 libraries with closed-stack policy, only 4 were college or university libraries; 3 were public or state libraries, and 1 a specialized historical collection. Furthermore, of the 4 college or university libraries with closed stacks, 2 were changing in the near future to open-stack policy.

The lack of comments on this question emphasized the taken-for-granted nature of open-stack policy in academic libraries. Any difficulties in maintaining open-stack collections for students (even devil's advocate arguments) were not mentioned.

Problems Met by Browser Users

Libraries were asked to make observations on "any problems met by users as they browsed in the stacks." This question was particularly significant in relation to the preceding one on open-stack access.

Response to the browsing question was light. Twenty-nine libraries volunteered observations; most comments implied that browsing was used for locating books with known call numbers. (Hoage's finding was similar.) Thus, a number of libraries reported that patrons had difficulty reading decimal notation, or that patrons were accustomed to Dewey rather than to LC. One library commented that two classification systems in the same library made it difficult for patrons to locate books. At least 2 libraries denied the published statement that browsing was not possible with LC.

One library reported that PZ was confusing to patrons, and that the library probably should not have used it. Another library reported that because it did not use PZ, browsing for fiction was impossible; the library accordingly assembled a fiction browsing collection. One library's patrons were confused by LC treatment of fiction and biography.

Few comments mentioned the role of browsing in subject exploration. One library felt that faculty had more difficulty than students in browsing with LC, because LC seemed to have more areas where disciplines crossed than did Dewey. One library complained that LC overlong class numbers put only a few books in each subject. One library commented that its browsers overlooked related materials classed elsewhere.

Generally, the answers to this question suggested a lack of librarian interest or of patron "feedback" in relation to the use of shelf classification for subject exploration in open-stack collections. So many of the comments indicated patron ignorance of the notation that more sophisticated problems of browsing for information retrieval were not even raised. This may suggest that most librarians are not particularly concerned with the theoretical validity of book classification systems. Also notable is the conditioning of academic library patrons by previous exposure to Dewey—probably in public libraries.

On the whole, the statements produced by the browsing question were not dissimilar to those of the S. L. Jackson *Catalog Use Study*.[12] Most patrons seemed concerned with call number identification of wanted items. One librarian, in fact, stated that the difficulties arose not in "browsing but in catalog use."

User Instruction on LC Classification

The answers to this question showed a general lack of special instructions to the patron on LC classification use. (This was also found by Hoage.) Sixty-five libraries answered this question. Thirty-seven (57 percent) gave no "special" instructions; 28 (43 percent) did. "Special instructions" was not defined by the questionnaire, and this might have given an even more optimistic picture than warranted. For example, 1 library considered its "Yes" justified because it prepared a printed sheet for students which gave the LC class equivalents to Dewey. On the other hand, 1 library which answered "No" added the comment: "Nothing beyond the usual printed instructions, handbook, etc." Since most "Yes" answers were unannotated, it may be that the "Yes" often referred to simple printed instructions or wall charts.

In any case, no library described in detail any elaborate formal program of instruction. This is especially serious since the previous question revealed elementary patron ignorance of LC notation, not to mention more sophisticated difficulties. Many other studies besides this one and Hoage's have drawn the same conclusion, but not very much seems to be done about it practically. Can it be that classification problems are of importance only to classifiers and not to users?

Difficulties with Assigning LC Classifications When Not on Cards

In general, libraries had no difficulties in assigning LC classifications when they did not appear on LC cards. Of 64 respondents, 46 (72 percent) had no difficulties, and 18 (28 percent) did. A strictly quantitative tally may be misleading, since the larger libraries, doing more original cataloging presumably than the smaller libraries, bear a heavier national bibliographic responsibility. Thus, the 28 percent may outweigh in significance the 72 percent.

By far the most common difficulty was the absence of a K schedule for Law. Next most common complaint was on the lack of instructions in some parts of schedules and of specificity in tables. Frequently complained of was the failure of LC to provide unique author numbers for some prolific authors, e.g., Sigmund Freud, whose works might otherwise be intershelved with those of his daughter, Anna Freud.

General Satisfaction and Specific Difficulties in Applying LC

Generally, most libraries (as found by Hoage) seemed satisfied with LC, though a considerable number indicated specific difficulties with (1) Instructions, (2) Mechanics, (3) Index, (4) Changes. Most of the difficulties have long been known.

Sixty-one analyzable responses resulted from this question. (Some libraries had more than one staff member answer, and each response was tabulated.) Forty-three answered "Yes" to the question, "In general, have you been satisfied with the LC classification?" Of these 43 responses, 27 (63 percent) indicated no specific difficulties, but 16 (37 percent) did. Sixteen responses listed specific difficulties without answering "Yes" to the main question, though probably this meant in most cases not an implied "No" but rather "Yes—but. . . ." Only 2 responses listed specific difficulties and also wrote "No" in answer to the main question. Thus, although this question was not overly precise, the answers seemed to indicate general satisfaction with LC even when specific difficulties were listed.

Libraries were asked to indicate specific difficulties in the following four categories: (1) Instructions, (2) Mechanics, (3) Index, (4) Changes. There were 26 complaints about Instructions, 20 about Changes, 15 about the Index, and 7 about Mechanics.

The questionnaire did not define the difference between Instructions and Mechanics; perhaps these two categories should be considered together. Most complaints were on lack of adequate and/or specific instructions in schedules or tables. There was much comment on the difficulty of constructing author numbers when the library chose not to use the PZ schedule. Some catalogers complained that they were not given the theory or plan behind certain sections or tables, so that they could not apply a principle to individual cases. A general manual of instructions was requested for guidance in practice and for instruction of new catalogers.

Complaints about Changes concerned their slowness and their not being made available on cards or loose-leaf sheets. Some libraries thought that new schedules incorporating changes were past due. Index complaints centered on the lack of one general, preferably relative, index for the whole classification scheme.

These complaints are not new. (The questionnaire format possibly may have conditioned them.) The present need seems to be for the library profession, in cooperation with the Library of Congress and any other interested groups, to institute a crash program on such problems. Computers possibly may facilitate production of a general index or of frequently issued cumulated changes. Might not a joint ALA-LC committee provide author numbers for the Literature schedules and print them as alternatives to the PZ classification on LC cards? Other common problems may be approached nationally.

Application of Machine Methods to LC Notation

Libraries were asked if they found it difficult to apply machine methods to LC notation for preparing book catalogs or processing. Check-off answers were "Yes," "No," and "Not applicable yet." This question may have been premature for most libraries. Of 62 respondents, 47 (76 percent) checked "Not applicable yet," 12 (19 percent) "No," and 3 (5 percent) "Yes." Of the 3 which checked "Yes," only 2 specified the difficulties. One library had to improve its filing techniques to assure a normal shelflist; the other reported difficulty on rare occasions with overlong classification numbers.

Reclassification

LC Used with Other Classification

Twenty libraries answered at least part of the question on the use of LC with some other classification:

Three institutions were using another classification (National Library of Medicine, and Lynn, *Alternative Classification for Catholic Books*) for special portions of their collections.

Four libraries changing to LC indicated no subject choice or cut-off date in their reclassification. Eleven reclassifying libraries were using LC for all new titles. These 11 did not specify how they treated retrospective materials, reference books, additions, and continuations. One library began to reclassify with its reference books.

The answers suggest a lack of carefully formulated reclassification plans and timetables. Some libraries seemed to be "playing it by ear." Perhaps precisely formulated plans are not feasible, but a number of libraries *have* developed systematic programs.

Total versus Partial Reclassification

Forty-one libraries indicated whether or not they would reclassify their entire collection; 24 (59 percent) would, and 17 (41 percent) would not. It is significant how relatively equally divided the opinion seems to be on so major a decision. What are the bases for a more standardized choice?

The most common exception to reclassification was juvenile literature. Some libraries had special or departmental collections, e.g., medical or theological, which were left in their own classification. Governmental and UN materials and periodicals were also cited as exceptions. Some libraries made the point that their criterion for reclassifying was not that of subject but of past and anticipated use. Little-used materials were left in the old classification. (These findings, and those on the use of more than one classification, are not the same as Hoage's.)

Another Classification Continued along with LC

Of 53 respondents, 28 (53 percent) would continue to use more than one classification system, while 25 (47 percent) would not. The relative closeness of these two opinions is consistent with the answers to the previous two questions: some libraries continue to classify juvenile literature in Dewey, medical collections in NLM, Catholic literature by a special Catholic classification scheme, government documents according to SDC, UN documents by UN number, and so forth.

Research might be desirable on multiple classifications, though evidently their convenience seems to justify any added work or cost. It may be that, in many cases, segregation of certain blocks of material (UN documents; scientific, medical, or theological groupings) is the goal sought by the library and its patrons.

Reclassification Process: Personnel, Budgeting, Quarters, Special
Equipment, Use of Old Cards

Thirty-seven libraries contributed analyzable responses relating to personnel,
budgeting, quarters, special equipment, or the use of old cards in the reclassifying
process.

Twenty-one (57 percent) added personnel in the reclassification process. Noteworthy was the low ratio of professionals to nonprofessionals and student assistants in this personnel expansion.

Only 8 (22 percent) reported special budgetary arrangements for reclassification. It is to be feared that too many reclassification programs rely on the
potential ability of present staff to reclassify "when there are no new books to
do." This never really happens, although there are lull periods. Crash programs of
the staff have been used.

Seventeen libraries reported space expansion, and 8 commented that added
space was needed but unavailable. Thus more than 67 percent indicated that
reclassification required special or extra space.

Twenty-seven (73 percent) of the 37 libraries acquired special equipment for
the reclassifying process. Relatively expensive items were frequently mentioned
electric typewriters, Sel-In labelers, Xerox 914 models. (It is not clear how often
the Xerox machine was already in the library, and, of course, the machine is
usually leased, not purchased. Even if only leased for the specific purpose, the
machine requires space and sometimes costly installation.) Also commonly listed
were electric erasers, book trucks, and desks. There seemed very widespread
acceptance of Xerox 914 and Sel-In.

Almost all libraries used self-adhesive labels for spine and book pockets.
Several libraries used these labels to put the new classification number on the
catalog card. Most libraries, however, used the old catalog card (or shelflist card)
in corrected and edited form to generate Xerox copies. In 1939–41, most libraries
reused old cards. In the 1966 study, very few libraries retained the old cards,
though one library reported success with erased and retyped cards. Another
library, however, described a contrary experience and was shifting to Xerox. One
library had tried retyping over a white correction fluid, but the method was
discontinued because the dried fluid flaked off and the cards could not be used in
the catalog. Other libraries have used this method prior to photographing. Two
libraries employed a Flexowriter for card production.

The accepted procedure for book marking and card production in the reclassification process seemed clear: self-adhesive labels for spine and book pocket,
Xerox copies of retyped catalog cards, new cards when necessary.

Reclassification Process: Types of Card Catalog

Thirty-three (83 percent) of 40 respondents did not divide their card catalog
into old and new parts; 7 (17 percent) did so.

Fourteen (36 percent) of 39 respondents placed newly classified materials into a divided catalog; 25 (64 percent) did not. Most who did already had a divided catalog, so the reclassification was not ordinarily the occasion for adopting this type of catalog. All the divided catalogs were described as author-title and subject. One library added, "Like Columbia," which would imply a topical subject section.

Reclassification Timetable

Twenty (54 percent) of 37 respondents had set a time plan for reclassification; 17 (46 percent) had not. Those with a timetable reported completion goals ranging from two to ten years; about a half set their goal beyond five years. Are such long-range goals realistic or necessary? Might it be sufficiently effective to keep a larger portion of the collection in the original classification?

Classification Procedures for Bibliography, Periodicals, Biography, Documents, Textbooks, Literature

Bibliography. Thirty-four (76 percent) of 45 respondents selected the Z schedule; 5 (12 percent) classed bibliography under subject; and 6 (12 percent) did both. Regardless of theoretical objections expressed in the literature to the Z schedule, libraries generally seem to accept it, perhaps as a matter of expedience. Still, almost a fourth of the respondents did not completely accept the Z schedules.

Periodicals. Twenty-three (56 percent) of 41 respondents classified periodicals by subject; 14 (34 percent) arranged them alphabetically by title; and 4 (10 percent) did both. Subject classification may seem surprisingly frequent, though it must be admitted that once a periodical is subject-classified, there is ordinarily no need to change for hundreds of future issues.

Biography. Fourteen (31 percent) of 45 respondents classed biography by subject; 1 classed by CT; 30 (69 percent) classed by subject and CT. There was occasional comment that this last procedure was also followed by LC.

Documents. Forty-two libraries indicated if they classed documents by subject or by the Superintendent of Documents classification system. Nine (21 percent) classed by subject; 24 (58 percent) by SDC; and 9 (21 percent) did both. In general, libraries seem to rely on SDC for most of their government document classifying, if they classify them at all.

Textbooks. Thirty-seven libraries noted procedures in classing textbooks by subject or by placing them in a separate file. Thirty-one (84 percent) classed them by subject; 4 (11 percent) placed them in a separate file; 2 (5 percent) did both. This question probably would have had more relevance for libraries of teachers' colleges.

Literature. Forty-four libraries indicated if they used the P or the PZ3 schedules for classifying works of literature. The answers confirmed the previously noted dissatisfaction with the PZ3 schedule. Only 1 library used the PZ3 schedule exclusively. Thirty-three (75 percent) used the P schedules; 11 (25 percent) both the P and the PZ3 schedules.

Reclassification by Osmosis or Other Plan

Libraries were asked whether they followed Ranganathan's principle of osmosis (i.e., reclassify only items for which new editions are ordered) or if they reclassified items as they returned from circulation. Most respondents indicated they followed neither method exclusively.

Thirty-eight responses were tallied for the "osmosis" part of the question. Only 6 (16 percent) followed Ranganathan's principle exclusively, and only 3 (8 percent) definitely rejected it. Six (16 percent) followed both plans; 23 (60 percent) followed neither Ranganathan's principle nor the alternative of reclassifying the books as they returned to the library. Some comments implied that those who said "Yes" to both and those who said "No" to both may have meant the same, i.e., they followed a combination plan of block reclassification plus osmosis plus reclassifying returned items.

Thirty-three responses were tallied for the second part of this question, i.e., did the library reclassify materials as they were returned from circulation? Only 4 (12 percent) gave an unequivocal "Yes"; only 1 (3 percent) an unequivocal "No." The other 28 (85 percent) followed neither plan exclusively.

Most libraries thus seem to have been unwilling to adopt any one formula in deciding when to reclassify which books. Is any one formula adequate? The implied opinion is no.

Summary

In a sense, the various sections of the questionnaire represent a summary of this report on developments among libraries in the country in respect to the adoption and use of the Library of Congress classification. A final word, which is supported by comments in the Holley[13] observations, indicates that fewer librarians are being overwhelmed by the reclassification aspects implied in changing to the LC system. Selective reclassification is a pattern that has been followed in some libraries, and the librarians have found that this creates, over a relatively short period of time, a basis for designating materials that should be reclassified quickly, and those which can be handled over a longer period of time. In academic libraries, faculty members have been found helpful in suggesting programs of order and selection.

Discussion

The questionnaire used for Chapter I was divided into three parts: one dealing with the Library of Congress classification in relation to certain characteristics of the institutions beginning to use it; a second, with general matters of classification in terms of the internal structure of LC from an overall basis; and the third, with reclassification.

The part dealing with reclassification concerns, first of all, the use of other classification systems along with the Library of Congress system. Of the 53 respondents who were among the first group of 66 libraries, 28 (or 53 percent) said they will continue to use more than one classification scheme, that is, the shifting to the Library of Congress classification does not mean that they are going to give up all of the old classification systems that they may have been using.

The relative closeness of these two observations about the use and nonuse—25 respondents would not be concerned with anything but LC—is consistent with the answers to several other questions which were asked with regard to periodicals, government documents, and juvenile literature. These represent areas which in some libraries are being left in their old arrangement. But, in addition to these being left in Dewey or some other classification, there are collections being reclassed into the National Library of Medicine scheme, Catholic literature into the Lynn classification, government documents shifted over into the Superintendent of Documents classification, and the United Nations documents going into the UN classification.

In the reclassification section general questions were asked; the questionnaire tried to get some idea of overall cost, personnel, quarters, special equipment, and the use of cards already in the catalog. Tentative findings of these responses may be of interest.

Thirty-seven libraries had a large number of significant responses that are not yet analyzed in detail regarding personnel, budget, quarters, and special equipment. Twenty-one percent, for example, added personnel in the reclassification process. Apparently, in the large library, it is almost essential that there be a separate staff. Along with this there is a tendency among many libraries, particularly those which have had good cataloging up to this point and do not need to recatalog, to use the time saved by introducing the Library of Congress classification to reclass much of the older material without increase in staff.

Only 8 of the libraries—and this is a surprising thing—reported special budgets being given for reclassification projects. In most cases, however, there is a high correlation between the shift due to the Library of Congress classification and increased acquisition backlog. This is one of the reasons why the LC scheme is being looked at as a possibility of helping to speed up new acquisitions.

Seventeen libraries reported space needs and 8 commented that additional space was needed but unavailable, which is not unusual in technical quarters in libraries.

Twenty-seven of the 37 libraries who answered the question said that they required special equipment for the reclassifying process. The items most frequently mentioned were electric typewriters and Xerox 914's. Also mentioned were electric erasers, book trucks, desks, and other essential equipment that libraries do not normally have with a staff that does not require new personnel.

Almost all the libraries use self-adhesive labels for spine and book pockets. Several libraries use these labels to put the new call number on catalog cards. Most libraries, however, use the old catalog card or the shelflist card, corrected and edited, to generate Xerox copies for the main catalog.

Notes

[1] With the valuable assistance of Richard J. Hyman, who tabulated the questionnaires and helped in preparing the report. Acknowledgment is likewise made to C. Donald Cook, Paul Fasana, Carlyle J. Frarey, T. C. Hines, Kay MacFarland, and Irlene Roemer Stephens for suggestions made in regard to the questionnaire. The writer is grateful also to the many libraries who sent information to him.

[2] Thelma Eaton, "Classification in College and University Libraries," *College & Research Libraries*, 16:168–76 (1955).

[3] Irene M. Doyle, "Library of Congress Classification for the Academic Library," in *The Role of Classification in the Modern Library*, ed. by Thelma Eaton and Donald Strout (Champaign, Ill.: Illini Union Bookstore, 1960, c1959), p.76–92.

[4] Leo La Montagne, *American Library Classification, with Special Reference to the Library of Congress* (Hamden, Conn.: Shoe String Press, 1961).

[5] Howard McGaw, "Academic Libraries Using the Library of Congress Classification," *College & Research Libraries*, 27:31–36 (1966).

[6] ———— "Reclassification: A Bibliography," *Library Resources & Technical Services*, 9:483–88 (Fall, 1965).

[7] Annette L. Hoage, "The Library of Congress Classification in the United States: A Survey of Opinions and Practices, with Attention to Problems of Structure and Application" (D.L.S. Dissertation, School of Library Service, Columbia University, 1961).

[8] Edward G. Holley, "The Trend to L.C.: Thoughts on Changing Academic Library Classification Schemes" (Paper given at Louisiana State University Library Lectures Series, May, 1966).

[9] These are included in the bibliography by McGaw, and also in the comprehensive bibliography included in this volume (p.227).

[10] Richard S. Angell, "On the Future of the Library of Congress Classification," in *Classification Research: Proceedings of the Second International Study Conference . . . Elsinore, Denmark, 14th to 18th September, 1964*, ed. by Pauline Atherton (Copenhagen: Munksgaard, 1965), p.101–12.

[11] Hoage, *op. cit.*, Chapter VI.

[12] Sidney L. Jackson, *Catalog Use Study: Director's Report*, ed. by V. Mostecky (Chicago: American Library Assn., 1953).

[13] Holley, *op. cit.*

Chapter 2

The Library of Congress Classification: Development, Characteristics, and Structure

Charles C. Bead

My observations on the development, characteristics, and structure of the Library of Congress classification are addressed primarily to practitioners, that is, to those who apply this classification system in their daily work or who may plan to do so in the future. It is not my purpose, therefore, to give a critical evaluation or a comparative analysis of the LC system and other library classifications. Instead, I am aiming chiefly to set forth some general criteria which may be useful for understanding the LC system as it is today and for applying it effectively.

A brief review of the origin and first development of the LC system may help to explain some of the characteristic features of this classification. In 1900, three years after the Library of Congress moved from the Capitol to its new building, it was decided to create a new classification for a more systematic and functional arrangement of the Library's collections. The development of the thirty volumes which make up the LC classification was the product of many minds. A great number of subject specialists and classifiers, working individually or in groups, set to work to prepare the schedules for the individual classes. The schedules so created are physically separate, but they form integral parts of the whole system.

It is important to note the method of work that the framers of the classification employed. First, a theoretical schedule was drafted for each subject class. This preliminary schedule was then applied to the existing LC book collection to reclassify it from the Jeffersonian classification which had governed the placement of the Library's holdings before. It was also used to classify newly acquired material. In this process of application the schedule of each class was modified and adapted to the collections of the Library of Congress by making necessary expansions for additional topics represented by books in the collections. Furthermore, on the basis of the examination of the Library's holdings, decisions were made on the collocation of certain topics and materials. For all schedules, this process of testing, molding, and development lasted several years. Finally, there emerged for each discipline the completed classification schedule which was tailor-made for LC's holdings and, in fact, reflected the nature of the LC collections, their strengths, and their weaknesses.

Characteristics of the LC Classification

From this history of LC's development it becomes evident that the details in each class were determined by the extent and character of the LC collections in the following two respects: (1) The holdings determined what topics were to be included since each topic in a schedule had to be warranted by material actually present in the Library of Congress. Today the same principle still prevails; except for certain form subdivisions, no new class number is inserted in a classification schedule unless a topic in a work requires it. (2) Particular arrangements of material by category of form and collocation of topics are provided as appropriate to the literature as published. In other words, the LC classification is based on what is often called "literary warrant," and it was constructed by application of an inductive method of development. In this manner a classification system was created in which each topic is justified by existing material, and the creation of empty classes is avoided.

Thus it is evident that the LC classification was originally designed with reference to the character and probable development of the collections of the Library of Congress and with regard to the Library's own reference needs. Today, of course, there is a keen awareness on the part of the Library of Congress of the interest of other libraries in the LC scheme. This is borne in mind at the Library of Congress both in the application and in the development of the classification. By publishing the schedules and thereby making them available for public distribution, the Library of Congress has demonstrated its desire to serve other libraries.

The LC classification, being completely based on the Library's collections, is coextensive in scope with the book stock of the Library of Congress. Therefore, the LC classification is comprehensive but not truly universal at the present time. Expansion of the classification is governed by and depends upon the acquisition of new material.

As a result, the Library's cataloging program and acquisition policy have a profound and direct effect upon the development of the classification. For example, an intensified cataloging program of Far Eastern material in the vernacular was responsible for the development of sections in the Class D (History) schedule for China, Japan, and Korea and for entirely recast schedules for Chinese, Japanese, and Korean literature in Class PL.

The acquisitions program under Public Law 480, which brings to the Library of Congress material from certain Asian and Arab countries, has led to a substantial revision of the schedules for Arabic and Hebrew literature, and has brought about the expansion of many subject areas, such as the provisions for Buddhism and Islam in subclasses BL and BP and for Philosophy in Class B.

In the immediate future, there can be no doubt that the currently initiated program of centralized or shared cataloging at the Library of Congress will have such a strong impact upon the further development of the LC classification that it will in time approach universality in scope.

While the LC classification, as a whole, constitutes a unitary system in the sense that certain fundamentals are common to all parts, each individual schedule was, as indicated before, devised and fashioned with reference to its own needs by application to that particular group of material rather than with reference to its relative part in the entire system. Consequently, there is no uniformity among the schedules in regard to subdivisions for form, geographic areas, or periods. Specifically, tables of subdivisions are unique to each schedule and are not applicable throughout the entire system.

Within separate classes, however, there are synthetic elements applicable to each class alone. They consist mostly of tables of geographic subdivisions, notably in Class H (Social Sciences) and tables of subject subdivisions which are found primarily in Class J (Political Science) and for languages in Class P (Language and Literature).

As the never ending flow of books brings about the continuous process of classifying at LC, the classification system is never static but thoroughly dynamic. The system is being updated and revised literally every day by LC's thirty subject catalogers who established more than 2200 new class numbers in the fiscal year 1965. Additions and changes to the classification schedules are published and made available to the other libraries in *LC Classification—Additions and Changes.* This quarterly publication contains not only the additions and changes but also specific instructions on how to annotate the schedules and indexes so that they reflect the changes accurately. When stock of the schedules is exhausted, they are reprinted, usually with cumulative supplementary pages which contain all additions and changes up to the time of publication of the reprint.

Overview of LC Classification Spectrum (Outline)

A broad overview of the LC classification spectrum will be found in the *Outline of the Library of Congress Classification.*[1] It begins with Class A (General Works and Polygraphy), which is followed by the humanities and social sciences in Classes B–P. Next in order are science and technology in Classes Q–V, and the scheme is concluded by Class Z (Bibliography and Library Science). The letters I, O, X, and Y have not been used.[2]

There are two major gaps in the LC system: Class K (Law) and a general index. Part of Class K, the schedule for the federal law of the United States, is now completed. Working copies of this schedule are in the hands of LC's law subject catalogers, and class numbers in cataloging entries for material on United States federal law are being assigned. Simultaneously, this partial schedule is being prepared by editors for publication as a provisional edition of this part of Class K. The next step is the development of schedules for the law of the states of the United States, which will be followed by a preparation of a subclass of Class K for the law of Great Britain. Schedules for other jurisdictions and legal systems will follow later.

In this connection particular attention should be called to the fact that class numbers for legal topics are still present in many LC schedules. For example, there are class numbers in HD (Industry) for labor law, in HG (Finance) for banking law, in HJ (Public Finance) for tax law, in subclasses for the J (Political Science) schedule for constitutional law, and in LB (Education) for educational law. All these class numbers are no longer in effect at the Library of Congress. They will be designated as alternatives in due course. Since 1949 all law materials, including books dealing with such special legal subjects as mentioned above, have been assigned to LC's Law Library and have simply been classed: LAW. This is the reason why LC call numbers have not appeared on LC catalog cards for law material. As the Class K schedule is completed, Class K numbers will be indicated on cards for newly cataloged materials. However, LC does not expect to reprint cards for previously classified law material when it is reclassed to Class K numbers. These retrospective changes connected with reclassification will be made internally only. Consequently, call numbers will not appear on cards for legal works cataloged prior to the fall of 1966 unless the cards are reprinted to replenish the stock of the Card Division or for some other reason.

The other major gap in the LC system is the lack of a combined index for all classes. Of course, there are now detailed indexes in most individual schedules which are kept up to date by the quarterly *Additions and Changes* and by supplementary pages in reprinted schedules. But these indexes refer, for the most part, only to class numbers in the schedules of which they are a part and do not refer to class numbers in other schedules. For example, when one looks up Automobiles in the Class H index, he will find a class number for the economic aspects of the automotive industry, but there is no reference to the technical or engineering aspects of this industry which are classed in TL, a subclass of Technology.

The importance of a combined index to the LC schedules, showing class numbers for all aspects of a subject, is evident. It must also be realized that the compilation of such an index is a task of considerable magnitude, since according to present tentative estimates a general index would comprise a volume of about 1400 pages with approximately 140,000 entries, all of which would have to be compiled, verified, and edited. It can be plainly seen that a major project is involved here.

Structure of the LC System

The discussion of the need for a combined relative index which indicates class numbers for all aspects of a subject leads directly to a discussion of the structure of the LC system.

The entire spectrum of this classification is arranged by major disciplines, such as Economics, Sociology, Political Science, Technology, etc. As a result, various aspects of a subject are generally not grouped together but are classed with pertinent disciplines. For example, the technical aspects of agriculture are classed in Class S (Agriculture), while Agricultural Economics is assigned to HD, a subclass of Economics; Railroad Engineering is classed in TF (Technology), while organization and management of railroads belong in HE (Transportation and Communication) and Railroad Law in Class K. Ragweed may be treated from the point of view of botany as in Class QK; from the point of view of medicine, that is, hay fever prevention, in Class RC; or from that of plant cultivation—weeds, in Class SB. Since this arrangement by discipline is basic in the LC system, a classifier in making the subject analysis of the work must determine which of several aspects of a subject is involved or which aspect predominates.

Within the framework of the LC classification several fields of study or categories of literature have been collocated in a way that is peculiar to LC. A few of these are discussed individually below.

Subject versus Country Collocation

Generally the arrangement in the LC classification is by discipline or subject, which may be subdivided, when necessary, by country or place. This order favors the comparative approach of study. The LC classification is, however, not rigid in this respect, and LC has adopted classification and collocation by country and then subdivided by subject where the reader's interest is primarily concerned with the institutions of the particular area. This provision for the area study approach is illustrated by the arrangement in Class J, where government and politics of individual countries are arranged by country which, in turn, are subdivided by subject. Material dealing with the governmental and political systems of the fifty states of the United States is grouped in the same manner: first by state and then by subject. Other examples of country collocation can be found in subclasses HE (Transportation and Communication), HG (Finance), and Class K (Law).

One of the major subjects affecting several disciplines is geography. General geography, mathematical and astronomical geography, physical geography, and anthropogeography are collocated in Class G (Geography). However, the topography and description of individual continents and countries are not classed in Class G but are placed in the history schedules (D–F). This collocation was considered desirable because "a knowledge of the geography of a country is essential to the understanding of its history."[3]

Furthermore, topical geography is not classed in Class G, but is grouped together with pertinent subjects, e.g., economic geography in HC, HD, and HF (Economics); geography of transportation in HE (Transportation and Communication); medical geography in RA (Medicine); military geography in UA (Military Science), etc. It is evident that topical geography was treated by the creators of the classification as an auxiliary branch of study, and was therefore placed with the main discipline which it was designed to assist.

Biography

A similar pattern of collocation has been followed for biography. General biography, that is, collective and individual biography without a specific subject orientation, is classed in CT (Biography) with the exception of collective local biography which always goes in the history classes D, E, and F. However, subject biography, that is, biography being illustrative of any special subject, has been considered important reference material which contributes to the understanding of the respective subject field and is classed by subject as provided in the schedules of other classes. Therefore, the biography of public figures, that is, persons who have played a prominent part in shaping the history of a country, state, or city, is assigned to the history classes; the biography of economists is classed in HB (Economics), that of mathematicians in QA (Mathematics), etc.

For other libraries wishing to class all biographical material in CT, a detailed alternative classification schedule for subject biography is available in CT (4150–9950). These class numbers are enclosed in parentheses which indicate their alternative character. They are not used by the Library of Congress.

Statistics

An extensive chapter entitled "Statistics" in Class HA provides for works on general statistical theory and method, for statistical organizations, and for general collections of statistical data. Works dealing specifically with the application of rigorous mathematics to statistical theory are classed in QA276–277 (Mathematics). However, topical or applied statistics, including methodology and data, are generally classed with the field to which they are applied, for example, agricultural statistics in Class HD (Agricultural Economics), educational statistics in Class L (Education), medical statistics in Class R (Medicine), etc. It is evident that this arrangement is based on the consideration that applied statistics are essentially a tool in the study of special subjects to which they are applied, and it was therefore decided to group subject statistics with the subject concerned.

Bibliography

While topical geography, subject biography, and topical statistics are classed by subject, the opposite course of action has been followed for subject bibliography, which is completely grouped together in Class Z and is not classed by subject. The only exceptions to this practice are music bibliography in Class ML (Literature of Music) and bibliography of law, which will be classed in Class K. This arrangement has been criticized by some who would prefer to group subject bibliography with the subject literature.

The Class Z schedule was completed in 1898, long before a decision on a new classification system was made. At that time it was felt that a strong and unified bibliography collection was essential to the new cataloging and classification program. It is questionable whether the original classification decision of the Library of Congress on subject bibliography, made about seventy years ago, would be the same today. However, the Library of Congress will continue to use Class Z for subject bibliography, and no major reorganization of subject bibliography in Class Z is planned at this time.

PZ3 and PZ4 (Fiction)

Perhaps no decision on collocation has produced more comment than the grouping of all fiction in English in PZ3 and PZ4. This material includes, of course, not only American and English fiction, but also foreign fiction translated into English, and so English translations of *The Magic Mountain* by Thomas Mann, *War and Peace* by Tolstoi, and *Dr. Zhivago* by Boris Pasternak are found in PZ3, together with American and English fiction.

The original purpose of classing all fiction in English in PZ3 was no doubt to bring together at the Library of Congress a special collection of fiction, arranged alphabetically by author, which a reader could easily use for browsing without first consulting the catalog. This method of grouping, however, separates fiction in English from other works by or about a literary author, which would be classed in PR, PS, PG, PT, etc. This arrangement is occasionally deplored in some college or university libraries where literary studies and research are carried on and where classification by literature and author is preferred. One may wonder whether the arrangement for fiction in English, made by the Library of Congress several decades ago, would be adopted today. At any rate, the assignment of an alternative class number—bracketed PR, PS, PT, etc.—on LC catalog cards will be investigated at the Library of Congress. This may help other libraries, which deviate from LC practice and do their own classifying of fiction in English, to avoid conflicts with call numbers which may be assigned by the Library of Congress to other works in the future.

Alternative Class Numbers

Alternative class numbers are those which other libraries may wish to use if they prefer a subject collocation differing from LC practice. They are identified by parentheses which enclose them. They occur throughout the LC classification system either in large blocks, as in CT for subject biography, or in single numbers in numerous cases where provision in the schedule is made for relationships and where *see* references to other disciplines are indicated in the schedules. For example, in the HM (Sociology) schedule, class number HM (31) indicates the topic "Relation [of sociology] to religion" *see* BL60 (Religion), or HM (32), "Relation [of sociology] to education" *see* LC189–191 (Education). In these cases other libraries may prefer to bring all material dealing with relational aspects of sociology together in HM (Sociology), and to assign the alternative class numbers instead of the numbers used by the Library of Congress. Another possibility is to accept in these examples the classification in BL and LC respectively, but to insert in the shelflist unit cards under HM (31) and HM (32) as "added entries." In this fashion the material is represented in the shelflist under *both* Sociology and Religion, or Sociology and Education, and can be found in both places by those who search systematically by subject in the shelflist record.

While alternative class numbers are not assigned by the Library of Congress in classifying material, the numbers enclosed in parentheses in the schedules are reserved and will generally not be used for other topics.

Subdivisions and Principles of Arrangement within Each Class

Within each class the arrangement of material follows a general pattern which is not identical but similar for most classes. First come the "external" form subdivisions, such as Periodicals, Documents, Societies, Collections, Encyclopedias, Dictionaries, Directories, etc. They are followed by "internal" subdivisions, such as Theory, Philosophy, Methodology, History, Biography, Study and teaching, and Research. Then come "Treatises" and "General works," to which are often added "General special" and frequently, for different intellectual levels, "Popular works" and "Juvenile works." There is some variation among the different classes because the provisions for form subdivisions are based on the requirements of the material in each case.

The captions "General works" and "Treatises" are, of course, for works dealing with a topic comprehensively, whereas "General special" is used for works on the general subject but dealing with it from a particular point of view or with respect to a particular relationship. For example, in the Class HF (Commerce) schedule, "Treatises" on advertising are followed by "General special" for works on advertising in foreign countries. In HE (Transportation and Communication), general works on transportation precede "General special" for those dealing with transportation from the point of view of public policy and state ownership. Another example can be found in Class HB (Economics), where general works on crises and business cycles are followed by "General special" for such topics as costs and profits and crises, consumption and crises, social aspects of crises, etc.

Subjects are followed by subject subdivisions or subtopics, progressing from general to specific, as far as possible in logical order. When a systematic sequence of coordinate subdivisions cannot be discerned, the classification schedules frequently provide for an alphabetical order (A–Z) in which topical Cutter numbers indicate the individual topic. Occasionally the same method is applied when there is a shortage of whole numbers.

In the systematic arrangement of main subjects and subject subdivisions the hierarchical relationship is not expressed by the notation. In particular, decimal numbers do not always indicate subordinate relationship. However, the relationship of topics is expressed by the indention of captions in the schedules.

Notation

In the mixed notation system of LC, a combination of capital letters and Arabic numerals is employed. Single letters indicate main classes; two-letter combinations designate subclasses, e.g., the capital letter H stands for Social Sciences, with subclasses HA (Statistics), HB (Economic Theory), HC (Economic History and Conditions), HD (Agricultural Economics and Industry), etc. The numerals are usually integers and can range from 1 to 9999 in each class and subclass. The average class number is compact, since it generally does not exceed two letters and four numbers.

Class numbers may be expanded indefinitely by the addition of decimals when it is necessary to insert a new topic systematically in a schedule and when whole numbers are not available. As mentioned before, however, decimal fractions do not always express hierarchical subordination. The symbol for a main topic may be a decimal number and that for a topic subordinate to it may be a whole number. Similarly, when there are two coordinate topics, one may be represented by a whole number and the other by a decimal; for example, DS904 stands for "Social life and customs" in Korea, and DS904.5 for "Ethnography" of Korea.

Another way of expanding a class number is, as mentioned before, by the use of topical Cutter numbers where a schedule provides for an A–Z arrangement. In these cases the topical Cutter number is part of the class number. For example, under HF5549.5, "Personnel management, By topic, A–Z," .J6 stands for "Job analysis," .J63 for "Job satisfaction," .L3 for "Labor discipline," etc. Topical Cutter numbers are used decimally and are constructed according to the same principles as Cutter numbers for author and works.

An important part of the notation is the book or author number which is added to the class number and completes the call number. The topic of book numbers is discussed in Chapters 6 through 8.

Hospitality of LC for Expansion

The capacity of the LC classification for growth and expansion, often called hospitality, is achieved by the use of vacant numbers and by the addition of decimal numbers. The LC system is laid out on a generous scale, and it is, therefore, usually possible to use a vacant whole number to fit a new topic in its systematic place. Expansion by use of decimal numbers, as just indicated, is resorted to when whole numbers for the logical place of a topic in the system are not available. This latter method of expansion is unlimited.

Apart from the accommodation of a single new topic or a few topics, the LC system can add many hundred thousand class numbers by establishing new subclasses. Classes E, F, and Z have never been subdivided by subclasses. Even in the most heavily populated classes such as H, subclasses can be established by using double letters which have not been used as yet, e.g., HK, HL, HR, etc. Many more subclasses are still vacant in other disciplines. Beyond that, it is quite possible to introduce, in the future, main classes identified by combinations of three letters which would make it possible to expand LC indefinitely or to rebuild certain parts of LC entirely.*

---

* The newly developed K schedule now being used at the Library of Congress employs the use of three letters for some subdivisions.—*Ed.*

Application and Development

At the Library of Congress the subject cataloger's work involves both application and development of the LC classification. In the area of application, the subject cataloger is concerned with subject analysis, that is, determination of the subject matter of a work, selection of the most specific class number, and, when necessary, number building when synthetic devices are provided.

A manual for the LC classification is not available as yet. Its compilation is on the agenda of the Library's Subject Cataloging Division, and work on such a manual hopefully is expected to begin as soon as additional staffing will permit. In the absence of a manual the subject cataloger is guided in making a classification decision by general principles of library classification as set forth in such works as Jack Mills' *Modern Outline of Library Classification*,[4] W. C. B. Sayers' *Manual of Classification*,[5] and W. S. Merrill's *Code for Classifiers*.[6]

In addition, he follows the directions given in the LC schedules. These directions are contained in specific instructions, usually in the form of notes and in cross references. For example, in Class JX (International Law) the classifier is instructed by a note at the beginning of the chapter "Foreign relations" to class here only "International questions treated as sources of or contributions to the theory of international law. All histories of ₁international₁ events, diplomatic history of wars, etc., go in History. In case of doubt, favor D–F (History)." In Class HB (Economic Theory) the classifier finds under the caption "History of economics" a note with directions to classify here works on the history of economic theory, but to assign works dealing with the economic history of a country to HC (Economic History and Conditions). In Class B (Philosophy), ₁p.5₁, the classifier is given specific instructions when to class works of classical philosophers with Greek and Latin literature (Class PA) and when to classify them by subject in Philosophy. Furthermore, under many subjects attention is called to related (coordinate or subordinate) topics by so-called "cf." notes (which are, in fact, *see also* references) and by *see* cross references.

The frequent notes and guideposts with which the LC system is equipped make this classification self-explanatory to a high degree; they furnish a partial substitute for the planned manual which will codify LC practices.

As stated before, the Library of Congress is revising its schedules every day as new material is added to the collections. After the subject cataloger receives his daily inflow of work, he studies each book, and on the basis of his findings determines whether an appropriate class number already exists within the system. If this is not the case, it is the cataloger's responsibility to suggest new class numbers for topics not yet represented in the LC classification, for example, a new discovery, invention, historic event, etc. The need for updating certain classes may also result in the proposal of more specific topics or revised captions. Research will be carried out to identify the exact nature and scope of the new topic and to determine its proper systematic place in the system in relation to other topics. The proposals are submitted on prescribed form cards to the Editor of Classification Schedules, who will give them editorial scrutiny.

The edited proposals are consolidated weekly, and a list of tentative additions and changes is duplicated for internal use. This weekly list, which is distributed to all subject catalogers for information and comment, serves as the agenda for a weekly editorial conference which is presided over by the Chief of the Division. During the conference, each of the proposals is considered and either approved, rejected, or returned to the subject cataloger for further research and consideration. Once the proposed class numbers have been approved, they will be used immediately and promptly appear on LC printed cards. Subsequently they are published in *LC Classification—Additions and Changes*.

In preparing a new class number the subject cataloger has to examine not only the new work to be classed, but also all pertinent material already in the collections, to determine whether some works should be reclassified under the new class number. This is often the case when a class number for a more specific topic is set up or when new period subdivisions are adopted. It is important to note that the Library of Congress generally does not undertake actual reclassification of old material that might be more appropriately classed in the new number, but simply makes a notation on the shelflist records: "Better ₍new class number₎." It is evident that this practice is the result of the need for economy. A consequence of this policy of not reclassifying is that cards for old material are not reprinted with the new class number. There is no guarantee, therefore, that LC class numbers on printed cards, particularly those printed several years ago, will correspond to the latest revision of the LC classification schedules.

In these situations the use of the old, more general class numbers is not critical. In general, the Library of Congress does not vacate and cancel class numbers or give them new meanings after a lapse of years; development consists for the most part of refinements, i.e., of the addition of new or more specific numbers to the schedules, often as subclasses of existing classes. However, there have been some major redevelopments, as in some subclasses of Class T (Technology). Again, LC cards printed before the redevelopment do not reflect the latest state of the classification. Incidentally, there is no LC master list indicating obsolete class numbers and their revised substitutes.

An outstanding recent development will affect the future of the LC classification. The program of centralized or shared cataloging on an international basis brings to the Library a greatly increased inflow of material, which may double or even triple cataloging production and will, in turn, be responsible for a substantial increase in the establishment of new class numbers.

Discussion

Question: Is warning given about old class numbers, that is, on older LC cards ordered by libraries, going into reclassification? Will libraries know that class numbers may not be up to date?

Dr. Bead: A library undertaking reclassification and ordering older LC cards for the changeover to LC will find that the call numbers do not completely correspond to the latest development of the classification. At this time there is no particular warning system to let other libraries know that a class number on old cards should be replaced by an updated and more specific class number.

Mr. Angell: When a new number is established, or an existing class number subdivided topically, the next general procedure is to mark the entries affected by the change in the shelflist "Better," followed by indication of the new class. In other words, a note is made of what *would* be done if work could stop and the old titles reclassified. The cards for these old titles are not reprinted to record the change. However, when the entries are changed and the books reclassified, the new numbers appear on the reprinted cards, so that a certain number of them are brought up to date, but only fortuitously.

Question: How are schedules kept up to date at LC?

Mr. Angell: Our practice is to write in the changes in the official copies used by the staff: the three general officers, specialists in various subject areas, and the Classification Record assistants. When revisions are extensive, we tip them in, either from the quarterly *Additions and Changes* or from the weekly list.

Question: Why were so many gaps left in numbers in classes? May other libraries use these gaps by inserting numbers of their own?

Mr. Angell: The capacity of the LC classification for expansion was put into the system by the original framers early in the century by means of leaving gaps at places presumed, guessed, or predicted to need them. This is a feature of an enumerative classification (of which LC is an example) that is very much criticized in the literature of classification theory. Manifestly it was impossible, gifted as the original framers of the classification were, to anticipate and provide for all future needs at the places where they would arise.

The blanks are there for expansion, and anyone who needs to expand at that place, can. This, of course, does not answer the question of what LC will do with that space and how LC will use it. The Library of Congress cannot predict that. If a library develops at a particular point, there is the evident possibility of LC using the space in a different way later. This, I take from the question, is something that those libraries who want to use LC's work as literally as possible wish to avoid. I do not know how to solve that problem.

Question: The Z class is objectionable to a number of libraries. Can nothing be done to class bibliographies of subjects with the subjects?

Mr. Angell: At the Elsinore conference I said "the schedule for bibliography was the first to be developed, for reasons having to do with the transition to the new system. A strong central bibliographical collection was needed and of course still is. The treatment of subject bibliography, however, has become particularly questionable: first, its extraction from the subject classes; second, its . . . arrangement in the bibliography class. A pattern toward which the system should strive is to represent bibliography systematically in the various disciplines with parallel representation in subject order in the bibliography class as an alternative."[7]

Some libraries are already doing the latter, using a prefix before the class number for the topic in the general schedules. Thus they would have a bibliography class which would duplicate or epitomize the class schedules as a whole. This is the less-preferred alternative, I feel sure, from information reaching LC.

The other alternative, the one that perhaps most people really want, is to place bibliography in the several classes. We at LC have given some consideration to how this might be done. Using Electronics as an example, we could find a place in the form classes for bibliography and add it in parentheses, this being the designation used in our schedules for alternative class numbers. Since no whole number is available, TK7804.5, between Dictionaries and Biography, would be a likely choice. This would be followed by a *see* reference to the class number for the general bibliography of electronics in the Z schedule, Z5836. In the Z schedule, itself, would appear the alternative TK number as a signal that this alternative was given in Class TK. The relevant sections of the two schedules would then appear as follows:

TK	Electrical Engineering and Industries	
	Electronics	
7800	Periodicals and Societies	
	. . .	
7804	Dictionaries	
(7804.5)	Bibliography *see* Z5836	
	Biography	
7806	Collective	

Z	Subject Bibliography	
	Electronics	
5836	General bibliography (TK7804.5)	

For special topics, however, this solution can become fairly complicated, even when there are reasonably close parallels between the schedule and the relevant portion of Z, for example:

TK	
	Electronics
7850	Patents
	. . .
	Apparatus
7870	General
7872	Special, A–Z
(.A2)	Bibliography *see* Z5853*
	. . .
.T73	Transistors

* If it is desired to class bibliography of a special topic with the topic, the Cutter .A2 may be used after the Cutter number for the topic. This use of .A2, however, could conflict in the places where .A2 has been assigned in the schedules.

<pre>
         Z
                    Electronics
       5838   Special topics, A–Z (TK7872.+)
                      .T7 Transistors (TK7872.T73+)
</pre>

What this example means to me is that I do not see any way in which we could get a bibliography number in any given class, either in a general or in a specific class basis, by means of a formula, such as the digit 9 added at whatever decimal place you need it, or the Cutter .A1 or .A2, or .Z9 or .Z99, because those Cutters appear too frequently in tables. It appears that there would have to be a separate solution in each case.

Question: Would you use the same classification tables for audio-visual materials as for books?

Mr. Angell: Generally, no. It is, of course, possible to do so by taking the class number that the work would have if it were in printed-text form and preceding it by or adding to it some code letter for the kind of audio-visual material, but we do not have specific tables for audio-visual materials.

Another problem category is phonorecords. The Library of Congress's collection of commercially available discs and tapes is arranged by manufacturer, and within manufacturer by disc or album number. This is an arbitrary arrangement, of course, but if it is one that suits any library's purposes, then the location number is derivable from the entry, although not printed in the entry as a call number. As to the possibility of subject classification of phonorecords, as far as music recordings are concerned, the Library has no expectation of developing one that would, for example, bring symphonies, concertos, or other forms and mediums together on the shelves.

Question: Are cooperative cataloging entries, printed in the *National Union Catalog* without a classification number, later reprinted in the *NUC* when LC has assigned a classification number?

Mr. Angell: The entry will have a classification number at such time as LC adapts a cooperative entry for a copy of the work acquired for its own collections. If this entry were reprinted as an LC card, it would appear again in the *NUC*. Cooperative copy not adapted for the LC collections is expected to decline under the centralized cataloging program of Title II. Therefore, fewer cards without class numbers will appear.

Question: Is there any possibility of revised LC schedules appearing more frequently?

Mr. Angell: We hope very much that the new electronic photocomposing technique being used for the subject-heading list will expedite the release and availability of new editions of the schedules, certainly from the printing and production point of view. At the moment I do not see any way in which this can expedite the editorial processes which must be gone through. Once schedules are ready, there is a long gap between dispatch of copy and availability of the printed schedules because of the extremely difficult composition and proofreading work done by the Government Printing Office.

There are four questions relating to LC publications:

1. Is it possible to include LC class numbers in *New Serial Titles?*
2. Could nonintegrated tables at the end of schedules be issued as fold-out sheets or even as separate supplements?
3. It would be most useful if the *Additions and Changes* were issued in loose-leaf form and in a larger size. Could this be done?
4. Could the quarterly issues of *Additions and Changes* be cumulated?

My answer to these can only be that we at the Library of Congress will certainly study them.

Notes

[1] U.S. Library of Congress, Processing Dept., Subject Cataloging Division, *Outline of the Library of Congress Classification* (Washington: Govt. Print. Off., 1942; reprinted 1965). 22p.

[2] The letter "W" has been used for the medicine classification of the Armed Forces Medical Library (now the National Library of Medicine); cf. U.S. Armed Forces. Medical Library, *Classification: Medicine . . . Prelim. ed., 1948* (Washington: Govt. Print. Off., 1949), p.ix; Leo LaMontagne, *American Library Classification, with Special Reference to the Library of Congress* (Hamden, Conn.: Shoe String Press, 1961), p.310, 369–70.

[3] U.S. Library of Congress, Classification Division, *Classification. Class D: Universal and Old World History* (Washington: Govt. Print. Off., 1916), p.4.

[4] Jack Mills, *A Modern Outline of Library Classification* (London: Chapman & Hall, 1960). viii, 196p.

[5] William Charles Berwick Sayers, *A Manual of Classification for Librarians and Bibliographers* (3d ed., rev.; London: Grafton, 1959). 346p.

[6] William Stetson Merrill, *Code for Classifiers: Principles Governing the Consistent Placing of Books in a System of Classification* (3d ed.; Chicago: American Library Association, 1954). xi, 177p.

[7] International Study Conference on Classification Research, 2d, Elsinore, Denmark, *Classification Research: Proceedings*; ed. by Pauline Atherton (Copenhagen: Munksgaard, 1965), p.106–7.

Chapter 3

Special Problems in Social and Political Sciences (Classes H and J)

Nicholas Hedlesky

Class H (Social Sciences)

Class H consists of major sections as indicated below:

SOCIAL SCIENCES
Synopsis

	ECONOMICS		SOCIOLOGY
H General Works	HB Theory		HM Theory
HA Statistics		History and Conditions	HN Social History
	HC	National Production	Social Groups
	HD	Land Agriculture	HQ The Family
		Industry	HS Associations
		Labor	HT Communities
	HE Transportation		Classes
		Communication	HV Social Pathology
	HF Commerce		HX Socialism
	HG Finance		Communism
	HJ Public Finance		

Another area of interest is the Tables of Geographical Divisions, I–X, shown in part in Figure 12 (p.46) (LC H schedule, p.527–32).

It may be seen that the classification is built on a hierarchical pattern, progressing from the general to the more specific in a logical order. This progression is illustrated by subclass HB (Economic Theory) in Figure 1. Some of the form subdivisions which appear in all subclasses are: Periodicals; Societies; Congresses; Collections; Encyclopedias and Dictionaries; History; and Biography.

From the form subdivisions the subclass moves on to those topics which are more specific in economic theory, such as: wealth, labor and wages, rent, capital and savings, etc., as underlined in Figures 2–3. These figures contain several examples of the cross references and the "Cf." notes with which the H schedule is

ECONOMIC THEORY

HB

Periodicals. Societies. Yearbooks.
1   English and American.
3   French.
5   German.
7   Italian.
9   Other.
21   Congresses. Exhibitions.

Collections.
       Cf. HB 151-179, Treatises.
    English.
31   Monographs by various authors.
33   Collected writings of individual authors.
         Prefer HB 151, 161, 171-172.
34   Essays, papers, etc.
35   Pamphlets.
36-40 French.
41-45 German (including Austrian). ⎫ Arranged like
46-50 Italian   ⎬ HB 31-35.
51-55 Other.   ⎭
61   Encyclopedias. Dictionaries.
71   Economics as a science. Scope, method, utility, etc.
72   Relation to philosophy, religion, ethics.
73   Relation to politics and law.
74   Relation to other special topics, A-Z.
        e. g. .M3 Mathematics.
              .P8   Psychology.
    Study and teaching, *see* H 62-67.

History of economics.
       History of economic theory. Economic history of countries
       in HC.
75   General works (including Modern general).

Biography.
    Collective.
76   General and Modern.
     Medieval, *see* HB 80.
    Individual, *see* HB 101-129.

By period.
77   Ancient.
79   Medieval.
80   Biography.

Figure 1

Economic theory.

Treatises, "systems," compends, textbooks.

    Medieval works with history in HB 79.

    Before Adam Smith (to 1776/89).

151	English and American.
153	French.
155	German.
157	Italian.
159	Other.
161–169	Classical period, 1776/89–1843/76.

        Subdivided like HB 151–159.   Cf. HB 171–179.

    Recent, 1843/76–

        Cf. HB 161–169.

171	English and American.
.5	Textbooks.

        Including outlines, syllabi, etc.

.7	Minor popular.
172	Pamphlets.
173	French.
175	German.
177	Italian.
179	Other.

General special.

195	Economics of war.

    Economics of distribution, *see* HB 771.

199	Other.

        e. g. Profit motive, economy of abundance, economic equality.

Value.

201	Theory.

    History of theory.

203	General.
205	By country, A–Z.

Price.

    Cf. HD 6977–7080, for works on cost of living.

221	Theory of price.
225	Index numbers.

        Cf. HG 223, Standard of value.

    History and collections of prices.

231	General (including Modern).
232	Early and Medieval.
233	Special, by subject, A–Z.

        For broad fields only.

        e. g.   .A3   Agricultural prices.

        Cf. HD 9000–9999, Special industries and trades.

235	By country, A–Z.

Figure 2

Economic theory.

    Price—Continued.

236   Regulation of prices.   By country, A–Z.

          .A3   General works.

          Cf. HB 845, Sumptuary laws.

251   Wealth.

301   Labor and wages.   Wage fund.

      Theory only; for Laboring classes, see HD 4801–8940.

401   Rent and land.

      Cf. HD 101–1395, Land and agriculture.

501   Capital. Saving.

      Including Capital and labor, but not Laboring classes.

      Cf. HB 301, Labor and wages.

      Biography of Karl Marx in HX 39.5.

  Interest and usury.

      Cf. HF 5681.I6, Commercial arithmetic.

      HG 1621–1639, Banking practice.

531   History.

535   Early works to Adam Smith, 1776.

539   Later works.

    Individual countries.

545   United States.

547   Individual states, A–W.

549   Other countries, A–Z.

601   Profit. Income.

      Prefer HC.

615   Risk and risk bearing.

  Property.

701   General works.   Ownership.

711   Private property.

715   Inheritance.

      Cf. HJ 5801–5819, Inheritance tax.

    Personal, see K; cf. HF 1263, etc.

    Public, see HD 3840–4730, State and municipal industries; HD 1266 and HJ 3803+, State domain, etc.; JK 1606–1686, etc.

751   Other special.

771   Distribution.

  Consumption.

801   General works.   Theoretical works.

805   Historical and descriptive works.

    Special.

821   Inequality of distribution of wealth.

831   Use of wealth.   Leisure classes, etc.

835   Ethics of wealth. "Mammonism."

838   Hoarding.   Misers.

Figure 3

furnished. These connections are made between H and other main classes as well as between the subclasses of H.

In addition to the above Synopsis, the H schedule includes a detailed outline (LC H schedule, p.vii–xxxiv) which provides the classifier with a guide to the organization of the classes and subclasses. Therefore, it will be most useful to devote major attention to the use of the principal tables with which Class H is provided, in particular to the means by which the literature of a class is subdivided: by country and, within each country, by category and topic.

Subdivision by country is achieved in Class H in two principal ways: first, by application of the Tables of Geographical Divisions (LC H schedule, p.527–32), and second, by special provision within the schedule itself. An example of special provision is found in HE2701–3560, "Railways, By country" (LC H schedule, p.121–29), part of which is shown in Figures 4, 5, and 6.

After the detailed provisions for material on United States railroads, a table appears for use with the class numbers provided for other countries: HE2801–3560 (Fig. 5). The assignable number range for each country is printed in the scheme, and the extent of this range (5 or 10 numbers) determines for each country which of the two columns of the table is to be used for subarrangement of material relating to it.

The detailed development of the United States numbers aids in interpreting similar specific captions in the "Other countries" numbers. Figure 4 illustrates this development. A comparison of "Directories" and "Guides" in HE shows that the United States has numbers HE2723 to HE2737, whereas for the same captions in "Other countries" (Fig. 5) there is only number 4 for a country with a 10-number range and number 2 for a country with a 5-number range. For instance, Canada has 10 numbers, HE2801–2810, and thus Canadian directories and guides are classed in HE2804 (Fig. 6). Honduras, on the other hand, has 5 numbers, HE2841–2845, and thus directories and guides of Honduras are found in HE2842.

Figure 7 reproduces part of another geographic division, this one in the HC subclass, "Economic History." Figures 8 and 9 show the table used for subarrangement of material in HC95–695.

To illustrate the use of this table, examples from Japan and Austria will be used. Japan has 5 numbers allocated to it in HC, 461 to 465 (Fig. 7). The 5-number column in Figure 8 is applied. Austria has 10 numbers allocated: HC261 to HC270 (Fig. 10). In the case of Austria the 10-number column of Figure 8 is applied.

A book about contemporary economic conditions in Austria, treated in a general way, is classed as shown in Figure 11a. Austria has 10 numbers: HC261–270. The call number in this case is HC265.K58. This is obtained by determining that the book is a "general" work in a "later" period, or number 5 in the 10-number column (Fig. 8), and therefore the fifth number of the range of numbers allocated to Austria, that is, 265. The Cutter number .K58 stands for the author.

Railways.   By country.
America.
United States—Continued.

2715	Associations. } Cf. HE 1003–1005.
2717	Congresses. }
2721	Directories of railroads.
	Cf. HE 1009.
2723	Directories of officials.
2725	Directories of stations.
	Guides for travelers, time tables.
2727	General.
2728	By railroad, A–Z.
2729	By place, A–Z.
	Guides for shippers.
2731	General.
2733	By railroad, A–Z.
2735	By place, A–Z.
2737	Special kinds of freight.
	e. g. Lumber, etc.
2741	Treatises (General).
	Administration, operation, etc.; for description, *see* HE 2751.
2751	History. Statistics, etc.
	Biography.
	Cf. HE 2723.
2752	Collective.
2754	Individual, A–Z.
2757	**Railways and the state. Public policy. By date.**
	Class here controversial and pamphlet material only. General works in HE 1051–1081. Cf. HE 2708, Note.
	By region.
2761	Atlantic to Mississippi. By date.
2763	Mississippi to Pacific. By date.
2765	To Canada. By date.
2767	To Mexico. By name of railroad.
2771	By state, A–W.
	Cf. HE 2709, Documents; HE 2710, Laws. .A1–19, Regions other than HE 2761–2767 Cf. HC 107.
2781	By city, A–Z.

Figure 4

Railways.   By country.
   America.
      United States—Continued.
2791   By railroad (or company), A–Z.
                     Under each: [1]
            2 nos.   3 nos.   7 nos.
               (1)   (1)   (1)   Charters.   By date.
                        (2)   (2)   Reports.
                                          (a) Directors.   President, etc.   (Serial).
                                          (b) Special.   By date.
                                 (3)   Regulations.
                                 (3b) Lists of officers, etc.
                                 (4)   Documents (Public documents and re-
                                          joinders, etc.)
                                 (5)   History.
               (2)   (3)[2]   (7)   Other (Nonofficial pamphlets, etc.).
                                          By date.

2801–3560   **Other countries.**
                     For Germany, *see* Note following HE 3560, p. 128–129.
            Under each:
            10 nos.   5 nos.
               (1)   (1)   Serial publications.
                                      Collections of documents: Statis-
                                          tics, laws, etc.
               .A1–6   Official.
               .A7–Z5   Nonofficial, other than (3).
               (2)   Separate documents.   By date.
               (3)   Laws, legislation, etc.   (other
                                      than serial publications).   By
                                      date.
                                      Including nonofficial compilations.
                                      Cf. (7) Public policy.
               (4)   (2)   Directories.   Guides.   Tables.
               (5)   (3)   General works.
               (6)   Administration.   Operation.
               (7)   Public policy.   (Railways and
                                      the state, and Railways and
                                      the public).

---

[1] If small railroads, use two or three successive Cutter numbers only.
[2] Not limited to nonofficial.   It is for anything other than charters or reports.

Figure 5

Railways. By country.
  Other countries.
    Under each—Continued.
      10 nos.   5 nos.

                    History. Statistics. Description, including preliminary surveys.
                         For serial publications prefer subdivision (1).

(8)		General.
		Biography.
.1		Collective.
.2		Individual, A–Z.
(9)	(4)	Local, A–Z.
		For Colonial railways use:
		Documents.
.Z4		Serial.
.Z5		Special. By date.
.Z6		Law. By date.
.Z7A–Z		Nonofficial. By author.
(10)	(5)	Special railroads or companies, A–Z.

(10)	2801–2810	**Canada.**
	2811–2820	**Mexico.**
(5)	2821–2825	**Central America.**
	2824.B7	British Honduras.
	2826–2830	Panama.
	2831–2835	Costa Rica.
	2836–2840	Guatemala.
(5)	2841–2845	Honduras.
	2846–2850	Nicaragua.
	2851–2855	Salvador.
	2856–2860	**West Indies.**
	2861–2865	Bahamas.
	2866–2870	Cuba.
	2871–2875	Haiti.
	2876–2880	Jamaica.
	2881–2885	Puerto Rico.
	2886–2890	Other.
	2891–2900	**South America.**
(10)	2901–2910	Argentine Republic.
(10)	2911–2920	Bolivia.

Figure 6

	By country.[1]
	Europe—Continued.
401–410	**Turkey and Balkan states.**
407	Balkan states, A–Z.
408	Turkish provinces or districts, A–Z.
409	Cities, A–Z.
411–415	**Asia.**
416–420	Afghanistan.
426–430	China.
431–440	India.
	Including the Republic of India.
439	Famines.
440.5	Pakistan.
441–445	Indochina.
446–450	Indonesia. Dutch East Indies.
451–460	Philippine Islands.
461–465	Japan.
466–470	Korea.
471–480	Persia. Iran.
481–490	Russia in Asia.
491–495	Turkey in Asia.
	Turkish Republic in HC 401–410.
497	Other Asiatic countries, A–Z.
	e. g. .A6 Arabia.
	.A7 Armenia.
	.M4 Mesopotamia. Iraq.
	.P2 Palestine.
	.S5 Siam. Thailand.
501–505	**Africa.**
511–520	British possessions.
517	Local, A–Z.
	e. g. .R4 Rhodesia.
	.S7 South Africa.
531–540	Egypt (Modern).
	Cf. HC 33, Ancient Egypt.
541–550	French possessions.
551–560	German possessions (Former).
561–570	Italian possessions.
571–575	Spanish possessions.
576–580	Portuguese possessions.

[1] For subarrangement, see Tables, p. 23.

Figure 7

HC

95–695   (*Change to* "95–710."   *Revise table below.*)   *p. 23*

Under each:

Cutter no.[1]	5 nos.	10 nos.	
1		1	Collections.
			Including periodicals, societies, documents.
.xA1–3	.A1–3	.A1–3	Periodicals. Serial documents. Separate documents.
.xA4	.A4	.A4	Administrative documents. By date. Other documents to be classed with general works.
		2	Dictionaries. Directories.
	.5	.5	Biography.
			Prefer specific industries.
		.A2	Collective.
		.A3–Z	Individual.
.xA5–Z	2	3	General works.
	.5	.5	Natural resources. By period.
			Period divisions vary for different countries. Cf. corresponding divisions in HF 3001–4040.
		4	Early, including Medieval.
		5	Later.
.x2A–Z	3		Local.
		7	By state, etc., A–Z.
		8	By city, A–Z.
			Annual (local) reviews of "Commerce," "Finance," "Trade," etc., HF 3163 and HF 3211–4040, subdivision (10) under each country; general, in HC 14.
	4	9	Colonies.
			Exploitation and economic conditions. Colonial administration and policy in JV.

---

[1]. X = cutter number.   Substitute the cutter number for the country for .X in the table, for example HC 337.P7–73, Poland.

Figure 8

HC

95–695   (*Change to* "95–710."   *Revise table below.*)   *p. 23*

               Under each—Continued

.x3   5   10   Special topics (not otherwise provided for), A–Z.

           .A8   Auditing and inspection of state enterprises.

                  Use limited to socialist countries.

                  Cf. HD 3840–4420, State industries.

           .A9   Automation.

           .C3   Capital.

           .C6   Consumer demand.

           .C7   Costs (Industrial).

           .D5   Distribution of industry.

           .D6   Diversification in industry.

           .F3   Famines.

                  Famines in India, *see* HC 439.

           .I5   Income.

           .I53   Industrial promotion.

           .I6   Inventories.

           .L3   Labor productivity.

           .P3   Patents.

           .P7   Profit.

           .S2   Sabotage.   Espionage.

                  Cf. HD 5473, Labor disputes.

           .S3   Saving and investment.

           .S6   Socialist competition. Stakhanov movement.

           .S8   Strategic materials.

           .S9   Subsidies.

           .T4   Technological innovations.

           .W3   Waste.

           .W4   Wealth.

           .Z6   Economic zoning.

Figure 9

By country.[1]
    South America—Continued.

231–235	Uruguay.
236–239	Venezuela.
240	**Europe.**
243	Northern Europe. Baltic states.
	British Empire.
245	Collections.
246	General.
247	Local (not elsewhere provided for), A-Z.

              e. g.   .C8   Cyprus.

251–260	**Great Britain.**
253	General comprehensive.
	By period.
254	Middle ages.
.3	Manorial system.
.5	1600–1800.
255	19th century.

              Including general modern.

256	20th century.
.2	European war, 1914–1918.
.3	Reconstruction, 1919–1939.
.4	World war, 1939–1945.
.5	Reconstruction, 1945–
261–270	**Austria. Austro-Hungarian Empire.**

              Including the Danube Valley.

267.A2	Hungary.
.B2	Bohemia. Czechoslovak Republic.
271–280	**France.**
274	To 1600.
275	1601–1900.
276	1901–
281–290	**Germany.**
286	20th century.
.2	European war, 1914–1918.
.3	Reconstruction, 1919–1939.
.4	World war, 1939–1945.
.5	Reconstruction, 1945–
287	States, A–Z. —————————.A2 Democratic Republic, 1949–

        e. g.   .A3   Alsace-Lorraine.
               .B2   Baden.
               .B3   Bavaria.
               .B7   Brunswick.
               .F8   Friesland, East.

---

[1] For subarrangement, unless otherwise provided for, *see* Tables, p. 23.

Figure 10

HC265
.K58

Kobatsch, Rudolf, 1868–
   Die österreichische Volkswirtschaft. Wien, C. Fromme
[°1918]

   93 p.   17 cm.   (Österreichische Bücherei; eine Sammlung auf-
klärender Schriften über Österreich. 4. Bdchn.)

1. Austria—Econ. condit.   (Series)

HC265.K58   52–53642

Library of Congress   [3]

HC462
.A614

Allen, George Cyril, 1900–
   Japan's economic recovery. London, New York, Oxford
University Press, 1958.
   215 p.   23 cm.
   Includes bibliography.

1. Japan—Econ. condit.—1945–   I. Title.

HC462.A614   330.952   58–1672 ‡

Library of Congress   [7]

Figure 11b

A similar work for Japan would receive the number for a "general" work (see Fig. 11b), or the second number under the 5-number table. This would lead us to the second number of the range of numbers for Japan (HC461–465) or HC462.

The other common method of subdivision by country in Class H is by application of the Tables of Geographical Divisions (LC H schedule, p.527–32), the first portion of which is shown in Figure 12. Indications for the use of these geographic tables are given at many points in the schedules. For example (Fig. 13), in HD (Economic History) at the spread of numbers 8101–8942 "Labor. By country. Other countries," geographic Table VIII is specified, "modified." The word "modified" indicates that following the "Under each" statement are special provisions to be used in the particular spread of numbers. At the end of Figure 14 is a modification note concerning the Pacific Islands.

Under VIII in the Tables (Fig. 12) there are two sets of numbers in parentheses. The first set (840) indicates that a total of 840 numbers has been allocated to "Other countries" for this topic. The second set (10; 20) indicates the number of subdivisions provided for use under each country (Figs. 13–14).

45

TABLES OF GEOGRAPHICAL DIVISIONS

The first number in curves (100), (200), etc., below the Roman numeral at head of column indicates the total number of divisions comprised in that table; the second number in curves (1), (2), (5; 10), etc., indicates the number of subdivisions assigned to any one country in a given table.

May be modified to meet the requirements of special subjects, where different order and different distribution of numbers is desired.

I	II	III	IV		V	VI	VII	VIII	IX	X
(100)	(200)	(300)	(400)		(130)	(200)	(830)	(840)	(420)	(1000)
(1)	(2)	(2)	(4)		(1; 4)	(2; 5)	(5; 10)	(10; 20)	(5; 10)	(5;10)
1	1	1	1	America	1	1	......	......	......	11
2	3	3	3	North America	2	2				21
3	5	5	5	United States	3-6	3				31
4	7	8	9	Northeastern (New England).						41
5	9	11	13	Atlantic						51
6	11	14	17	South (Gulf, etc.)						61
7	13	17	21	Central						71
8	15	20	25	Lake region (St. Lawrence Valley).						81
9	17	23	29	Mississippi Valley and West.						91
10	19	26	33	Southwest (south of Missouri and west of the Mississippi River).						101
11	21	29	37	Northwest, and Rocky Mountains.						111
12	23	32	41	Pacific coast						121
	----	----	----	Colonial possessions						-----
13	25	35	45	States, A–W (see p. 537)		8				131
14	27	38	49	Cities, A–Z (see p. 539)		9				141
15	29	41	53	Canada, British N. A.	7-10	10	11-20	1-10	1-10	151
	----	----	----	Provinces, A–Z						-----
16	31	44	57	Mexico	11	12	21	11	11	161
	----	----	----	States, A–Z						-----
17.A1-5	33	47	61	Central America	13.A1-5	14	31	21	16	171
17.A6-Z	35	48	65	British Honduras	13.A6-Z	......	36	26	19	181
18	37	49	69	Costa Rica	14	......	41	31	21	191
19	39	52	73	Guatemala	15	......	51	41	26	201
20	40	55	75	Honduras	16	......	61	51	31	211
21	41	57	77	Nicaragua	17	......	71	61	36	216
22	42	59	79	Panama	18	......	81	71	41	221
22.5	43.5	61	80	Panama Canal Zone	18.5	......	86	76	45 5	226
23	44.	62	81	Salvador	19	......	91	81	46	231
I	II	III	IV		V	VI	VII	VIII	IX	X

Provinces, A–Z:

Alberta.	Newfoundland.
Assiniboia.	Northwest Territories.
Athabasca.	Nova Scotia.
British Columbia.	Ontario (Upper Canada).
Franklin.	Prince Edward Island.
Keewatin.	Quebec (Lower Canada).
Labrador.	Saskatchewan.
Mackenzie.	Ungava.
Manitoba.	Yukon.
New Brunswick.	

Figure 12

    Labor. By country.
      <u>United States</u>—Continued.

	Labor in politics.
8076	General works.
8079	Local, A–Z.
(8080)	Negro labor, *see* E 185.8.
8081	Immigrant labor, by race, A–Z.

          .A1–5 General.
          .A5   Nonofficial works.
          Under each (using successive Cutter numbers):
            .A1–5 General.
                    Documents.
            .A15   Serial.
            .A2   Other. By date.
            .A6–Z Nonofficial works.

| 8083 | By state or region, A–W. |
| 8085 | By city, A–Z. |

          Under each:
            (1) Associations (General).
            (2) Directories.
            (3) Other.

8101–8942   **Other countries. Table VIII,[1] modified.**

          In connection with HD 8455, compare HD 7887–7889 and
          HX 279.
        Under each:

20 nos.	10 nos.	5 nos.	
			Documents.
(1)	(1)	(1)	General.
			Department of labor.
			e. g. "Ministère du travail."
.A1–3			Serial publications, in order of priority of first issue.
.A4–9			Special bureaus.
			Legislative documents.
.B1–4			House.
			Serial.
			Special.
.B5–8			Senate.
			Serial.
			Special.
.C			Commissions. By date.
(2)			State.
(3)	(2)	(2)	Associations and periodicals.

               To include non-technical reports of
                  mechanics institutes, Gewerbever-
                  eine, etc. Technical publications,
                  in T.

---

[1] For Table VIII, *see* p. 527–532. Add country number in Table to <u>8100</u>.   **Base number**

Figure 13

Labor. By country.

8101–8942   **Other countries.   Table VIII.** [1]

Under each—Continued.

20 nos.	10 nos.	5 nos.	
(4)			Conferences.
(5)	(3)		Annuals.
(6)			Directories.
(7)			Statistics.
(8)	(4)	(3)	History (General).
			General works and history. By period.
(9)	(5)		Early to 1848.
(10)	(6)		Later, 1849–
(13)	(7)		Biography, A–Z.
			.A1 Collective.
	(8)		Labor in politics.
(15)			General works.
(16)			Chartist movement (Great Britain).
(17)			Local, A–Z.
(18)	(8.5)		Immigrant labor, by race, A–Z.
			e. g. .A2 General works.
			.N5 Negro.
(19)	(9)	(4)	By state, A–Z.
			Under each:
			(1) Collections. (Documents in subdivisions (1)–(2) above).
			(2) General works. History.
			(3) Other.
(20)	(10)	(5)	By city, A–Z.
			Under each:
			(1) Early to 1848.
			(2) 1848–

(Modification)

NOTE.   For Pacific islands use:

8931	General.	
8933	American possessions.	
8934	Hawaii.	
8935	Other.	
8936–8937	British possessions.	Under each:
8938–8939	French possessions.	(1) General.
8940–8941	German possessions (Former).	(2) Local, A–Z.
8942	Other.	

---

[1] For Table VIII, *see* p. 527–532.   Add country number in Table to 8100.

Figure 14

Europe—Continued.

I	II	III	IV	Name	V	VI	VII	VIII	IX	X
47	91	136	181	Austria	49–52	66	331	301	151	471
				States and Provinces A–Z	....	......	......	......	......	.....

States and Provinces (Austria):

Austria, Lower.	Görz and Gradiska.
Austria, Upper.	Istria.
Bohemia.	Moravia.
Bosnia and Herzegovina.	Salzburg.
Buckowina.	Silesia.
Carinthia.	Styria.
Carniola.	Trieste.
Dalmatia.	Tyrol.
Galicia.	Vorarlberg.

I	II	III	IV	Name	V	VI	VII	VIII	IX	X
				Czechoslovak Republic[1]	....	......	......	......	......	.....
	....	....	....	Hungary [1]	....	......	......	......	......	.....
	....	....	....	Croatia and Slavonia [1]	....	......	......	......	......	.....
	....	....	....	Transylvania [1]	....	......	......	......	......	.....
	....	....	....	Liechtenstein [1]	....	......	......	......	......	.....
48	93	139	185	France	53–56	70	341	321	161	481
	....	....	....	Colonial possessions in general.	....	......	......	......	......	.....
	....	....	....	Andorra	....	......	......	......	......	.....
	....	....	....	Monaco	....	......	......	......	......	.....
49	95	142	189	Germany	57–60	75	351	341	171	491

States (Germany):

Alsace-Lorraine.	Oldenburg.
Anhalt.	PRUSSIA.
BADEN.	Reuss, Elder branch.
BAVARIA.	Reuss, Younger branch.
Bremen.	Saxe-Altenburg.
Brunswick.	Saxe-Coburg-Gotha.
Hamburg.	Saxe-Meiningen.
Hanover.	Saxe-Weimar.
Hesse.	SAXONY.
Lippe.	Schaumburg-Lippe.
Lübeck.	Schwarzburg-Rudolstadt.
Mecklenburg-Schwerin.	Schwarzburg-Sondershausen.
	Thuringia.
Mecklenburg-Strelitz.	Waldeck.
	WÜRTTEMBERG.

I	II	III	IV	Name	V	VI	VII	VIII	IX	X
	....	....	....	Colonial possessions in general.	....	......	......	......	......	.....
50	97	145	193	Greece	61	80	361	361	181	501
51	99	148	197	Italy	62–65	85	371	371	186	511
	....	....	....	San Marino	....	......	......	......	......	.....
52	101	151	201	Netherlands (Low Countries)	....	90	381	391	196	521
53	103	154	205	Belgium	66–69	95	391	401	201	531
54	105	157	209	Netherlands (Holland)	70–73	100	401	411	206	541
54.5	106.5	159.5	212.5	Luxemburg	73.5	104.5	410.5	420.5	210.5	550.5
55	107	160	213	Russia	74–77	105	411	421	211	551
55.2	108.2	162.2	216.2	Estonia	77.2	109.2	420.5	430.2	215.3	560.5
55.3	108.3	162.3	217	Finland	77.3	110	421	431	215.5	561
55.5	108.5	162.5	217.5	Latvia	77.5	110.5	425.5	435.5	215.6	565.5
55.6	108.6	162.6	217.6	Lithuania	77.6	110.6	425.7	435.7	215.65	565.6
55.7	108.7	162.7	218	Poland	77.7	111	426	436	215.7	566
56	109	163	219	Scandinavia	78	112	430	440	216	570
57	111	166	221	Denmark	79	115	431	441	221	571
58	113	169	225	Iceland	......	120	441	451	226	581
59	115	172	229	Norway	80	125	451	461	231	591
60	117	175	233	Sweden	81–84	130	461	471	236	601
I	II	III	IV		V	VI	VII	VIII	IX	X

[1] May be arranged with "States and Provinces."

Figure 15

The number of such subdivisions can also be derived from each of Tables I–X by observing the size of the gap or gaps left between the numbers for the countries. In the case of Table VIII, gaps of 5, 10, and 20 are used; accordingly (see Figs. 12 and 15), the second line at the head of the column should have read (5; 10; 20), as confirmed by the table in Figures 13 and 14), which has columns for 5, 10, and 20 numbers. In short, the number span for a country specified in or derived from the designated Tables I–X will match one of the provisions of the "Under each" table given in the schedule proper.

The procedure for deriving a class number from the geographic divisions is the following: select from the range of numbers assigned to a country the appropriate number by applying the topical table, and then add this number to the base number which is indicated in a footnote in each case.

A book dealing with labor in Austria in recent times will illustrate the procedure. HD8101–8942 are the numbers for "Labor. By country. Other countries. Table VIII." It will be seen that Austria has 20 numbers, 301–320 (Fig. 15). The

Figure 16a

```
HD8410
.G3
            Garzarolli, Grete, 1900–
                    Erbarbeiter der Ostmark.  Geleitwort von Hans Mal-
                zacher.  Wien, A. Luser, 1940.

                67, [1] p.  illus.  19 cm.

                Bibliography: p. [68]




                1. Labor and laboring classes—Austria.      I. Title.

                                          Full name: Margarethe (von Scheuer)
                                                        Garzarolli von Thurnlackh.

                HD8410.G3                 331.8                  A 51–1862

                New York.  Public Libr.
                for Library of Congress         [3]†
```

```
HD8419
.H92S9
            Szántó, Béla.
                    A magyar munkásmozgalom 1914-ig.  Budapest [Athe-
                naeum, 1947]

                204 p.  18 cm.  (Athenaeum könyvek)

                Bibliographical footnotes.




                1. Labor and laboring classes—Hungary.      I. Title.

                HD8419.H92S9                                     59–53121

                Library of Congress              [8]
```

Figure 16b

number 320 is not printed under column VIII in Figure 15. but since France begins with 321, the inference is clear that Austria ends with 320. By looking at the directions under "Other countries" (Figs. 13–14), it will be seen that there are provisions for 5, 10, and 20 numbers; Austria, having 20 numbers, must use the 20-number column. The book deals with labor in Austria after 1850; by going through the captions and their numerical equivalents under the 20-number spread, the classifier would find "History. By period. Later. 1849–   " with the numerical equivalent of 10. Since Table VIII has shown that Austria has numbers 301–320, the tenth number of the sequence is selected, i.e. 310, and this is added to the base number indicated at the bottom of Figure 13: 8100. By adding these, 8100 + 310, the classifier arrives at the correct class number for the book— HD8410.

Another example may prove helpful. The classifier has a similar title on the contemporary history of labor in Hungary. Hungary is shown (Fig. 15) in Table VIII, under Austria, with a footnote indicating that it is to be classed as "States

ILLUSTRATION OF USE OF GEOGRAPHICAL AND TOPICAL TABLES

HD	Economic History
	Labor
8101–8942	Other countries. Base number: 8100
	Austria: 301–320 (20 numbers) in Table VIII
8401	General documents
8402	State documents
8403	Associations and periodicals
8404	Conferences
8405	Annuals
8406	Directories
8407	Statistics
8408	History (General)
8409	Early to 1848
8410	Later. 1849–
(8411)	
(8412)	
8413	Biography. A–Z
(8414)	
	Labor in politics
8415	General works
8416	Chartist movement (Great Britain)
8417	Local, A–Z
8418	Immigrant labor, by race. A–Z
8419	By state, A–Z
8420	By city, A–Z

Figure 17

Agriculture. By country—Continued.

1781–2206 Other countries. Table IX,[1] modified.
Under each:
10 nos. 5 nos.

Cutter no.	no.	10 nos.	5 nos.	
.X	A1-5	(1)	(1)	Documents.
				Law in HD 311–1130, subdivision (2).
.X2	A6-Z7		(2)	History and description.
		(3)		General.
		(4)		Medieval.
		(5)		Modern.
.X3	Z8	(7)	(3)	Policy. By date.
		(10)	(5)	Local, A–Z.

NOTE. Pacific islands.
Under each:
(1) General.
(2) Local, A–Z.

2196	General.
2198	American possessions.
2199	Hawaii.
2200	Other.
2201–2202	British possessions.
2203–2204	French possessions.
2205–2206	German possessions (Former).

Figure 18

and Provinces," since Hungary was considered as a territorial division of Austria when the H Class was originally drawn up. From the captions in Figure 14 the classifier notes that "By state, A–Z" has the numerical equivalent of 19; the nineteenth number of Austria's spread would be 319. Added to the base number of 8100, 319 would give the correct class number of HD8419. Since states and provinces are arranged A to Z, a Cutter number for Hungary must be added: .H92 in this instance, so that the class number is HD8419.H92.

Figures 16a and 16b illustrate examples of two works on labor and laboring classes in Austria and Hungary, respectively. The complete class numbers for these books are HD8410.G3 (.G3 represents the author notation) and HD8419.H92S9 (.H92 represents Hungary and S9 is the author notation). Figure 17 is a representation of the complete sequence of 20 numbers as written out for Austria.

To give another illustration of the use of the Tables of Geographical Divisions, Figure 18 shows that in HD1781–2206, "Economic History. Agriculture. Other

TABLES OF GEOGRAPHICAL DIVISIONS

I	II	III	IV		V	VI	VII	VIII	IX	X
				Europe—Continued.						
	----	----	----	Spain and Portugal ----						
61	119	178	237	Spain	85–88	135	471	481	241	611
62	121	181	241	Portugal	89	140	481	491	246	621
63	123	184	245	Switzerland	90	145	491	501	251	631
				CANTONS:						
				Aargau. Schaffhausen.						
				Appenzell a. R. Schwyz.						
				Appenzell i. R. Solothurn.						
				Basel Land. Thurgau.						
				Basel Stadt. Ticino.						
				Bern. Unterwalden, Lower.						
				Fribourg. Unterwalden, Upper.						
				Genève. Uri.						
				Glarus. Valais.						
				Graubünden. Vaud.						
				Luzern. Zug.						
				Neuchâtel. Zürich.						
				St. Gallen.						
64	125	187	249	Turkey and Balkan States (and Turkey alone).	91	150	501	511	256	641
	----	----	----	Albania	91.4	----	----	----	260.5	----
65	127	190	253	Bulgaria	91.5	----	511	521	261	651
65.5	128.5	192	255	Yugoslavia	91.6	----	521	531	265.5	661
66	129	194	257	Montenegro	91.7	----	526	536	266	666
67	131	196	261	Rumania	91.8	----	531	541	271	671
68	133	199	265	Serbia	91.9	----	541	551	276	681
	----	----	----	Near East		----	----	----	280.5	----
69	135	202	269	Asia	92	155	551	561	281	691
70	137	205	273	China	93–96	157	561	571	286	701

Before expansion

Figure 19

countries," Table IX, modified, is to be used. (The modification again is shown at the bottom of Fig. 18.) For a work on the economic aspects of agriculture in Austria, the classifier refers to Table IX (Fig. 15) to secure the country numbers, 151–160. Since there is a 10-number spread for Austria the classifier must use the 10-number column in Figure 18. For a history of the topic in modern times, the classifier would locate the caption "Modern" under "History and description," note the numerical equivalent of 5, use the fifth number of Austria's spread, 155, add it to the base number for "Other countries" which is 1780, and arrive at the correct class number for the book: HD1935.

Expansion of Class H may take place within the geographic tables as well as in the schedules proper. To illustrate the method of expansion through the Tables of Geographical Divisions two illustrations may be compared: Figures 19 and 20. Figure 19 shows blank spaces available for possible numerical expansion (dotted lines), and Figure 20 shows new numbers provided for Albania and the Near East. Note also the single number and Cutter expansion provided for some minor

Nicholas Hedlesky

ADDITIONS AND CHANGES TO JANUARY 1964

(*Add to* "Tables of Geographical Divisions" *as indicated*.)   p. 528–532

I	II	III	IV		V	VI	VII	VIII	IX	X
			85	West Indies. Caribbean area...						
			185	France_____						
				Andorra, *see* Other European, A–Z (68.5.A5, etc.)						
				Monaco, *see* Other European, A–Z (68.5.M6, etc.)						
			197	Italy_____						
				San Marino, *see* Other European, A–Z (68.5.S7, etc.)						
			201	Netherlands (Low Countries)².	65.5					

After expansion

(*Align with footnote*, p. 529.)

² Including Benelux Economic Union where applicable.

I	II	III	IV		V	VI	VII	VIII	IX	X
64.5	126.5	189.5	252.5	Albania_____	91.4	154.4	510.5	520.5	260.5	650.5
				Bulgaria_____		154.5				
				Yugoslavia_____		154.6				
				Montenegro_____		154.7				
				Rumania_____		154.8				
				Serbia_____		154.9				
68.5	134.5	201.5	268.5	Other European, A–Z_____	91.95	154.95	550.5	560.5	280.4	690.5
				.A5 Andorra_____						
				.G5 Gibraltar_____						
				.M3 Malta_____						
				.M6 Monaco_____						
				.S7 San Marino_____						
68.8	134.8	201.8	268.8	Near East_____	91.98	154.98	550.8	560.8	280.5	690.5

Figure 20

European areas. The full impact of these additional expansion numbers found in the Tables of Geographical Divisions lies in the fact that each new number results in many classes when applied throughout the H schedule. Figure 21 contains a list of the pages in the H schedule in which directions to use one of the Tables I–X appear. From it the number of classes generated by the addition of a country may be ascertained for each of the tables. For example, a single new number appearing under column I of the geographical tables may, in fact, represent 15 new and different numbers throughout Class H. There may be as many as 34 new numbers appearing throughout Class H by means of providing a single new number under column V in the Table of Geographical Divisions. In sum, a new country could generate 89 new classes.

Among the special provisions in Class H for geographical and topical subdivision attention might be called to those for material on special industries and trades in economic history: HD9000–9999. The four tables of subdivisions A–D, (LC H schedule, p.96–98), as shown in Figures 22, 23, and 24, are to be applied to each class according to the number range provided for the class: 20, 11,

PAGES WHERE GEOGRAPHICAL DIVISION TABLES I–X
ARE USED IN THE H SCHEDULE

Table I (15)	71, 73, 74, 99, 101, 112, 117, 119, 134, 135, 169, 171, 219, 499, 509
Table II (10)	17, 18, 19, 113, 120, 133, 156, 167, 191, 396
Table III (2)	174, 501
Table IV (2)	130, 161
Table V (34)	48, 49, 50, 51, 54, 58, 59, 60, 61, 62, 64, 72, 74, 76, 104–106, 166, 222, 230, 394, 395, 400, 404, 406, 409, 413, 426, 466, 468, 469, 471, 507, 519, 520, 526
Table VI (3)	221, 233, 238
Table VII (5)	35, 150, 153, 168, 172
Table VIII (5)	85, 202, 215, 228, 391
Table IX (12)	44, 53, 69, 405, 446, 455, 461, 465, 480, 497, 522, 525
Table X (1)	143
Total number of pages (89)	

Figure 21

1, or a Cutter number. The instructions in the schedule, together with the foregoing exposition on the use of other tables, should clarify the manner of class
number construction in this area.

Class J (Political Science)

The principal subclasses of Class J (Political Science) are as follows:

J	Official documents
JA	Collections and General works
JC	Political theory
	Constitutional history and administration
JF	General. Comparative
JK	United States
JL	British America. Latin America
JN	Europe
JQ	Asia. Africa. Australia. Pacific Islands
JS	Local government

JV   Colonies and colonization
     Emigration and immigration
JX   International law. International relations

Except for the placement of Civil Service at the end of JF, the same general
sequence of topics is used for all of the subclasses of "Constitutional history and
administration": JF (General and comparative); JK (United States); JL, JN, JQ
(Other countries); JS (Local government).

Tables of subdivisions under Industries and Trades
(HD 9000–9999)

Under each:

A	B	
20 nos.	11 nos.	
0	0	General.
.1	.1	Periodicals. Congresses. Associations of dealers (International). International boards, etc.
		Manufacturers' associations formed with particular reference to labor questions in HD 6515, etc.
.2	.2	Annuals.
.3	.3	Directories.
		Prefer T for manufactures.
.4	.4	Statistics, prices, etc.
.5	.5	General works. History.
.6	.6	Policy.
.65	.65	Manuals.
		Law and legislation.
		Cf. HD 7801–8023.
.7	.7	General.
		.A1A–Z General works.
		.A2–Z By country.
		Under each:
		(1) Documents.
		(2) Monographs. By author.
.8	.8	Taxation.
		Subdivided like .7.
		Cf. HJ, and HF 2651 (Industries and tariff) preferring HF in doubtful cases. If here, .85 may be used for customs taxation.

Figure 22

Tables of subdivisions under Industries and Trades
(HD 9000–9999)

Under each:

A   B
20 nos. 11 nos.

General.

Law and legislation—Continued.

.9	.9	Inspection.
		Subdivide like .7.
		Inspection of product; factory inspection in HD 3656–3790, etc.
.95	.95	Bounties.
		By country.
		Colonies with mother country.
	1	United States.
1	.1	Collections, associations, etc.
		.A4–49 Associations of dealers.
2	.2	Annuals.
3	.3	Directories.
		Prefer T for manufactures.
4	.4	Statistics, prices, etc.
		May be subdivided: 4.3 or .43, Export trade; 4.5 or .45, Import trade.
5	.5	General works. History.
		May be subdivided: 5.3 or .53, Early; 5.46 or .46, 1860–1866; 5.5 or .55, 1866–1900; 5.6 or .56, 1900–
6	.6	Policy.
7	.7	By state, A–W.
		May be divided as under HD 9757.
8	.8	By city, A–Z.
9	.9	By firm, etc., A–Z.
10	.95	Biography.
11	2	Great Britain.
.1	.1	Collections, associations, etc.
		.A4–49 Associations of dealers.
.2	.2	Annuals.
.3	.3	Directories.
		Prefer T for manufactures.
.4	.4	Statistics, prices, etc.
.5	.5	General works. History.
.6	.6	Policy.
.7	.7	By state, A–Z.
		May be subdivided: .A3, Scotland; .A5, Ireland; .A7, Wales; .A8–Z, Counties.
.8	.8	By city, A–Z.
.9	.9	By firm, etc., A–Z.

Figure 23

Tables of subdivisions under Industries and Trades
(HD 9000–9999)

Under each:

  A   B

20 nos. 11 nos.

             By country—Continued.

  12   3   France.
                 Subdivided like Great Britain.

  13   4   Germany.
                 Subdivided like Great Britain.

             Other countries.
                 Under each:
                   (1) Collections   Serials.
                   (2) General works.
                   (3) Local, A–Z.
                   (4) Firms, etc., A–Z.

  14   5   America, A–Z.
  15   6   Europe, A–Z.
  16   7   Asia, A–Z.
  17   8   Africa, A–Z.
  18   9   Other.
  19 10   Special, A–Z.
                 Under each (using successive Cutter numbers):
                  Four numbers: (1) Serials, (2) General, (3) Local, A–Z,
                    (4) Firms, A–Z.
                  Three numbers: (1) Serials, (2) General, (3) Local, A–Z.
                  Two numbers: (1) General, (2) Local, A–Z.
                  In case only two or three numbers are indicated, others
                    may be established. If desired, "Local" may include
                    "Firms."   The practice of omitting Cutter numbers
                    ending in "one" is generally observed at the Library
                    of Congress. For example HD 9019.H7–72, Hops,
                    is read: .H7, General; H72, Local; .H71 is not used;
                    .H69 may be established for "Serials" and .H73 for
                    "Firms."

C (One number).
      .A1   Collections.
      .A2   General works.
      .A3   Law and legislation.   By country, A–Z.
      .A4–Z By country.
             Under each:
                (1) Collections.
                (2) General works.
                (3) Local, A–Z.
                (4) Firms, etc., A–Z.

D (Cutter numbers), *see* note to HD 9999, p. 94.

Figure 24

The synopsis for the United States which follows is representative of the subdivisions under JL–JQ:

> Constitutional history
> Federal and state relations
> Government. Administration
>> The Executive
>> The Departments. The Civil Service
>> Congress. The Legislative department
>> The Judiciary
>> Government property
> Politics. Civil rights
>> Citizenship
>> Naturalization
>> Suffrage
>> Electoral system
> Political parties
> State government

The Library of Congress now classifies material on the judiciary in Law (Class K).

Two sections of the JK subclass depart from the general pattern slightly. The first, state government of the United States (JK2403–9593), begins with a general section applicable to all the states; then a section follows with the special states, which includes a table of subdivisions for use under them—a table which might be called a miniaturization of the general pattern outlined above.

The terminal section of JK (9661–9995) is a special scheme developed to handle the documents and constitutional history of the Confederate States of America.

Subclasses JL, JN, and JQ (constitutional history in countries other than the United States) have general tables at the end of the JQ subclass, which are applied in the three subclasses unless special schemes are provided within the schedules. JS (Local government) also includes tables of subdivisions under states and cities; all local government of states and cities is treated in JS, not in the preceding subclasses. These tables for JL–JS are applied in the same way as are those of the H schedule and do not represent new practices or problems.

Discussion

Question: How sensitive is H to political change?

Dr. Bead: The Library of Congress makes an attempt to adjust all classification schedules to the political changes that have taken place. For the most part, we cannot completely redevelop all geographical arrangements to reflect these changes, because in many areas this would lead to a complete reorganization of the classification. Generally, we proceed on the following basis: If a new jurisdiction emerges, as in some regions of Africa, and if that jurisdiction is substantially identical in territory and population with its predecessor—for example, Ghana as a successor to the Gold Coast—we continue using the same span of class numbers. However, we expand the caption in the classification schedule so that it will show the name of the old and the new country, e.g. Ghana (Gold Coast), and, furthermore, we may add a new subdivision indicating the period for the newly emerged state.

When a new country comes into existence that is not substantially identical with a previous jurisdiction, we have to make special provision for it by inserting a new caption and class number.

This summary is a brief description of what we do to keep the schedules up to date. It is true that we have not been able to achieve this goal in all fields. Some updating remains to be done in several history classes and particularly in Classes H and J. However, as I said, this will not be accomplished by complete recasting, but rather by adapting the schedules to the new situation, so that we have a continuation of the existing classes with new terminology unless we make special provision for a newly created jurisdiction.

Question: In regard to the geographical tables, Hungary has not belonged to Austria for the last fifty years, as is true of the Czechoslovak Republic and others. In the same way the United States is not called Great Britain. Why doesn't LC change their schedules accordingly?

Mr. Angell: Hungary turns up in our schedules as a province of Austria not because we like tradition, but because at one time Hungary was a province of Austria. It is perfectly true that much of the general shape of Class D reflects the state of Europe at the time of the First World War. The preface to the second edition of the D schedule attempts to say something like this: If we left Europe as it was in 1919, this would be obviously intolerable. If we attempted to change everything in accordance with that and subsequent treaties, we would be exposing ourselves and other libraries to an amount of change that they and we would find unacceptable.

You may very well have heard this problem expounded in connection with another classification. This is the geographical and political windmill that classifiers are tilting at. As long as Hungary has its own designation, its placement, it does not mean that we do not know what has happened, or that we like it; in our best judgment, we have spent our time on more important changes.

Question: Does the history of a particular bank warrant its being classed with local history? For example, is the history of the First National Bank of Mobile classed with the history of Mobile?

Mr. Hedlesky: In all probability it is not classed with local history. However, there is always the possibility that it may go into local history depending on the intent of the author or the emphasis of the book.

Let us take, for an example, cattle trade in the Far West, with emphasis on the trade in the early nineteenth century and the movement westward. In many instances those books on cattle trade in the Far West have been classed in local history because the emphasis was on the history of the West rather than on the cattle trade. The same thing might happen to the history of a bank in its specific area. It might be classed in local history, but in all likelihood it should be classed in HG under the history of banking.

Chapter 4

Special Problems in Literature (Class P)

Patricia S. Hines

Class P (Language and Literature) and subclasses PA–PZ are designed and developed for the classification of the world's languages and literatures. Languages in use today by a few or by millions of people; the languages of the past, now extinct or even half-forgotten; dialect languages and artificial languages; television plays; simple rhymes of rural troubadours; literary treasures of antiquity; the trivia from a would-be poet; even the best seller on the whodunit list—all these are encompassed in the Classes P–PZ. Following is an overview of the P–PZ classification:

LANGUAGE AND LITERATURE

P	Philology and Linguistics (General)
PA	Classical Languages and Literature
	Greek and Latin language (Ancient, Medieval, Modern)
	Greek and Latin literature (Ancient, Medieval, Modern)
PB–PH	Modern European Languages
PB	General works. Celtic languages and literature
PC	Romance languages
PD	Germanic (Teutonic languages)
PE	English. Anglo-Saxon. Middle English
PF	Dutch. Flemish. Afrikaans. Friesian language and literature. German. Low German
PG	Slavic. Lithuanian-Lettish. Albanian
PH	Finno-Ugrian and Basque languages and literature
PJ–PL	Oriental Languages and Literatures including Eastern Asia, Oceania, and Africa
PM	Hyperborean, American (Indian) and Artificial languages
PN–PZ	Literature
PN	Literary history and collections (General)
PQ	Romance literatures
PR	English literature
PS	American literature

62

PT   Teutonic literature
PZ   Fiction and Juvenile literature

Class P presents the origin, development, and structure of language in general. It includes general comparative philology; the Indo-European language family; and the extinct, ancient, and medieval languages of Asia and Europe.

PA is devoted to Classical Latin and Greek, and it encompasses also the medieval and modern versions of those languages.

In PB–PZ are found modern European, Asiatic, African, and all other languages and dialects of the world. With the exception of Classes PQ, PR, PS, and PT (Romance, English, American, and the Teutonic literatures) language and literature will be treated together.

PN, besides containing literary history and collections of world literature, embraces the allied arts of theater, journalism, radio, and television. The famous PZ class will be discussed in more detail later.

Language Classification

Language classification tables range from a minutely detailed 900-number table to a simple single-number or a Cutter-number table. Complete development for each language is not spelled out within the body of the scheme, but in every case the table to be used is indicated in parentheses in the caption for the class and printed in its entirety at the end of the schedule. In some cases, especially with the major languages, a skeleton development listing the most frequently used numbers is given. The intervening numbers can be filled in when needed by applying the indicated table.

Literature Classification

Classification of literature follows a basic pattern, whether the development involves a whole schedule, as in the case of PQ (French literature), or whether it involves simple tables. The basic pattern for the development of literature is as follows:

History and criticism
  General
  By period
  By literary form
Collections
  General
    Translation
  By period
  By literary form
Individual authors
  By period
Local, colonial, provincial

"By period" under Individual authors is underlined because this is quite important. There is only one exception to this arrangement by period, and that is in the PR (English literature) schedule, where material of individual authors of the English Renaissance (from 1500 to 1640) is found. English Renaissance literature *is* a period division, but within the period division there is an arrangement by literary form; one finds, on the one hand, writers of prose and poetry together and, on the other, dramatists together.

The table to be followed for each literature is always clearly indicated in parentheses or spelled out in full, and should present no problem. What may be of interest is a combination of tables used together for a particular language and literature. One example of this type of combination, taken from the PJ–PM schedule, is the Bengali language and literature table, a 50-number table, as shown in Figure 1. The literature table (indicated as Table XXIII) appears in Figure 2, showing a span of 18 numbers. Any deviation from the scheme should be written in; thus the deviation "Folk literature" is inserted.

```
                              Bengali (V).
PK1651-1696                     Language (V).
  1700-1718                     Literature (XXIII).
                                  Individual authors.
                                    Through 1960.
      1718                           A - Tag.
  1719-1727                           Tagore, Sir Rabindranath, 1861-1941.
                                        Collected works.
      1719                                By date.
      1720                                By editor.
      1721                                Selections.
      1722                                Translations (Collected works).
         .A2A-Z                              English.  By translator.
         .A3-Z                               Other, by language, subarranged by translator.
      1723                                Separate works.
      1724                                Apocryphal, spurious works, etc.
  1725.A1-19                              Periodicals.  Societies.  Collections.
       .A2-3                               Dictionaries, indexes, etc.
       .A5-Z                               Biography and criticism.
                                          Criticism.
      1726                                    General.
      1727                                    Special topics, A-Z.
                                                .B4    Beauty.
                                                .D7    Drama
                                                .E8    Essays.
                                                .F5    Fiction.
                                                .H8    Humor.
                                                .L6    Love.
                                                .P6    Poetry.
                                                .S3    Science.
      1729                            Tag - Z.
  1730.1-46                           1961-    (Table G).
```

Figure 1

LITERATURE

XX	XXI	XXII	
			Special subjects—Continued.
235	135	85	Literature (Literary history: General and special).
			Science.
236	136	86	Mathematics. Astronomy. Physics. Chemistry (Q–QD).
237	137	87	Geology. Natural history. Botany. Zoology. Human anatomy. Physiology. Bacteriology (QE–QR).
238	138	88	Medicine.
239	139	89	Agriculture.
240	140	90	Technology. Manufactures. Trades (T, TS–TT).
241	141	91	Engineering and Building (TA–TJ).
242	142	92	Mineral industries. Chemical technology (TN–TP).
243	143	93	Photography.
244	144	94	Domestic science.
245	145	95	Military science.
246	146	96	Naval science.
248	148	98	Bibliography.

XXIII	XXIV	XXV	
			History.
0	0.A1–5	0. A1–5	Periodicals. Societies. Collections.
1	0.A6–Z	0. A6–Z	General works. Compends.
2	0. 5	0. 05	General special. Minor.
3			Collected essays.
4	1	. 1	Biography. Collected.
5			Origins.
6			To 1800.
7			19th century.
8			20th century.
(9)			Local, *see* 17.
10	2	. 2	Poetry.
11	3	. 3	Drama.
12	4	. 4	Other. *Folk literature*
			Collections.
13	5	. 5	General.
14	6	. 6	Poetry. .A2, Early.
15	7	. 7	Drama.
16	8	. 8	Other.
17			Local.
18	9	. 9	Individual authors.

Figure 2

PJ–PM

(*Add* table, p. 246.)

TABLE G

Individual authors.
The author number is determined by the letter following the letter or letters for which each class number stands.

.1	Anonymous works.	→ .29	Mb–Mz.
.12	A.	.3	N.
→ .13	Ba–Bg.	.31	O.
→ .14	Bh.	.32	P.
→ .15	Bi–Bz.	.33	Q.
→ .16	Ca–Cg.	→ .34	Ra.
→ .17	Ch.	→ .35	Rb–Rz.
→ .18	Ci–Cz.	→ .36	Sa.
.19	D.	→ .37	Sb–Sg.
.2	E.	→ .38	Sh.
.21	F.	→ .39	Si–Sz.
.22	G.	.4	T.
.23	H.	.41	U.
.24	I.	.42	V.
.25	J.	.43	W.
.26	K.	.44	X.
.27	L.	.45	Y.
→ .28	Ma.	.46	Z.

L. C. Classification—Additions and Changes. **List 138**

Figure 3

The Bengali table demonstrates a variant pattern in that a fuller breakdown under the eighteenth number is given in the schedule. Under normal application, PK1718 would be used for all individual authors; however, the schedule shows the classifier that a further breakdown has been developed which is not indicated in Table XXIII.

The development is as follows: All authors writing before 1960 whose names begin with A to Tag are classed in PK1718; the writings of Rabindranath Tagore are classed in PK1719 to 1727; then are classed all authors writing before 1960 whose names begin with Tag through Z.

For authors writing after 1961, PK1730.1 to PK1730.46 is used. Here, in order to save space, Table G, developed decimally, is used. Table G (Fig. 3) was designed and developed because of the great amount of material that LC was receiving in the vernacular as a result of the Public Law 480 Program. It was also noted from previous experience that there were certain letters or combinations of letters in which large numbers of authors with the same name were found. In order to give more room, instead of a straight alphabetical arrangement from A to Z by decimal breakdown, special combinations of letters and letter groups were set aside and allotted a single Cutter. Some of these special combinations are indicated by an arrow in Figure 3. This is only one example, but similar combinations for literatures that need further expansion will often be found.

The specific treatment of an individual author is again reduced to a simple pattern. The pattern is basic and, when reduced, looks like the following:

Collected works / Selections
    Original language
    Translations
Individual works
    Original language
    Translations
    Criticism
Biography
Criticism

First, are an individual author's collected or selected works in the original language and in translation; then individual works in the original language, in translation, and as subjects of criticism. Following individual works is the biography and criticism and/or interpretation of the author and his works in general. Regardless of the table applied, or the classification numbers allotted, the pattern works out this way.

Authors such as Shakespeare, Dante, and Cervantes, because of the amount of creative writing produced and number of books written about them, are provided with elaborately detailed tables. Shakespeare, for instance, has a span of numbers from PR2750 to PR3112. Of this great span of numbers, PR2885 to PR3112 are reserved for biography, criticism, and interpretation.

Less-prolific authors are given fewer numbers, or just Cutter numbers. Further explanation and application of the specific tables for individual authors will be discussed in the section on subclassification and shelflisting procedures and practices (Chapter 7).

Fiction Classification

PZ1 through PZ4 is not a classification development in the true sense of the word. It is, rather, a sort of shelf control similar to the arrangement found on browsing shelves in public libraries.

PZ as a whole is divided into three main parts: PZ1 for collections of novels and short stories in English; PZ3 and PZ4 for works of fiction by individual authors in English as the original language or translated into English; and PZ5–PZ90 for juvenile literature.

To illustrate, PZ1 contains collections of novels or short stories by more than one author written originally in English or translated from foreign languages into English. Figure 4a is the catalog card for a collection of Soviet science fiction translated into English and classified in PZ1. A collection of short stories from the Chinese translated into English is also classed in PZ1 (Fig. 4b).

```
PZ1
.D6595
So
```
Dutt, Violet L   *tr.*
　　Soviet science fiction. ₍Translated from the Russian by
Violet L. Dutt₎ With a new introd. by Isaac Asimov. New
York₍ Collier Books ₍1962₎
　　189 p. 18 cm. (Collier books, AS279V)
　　First published under title: A visitor from outer space.

　　1. Science fiction, Russian—Translations into English. 2. Science
fiction, English—Translations from Russian. ɪ. Title.

　　PZ1.D6595So　　　　　　　　　　　　62–14004 ‡

　　Library of Congress　　　　　₍2₎

```
PZ1
.F3813
St
```
Fêng, Mêng-lung, 1574?–1645? *supposed comp.*
　　Stories from a Ming collection. Translations of Chinese
short stories published in the seventeenth century, by Cyril
Birch. London, Bodley Head ₍1958₎
　　205 p. illus. 23 cm. (UNESCO collection of representative works :
Chinese series)
　　Translation of selections from 古今小説 (romanized: Ku chin
hsiao shuo)

　　1. Short stories, Chinese — Translations into English. 2. Short
stories, English—Translations from Chinese. ɪ. Birch, Cyril, 1925–
tr. ɪɪ. Title.

　　PZ1.F3813St　　　　　　　　　　　　59–54286 ‡
　　Library of Congress　　　　　₍2₎

```
PQ4254
.H3
```
Hall, Robert Anderson, 1911–   *ed. and tr.*
　　Italian stories. Novelle italiane. Stories in the original
Italian. With translations, critical introductions, notes and
vocabulary by the editor. ₍New York₎ Bantam Books
₍1961₎
　　354 p. 18 cm. (A Bantam dual-language book, S2189)

　　1. Short stories, Italian — Translations into English. 2. Short
stories, English—Translations from Italian. ɪ. Title. ɪɪ. Title:
Novelle italiane.

　　PQ4254.H3　　　　　853.082　　　　　61–5104 ‡

　　Library of Congress　　　　　₍2₎

However, Figure 4c is a collection of Italian short stories classed not in PZ1, but in PQ. The reason is that along with the English translation is the original text. Where the original language text is printed with the English translation, the classification moves from PZ to the particular literature involved and to the particular classification number, which may be general, by period, or by form; in this case, Italian short stories, classed in PQ4254. The original language takes precedence over the English translation.

PZ3 and PZ4 are used for fiction in English, by individual authors, whether English is the original language or the translation. The same author will not be found in both PZ3 and PZ4, but either in PZ3 *or* in PZ4.

PZ4 is used for authors who began to publish fiction in English in 1951 or later. If an author is currently publishing and yet has entries in PZ3, the classifier continues to classify him in PZ3. If he is not located in PZ3 and the classifier has a book by him, he consults the book jacket first or tries to find lists of the author's published works if possible, to see if the author has published any fiction before. If no fiction is advertised as having been published before 1951, the author is classified in PZ4.

It is not intended that the author's works be separated between the two classes. For example, Bertrand Russell wrote his first work of fiction, *Satan in the Suburbs*, in 1953 at the age of 81, and another, *Nightmares in Eminent Persons*, in 1954; therefore, he is classified in PZ4 although he had written many other nonfiction works before 1951.

Foreign fiction in translation is found in PZ3 and PZ4. The first example (Fig. 5a) shows the German original by Erich Maria Remarque, *Arc de triomphe*, PT2635.E68A67. The .E68 is the author notation, and A67 is the number for this particular title.

The second example (Fig. 5b) is the English translation of this novel classed in PZ3. Line 2 contains the author notation, .R2818; line 3 contains the two letters "Ar" standing for the title.

```
PT2635
.E68A67
        Remarque, Erich Maria, 1898–
           ... Arc de triomphe; roman.   Zürich, F. G. Micha [1946]
        429 p.   21½ cm.

        "v. auflage, 14.–16. tausend."




        I. Title.

        PT2635.E68A67                              A 47—3302
        Harvard Univ.  Library
        for Library of Congress        [a61c¼†]
```

Figure 5a

```
PZ3
.R2818
Ar      Remarque, Erich Maria, 1898–
             Arch of triumph [by] Erich Maria Remarque, translated
          from the German by Walter Sorell and Denver Lindley.
          New York, London, D. Appleton-Century company, inc.
          [1945]
             3 p. l., 455 p.  20½ cm.




             I. Sorell, Walter, 1905–     tr.  II. Lindley, Denver, 1904–     joint
          tr.  III. Title.

             PZ3.R2818Ar               833.91              45—9381

             Library of Congress          [57t½]
```

All fiction in English or translations into English are not necessarily classed in PZ3 or PZ4. Occasionally editions with commentaries and critical notes, and editions that are considered rare by LC because of author signature, age of the book, or for some other reason, are not classed in PZ3 or PZ4, but in the regular literature classes from PA to PT. As an example, Jules Verne's *Le tour du monde en 80 jours* (Fig. 6a) is classed in PQ2469, with .T7 as the Cutter number assigned to the title, and 1943 as the date of imprint. The next example (Fig. 6b) is also classed in PQ2469 along with the original, with the Cutter number .T7E58. The E5 is for English and the 8 is for the translator. This book is assigned to the Rare Book Collection. The designation "Rare Book Collection" appears only on the set of cards in the LC card catalog; a library purchasing this set of cards for their own use would find only the PQ class number at the bottom of the card, with no mention of the rare book location, and therefore no explanation why this particular book was classed in PQ instead of PZ.

The third example (Fig. 6c) is a translation into English but classified in PZ3.

Juvenile Literature

PZ5–PZ90 is set aside for juvenile literature. Juvenile fiction and other literary forms for readers through age 16 are classified here. Juvenile nonfiction (generally for ages 12 and up) is not classed in PZ5–PZ90, but classified according to the subject matter and in the appropriate subject class; however, *all* juvenile nonfiction, *regardless of age group*, is classed by subject in the following: biography, history, ethics, music, and language. For example, a biography of Joan of Arc would not be found in PZ5–PZ90 but rather in DC (French history) although designed for fifth- and sixth-grade readers.

In most of the juvenile nonfiction cases, however, special numbers are provided for juvenile works classified in the specific subject disciplines.

Multilingual Authors

Works by multilingual authors, who write in more than one language, are classed with the original language of the book in hand. For instance, works written by Lin Yutang in Chinese will be classed in Chinese literature (PL2781); works written by him in English (not a translation) will be classed in PR6023, English literature. Tagore's works written in the Bengali language will be found in PK, but his literary works originally written in English will be classed with English literature in PR6039.

Another example is Taras Shevchenko, whose works in Russian will be found in PG3361, but those written in Ukrainian will be in PG3948. Since Shevchenko was also an artist, some of his works will be found in N (Fine Arts) as well.

Classical and Sacred Texts

Classical and sacred texts when considered as literature are treated as literature and classed accordingly; when considered as other than literature, they will find a place outside of the literature schedule. Some examples will make this a little clearer. Original texts written in Sanskrit prior to about 1500 are considered literary and when in the vernacular will be classed in PK, but modern translations and commentaries on the textual content will not be classed as literature; instead they will be found in BL (Religion) or in the appropriate class.

The original Latin text of Caesar's *Gallic Wars* is considered as literature and classed in PA; the English translations are considered as history and are classed by subject in DC62.C2+ in the number for Gaul. However, works about Julius Caesar as a political figure in Roman history and as a great military general are classed with the history of Rome in DG261 and following numbers.

Aesop's *Fables* shows some varieties in classification. The original Greek of Aesop's *Fables* is classified in PA (Greek literature) as the first example (Fig. 7a). The second example (Fig. 7b) shows a translation of the *Fables*. This is a translation which follows the original text and is classified in the appropriate number given in the PA schedule. The number .E5 is for English translations, and A3 is for the translator, Abbe. The same *Fables* retold for children (Fig. 7c) are classed in PZ8.2, the number for *fables* retold for children. In Figure 7d the same Aesop's *Fables* are reworked into a creative, artistic work. They are no longer classed as translations of *fables,* but as American literature by a particular author in PS. La Fontaine's *Fables* (Fig. 7e) are also considered creative and have a place in French literature (PQ).

As a last example, Plutarch's *Lives* in the original would be in PA (Fig. 8a); the German translation would be under the classification number for German translations (Fig. 8b); the Hebrew translation would still be classified under its appropriate number in PA (Fig. 8c); but an English translation of his complete works is classified in DE because it is considered as collected biography of the Graeco-Roman world (Fig. 8d).

PS3535
.I658A7

Riley, Alice Cushing (Donaldson) 1867–
    Aesop in modern dress, done in verse by Alice C. D. Riley.
[1st ed.] Claremont, Calif. [H. L. Fraser]; distributed by
Saunders Press, 1953.

    137 p. illus. 24 cm.

    1. Fables.   I. Æsopus. Fabulae. II. Title.

    PS3535.I 658A7   811.5   54–127 ‡

    Library of Congress   [2]

PQ1808
.A1
1965   **La Fontaine, Jean de,** 1621–1695.
        Fables mises en vers. [Paris, J. Tallandier, 1965]

        409 p. port. 21 cm. (Le Trésor des lettres françaises)

        1. .Esopus.   I. Title.

    PQ1808.A1 1965   65–67296

    Library of Congress   [½]

Figure 7e

Figure 8e shows an individual biography of Pyrrhus, classified not as literature but with the man about whose life it is written. It becomes part of Greek history and is included among many biographies on Pyrrhus in DF. The same is true of the last example, the life of Brutus (Fig. 8f). As single works the individual "life" is classified with the man about whom it was written and joins the other works about him in the appropriate class.

Discussion

Question: Can you suggest an accurate classification for authors from former British colonies, especially those from Africa?

Mrs. Hines: We have different ways of treating colonial literature. Most of the schedules have a provision for colonial literature and literature outside of the country itself.

Figure 8a

```
PA4369
.A2
1873      Plutarchus.
              Plutarchi Vitae parallelae ... Recognovit Carolus Sinte-
          nis. Lipsiae, sumptibus et typis B. G. Teubneri, 18

              v. 17½ cm.

              Paged continuously.




              1. Greece—Biog.  2. Rome—Biog.   I. Sintenis, Karl Heinrich
          Ferdinand, 1806–1867, ed.

              PA4369.A2   1873                          38M3706T
```

```
PA4376
.V6
1954     Plutarchus.
              Grosse Griechen und Römer; eingeleitet und übers. von
          Konrat Ziegler.  Zürich, Artemis-Verlag ₁1954–

              v. illus. 18 cm. (Die Bibliothek der alten Welt. . Griechische
          Reihe)

              CONTENTS.—Bd. 1. Theseus und Romulus. Lykurgos und Numa.
          Solon und Poplicola.  Aristeides und Cato.  Themistokles und
          Camillus.



              I. Title.

              PA4376.V6   1954                          54–26381

              Library of Congress        ₁²₁
```

Figure 8b

```
PA4381
.H5A3
1954     Plutarchus.
              חיי אישים.  תרגם מהמקור היווני והוסיף מבוא והערות, יוסף
          ג. ליבס.  ירושלים, מוסד ביאליק.   ₁Jerusalem, 1954–

              v. 24 cm. (ספרי מופת מספרות העולם)

              CONTENTS.—

                                                      נכרך ב₎ אנשי רומי.



              1. Rome—Biog.    I. Liebes, Gerhard Joseph, tr.    (Series:
          Sifre mofet mi-sifrut ha-'olam)    Title transliterated: Ḥaye ishim.

              PA4381.H5A3   1954                        57–51309

              Library of Congress        ₁⁸₁
```

Figure 8c

75

In the case of French literature, for instance, there is a fully developed plan arranged by country, area, or region for French literature outside of France. (The term "outside of France" should be explained. There is "outside of France" but within the confines of continental Europe, and there is "outside of France" meaning former colonies and other areas.) Within the continent of Europe, all French literature is classified under appropriate numbers found in PQ1–2686, but for authors outside of continental Europe, special tables are devised with a place for individual authors.

With English literature the arrangement is slightly different: there is provision for colonial literature, but with a warning: "Here are classified literary history, collected biography, collections of the literature of the following . . . The works and biography and criticism of individual authors are to be classified in PR1800 to 6076 . . ." In other words, the answer would be that individual authors who use English as their medium, whether they are colonial or whether they are within the boundaries of England or continental Europe, will be classed with the period of English literature in which they write, not in the local arrangement.

Question: Why is it that occasionally, when an author has been assigned a P schedule number, some of his nonfiction literary works are classed elsewhere? What determines whether they will be classed in P or not?

Mrs. Hines: An illustration of this would be an author's collection of assorted essays with no specific literary focus. On the assumption that these essays are the first published work of the author, the first class to be considered would be AC, collections by individual writers arranged by language. Works usually classed here are by people who have not previously written fiction, poetry, or plays and whose work has no particular subject focus. No subject heading will be assigned to the work classed in AC.

If the author has written previously and has poetry, plays, or fiction to his credit, and if the work to be cataloged is of a literary nature and not a treatise on a particular subject, that book will be classed under the author's literature number in P. If the book has subject value and can be assigned a subject heading, the book will be classed with the subject in the appropriate discipline.

Question: Is there an index to PQ?

Mrs. Hines: I imagine you mean an author index. We do not have that, but it should not be difficult to find your way through PQ if you remember that everything follows a specific pattern: starting out with history and criticism, moving to collections, and then to individual authors, always arranged by period.

Question: Where should one put a literary author who has lived in a number of countries? LC does not always seem to use the country of birth.

Mrs. Hines: We try to determine the country of birth of an author who has written in one language and we classify accordingly, e.g. a writer in Spanish might be Uruguayan, yet may have published in Argentina. Sometimes, however, the reference sources are so meager that, with proper regard to economy in cataloging, it is not practical to attempt to ferret out the birthplace of a relatively obscure author. In such a situation we may use the place of publication as a last resort, but generally we make an effort to ascertain an author's nationality and we classify on this basis.

Question: When dates are indicated for classification under individual authors, does the date apply to the period in which the author flourished? If so, how can one ascertain in which category to put borderline authors, those who flourished both before and after 1951, for example?

Mrs. Hines: We try to determine not only when an author began to write but when his production actually flourished, when he became a well-known author. This factor guides the classification. In some borderline cases the classification may involve a somewhat arbitrary decision. But once the decision has been made, further works are classified in the same chronological period. If an author flourished before and after a dividing date, he will be classed with the previous period.

Question: Does a foreign author who has written before 1951 but not been translated until after 1951 go in PZ3 or PZ4?

Mrs. Hines: The author would be classed in PZ4 because the translation came in then, regardless of the fact that he wrote in his own language before 1951.

Question: Since the language tables sometimes offer problems in use, would you please explain them, using the verb in Spanish as an example?

Mrs. Hines: First of all, the cataloger must turn to the Spanish language in the PC schedule (Romanic philology and languages). Under "Language" he will find that the Spanish language has numbers 4073–4693 (among others). Under the word "Language" he will also find the note: "(Subdivided like PC1073–1693)" and, further, that the Spanish language uses Table I at the end of the PB–PH schedule. If the cataloger turns first to PC1073–1693 (Italian language) and runs down the list of captions to "Grammar," under "Grammar" he will find "Parts of speech" and there "Verb" with the numerical equivalent of 1271 for the Italian verb. Since he should also have observed that the Italian language starts with 1073 in this section, he may readily see that the Spanish language is exactly 3000 numbers farther along in the schedule, therefore the number wanted is PC4271.

Had the cataloger gone from the Spanish language 4073–4693 directly to Table I, he would have had to look through the captions to find "Parts of speech," and "Verb" with the tabular equivalent of 271, then return to PC1073–1693 to locate 1271—which would, of course, be the number for verb in Italian—and add his 3000 numbers to arrive at PC4271, verb in Spanish.

By using a schedule to follow the two procedures, it appears much simpler. In application of tables, the cataloger must follow the information through; when given directions such as "divide like" or "treated like," he must follow them as well.

Question: Does LC plan to abolish PZ3 and PZ4?

Mr. Angell: It is impossible to conceive that LC would abandon a class that it has been using for nearly seventy years. The amount of reclassification would be staggering. LC will, however, consider the possibility of adding an alternate class number that PZ3 and PZ4 books would otherwise have. If LC can provide the alternate number in brackets, in many cases the author Cutter will appear also, since that is part of the class number in some literature schedules.

Question: Juvenile literature is classed in PZ5–PZ90. Some of this material is used in children's rooms for informational value or other reasons. Has any thought been given to the special problems of classifying juvenile works held by LC in a way more useful for children's libraries?

Mr. Angell: Quoting again from the Elsinore conference: "The Library's materials for juvenile readers are now disposed in part in the subject classes A–J and L–Z, with many specific subclasses for juvenile works, or juvenile and popular works combined, and in part in PZ, the literary forms of juvenile works in all languages. Uniformity in the classification of all juvenile literature and the adoption of specific criteria, particularly with respect to age limits, are required. What needs to be particularly borne in mind is that in relation to this material the Library of Congress' approach and that of most other libraries is basically different: our collection should be assembled to serve, not the juvenile reader, but those who study to serve and write for and illustrate books for the juvenile reader."[1]

If there is agreement with this proposition, then what would be assembled at the Library of Congress in the juvenile collection would not, it seems to me, be matched elsewhere except in a comparable research situation, not a service situation.

As to what those who do not find our provisions useful might do, it would be, of course, a simple matter to add a designation like JUV to all juvenile works in the classes A–Z, except for PZ5–PZ90 or even there if you want to have every book specifically with JUV on it.

This does not answer the needs of most collections, that is, service collections of juvenile literature and materials. And because books of informational value, as the questioner states, are in PZ5–PZ90, I can only suggest at this point that, if you want them outside of PZ, then you would have to class those books where so desired. This would principally apply, I would think, to such works for the earlier age group as we class in PZ5–PZ90, for example, titles such as *Let's Go to the Supermarket*. This we treat as a story for the lower age group. I take it this is wanted by many libraries in H somewhere, along with juvenile works for the upper ages.

Notes

[1] International Study Conference on Classification Research, 2d, Elsinore, Denmark, *Classification Research: Proceedings*; ed. by Pauline Atherton (Copenhagen: Munksgaard, 1965), p.107.

Chapter **5**

Special Problems in Science and Technology (Classes Q–V)

Edward J. Blume

The world of science and technology as represented by classes Q through V in the Library of Congress classification system is indeed a world of breadth and variety. It takes in the early Q classes; the physical and mathematical sciences; a transition class, QE (Geology), divided between the nonliving world of the rocks and the once-living world of fossils; and the late Q classes of natural history and biology. These are the pure sciences, the once-upon-a-time "hard" sciences which recent interdisciplinary philosophies, techniques, and interpretations have softened up. Then, in somewhat reverse order, follow the applied sciences of R (Medicine) and S (Agriculture), representing biology put to use. The T (Technology) schedule is vast in range but may be conveniently divided into four subclasses: the civil engineering group, TA through TH; the mechanical engineering group, TJ through TL; the chemical engineering group, TN through TR; and, finally, a composite group representing manufactures, mechanic arts and crafts, and home economics. The arts of war in classes U and V continue the sciences.

As a matter of fact, when one tries to integrate the military sciences into a classification system, one has the choice of attaching them on the basis of their administration, which is a governmental function, or their technology. In the LC system the bond is the bond of technology, and as things have developed, the attachment is fortuitous.

For working purposes at the Library of Congress the science group in the Subject Cataloging Division has also taken over Class BF1–990 (Psychology), because of its overlap with Neurophysiology in QP and with Psychiatry in RC; Class GB (Physical Geography), a near neighbor of QE (Geology) and included with QE in the concept of geomorphology; and finally Class GC (Oceanography), because of its inclusion in joint research with marine biology in the late Q classes.

The first thing that a classifier has to do, when he opens a classification schedule in search of the right number for the work in hand, is to read a caption. The numbers themselves can be manipulated several ways once he has a grip on them, but the key to finding them is a caption. The technical captions are endless

ASTRONOMY

QB

1	Periodicals, societies, etc.
2	Exhibitions. Museums.
3	Collections (nonserial).

41   Early works (to 1700).
        Cf. GA 6–7, Cosmography.
            QB 85, Early astronomical instruments.
            QB 215, Dialing.
            VK 551, Navigation (Early works).
    General works, 1701–
        Descriptive astronomy, *see* QB 461–991.

42	18th century.
43	1801–
44	Popular works.
45	Elementary textbooks.
46	Rudiments. Juvenile works.

        Cf. QB 63, Stargazers' guides.

47	Miscellaneous aspects of astronomy.

        e. g. Uses in military science.

51	Essays, lectures, addresses, etc.
.5	Astronomy as a profession.
52	Miscellaneous speculations.
54	Plurality of worlds.
55	Astronomical myths, legends, and superstitions.
61	**Study and teaching.**
62	Outlines, laboratory manuals, etc.
.5	Problems, exercises, etc.
63	Stargazers' guides.
64	Observers' handbooks.
65	Atlases and charts.
66	Use of globes (Astronomical).

        Cf. GA 12, Manuals for globes.

67	Miscellaneous models.
68	Pictorial works, etc.

Figure 1

PZ10
.J47
As

Johnson, Robert Ivar, 1933–
    Astronomy; our solar system and beyond.   Illustrated by
George Bakacs. Racine, Wis., Whitman Pub. Co. ₍1963₎
      58 p. illus. 22 cm. (A Whitman learn about book, 16)

    1. Astronomy—Juvenile literature.

PZ10.J47As   j 523   63–7177 ‡

Library of Congress   ₍5₎

QB46
.G89

Guillot, René, 1900–
    Astronomy. Pictures by Giannini. Racine, Wis., Whit-
man Pub. Co. ₍1963₎
      104 p. col. illus., col. map. 32 cm. (Whitman world library)
      Translation of L'espace.

    1. Astronomy—Juvenile literature. 2. Astronautics—Juvenile lit-
erature.

QB46.G89   j 523   63–14672

Library of Congress   ₍5₎

QB45
.B15
1964

Baker, Robert Horace, 1883–
    Astronomy. 8th ed. Princeton, N. J., Van Nostrand
₍1964₎
      viii. 557 p. illus., diagrs. 24 cm.
      Includes bibliographies.

    1. Astronomy.

QB45.B15   1964   523   64–9606

Library of Congress   ₍7–1₎

and are demanding of specialized knowledge; the form captions, however, are limited in number and are demanding rather of interpretation. It might be useful to discuss a few interpretations.

Form Divisions in Science

Figure 1 shows some excerpts from the QB schedule for astronomy. The classifier has in hand a work on general astronomy. He has to ask himself if he has a general work (and of what period); a popular work; an elementary textbook; a rudimentary or juvenile work; a collection of essays, lectures, and addresses; or a nonserial collection.

Examination of these captions may eliminate some confusing aspects by comparison of the terminology and what it stands for in the science section at LC. For purposes of simplicity the juvenile works should be eliminated first. QB46 reads "Rudiments. Juvenile works." What does this mean? Webster defines rudiment as an "element or first principle in any art or science; a beginning of any knowledge." Taken alone this would not be at all helpful, particularly since if the geology schedule is inspected, one will see "QE28 Elements. QE29 Rudiments. Juvenile works." Fortunately the caption "Rudiments" at no time stands alone in the science schedules; it is always associated with "Juvenile works." Figures 2a–2c show three examples of the two juvenile classifications.

What about an elementary textbook? At LC no textbook is to be classed as juvenile literature; so if the book is clearly labeled for school use, the classifier must consider the concept of textbooks. But what is an elementary textbook in a science, astronomy, perhaps, to be consistent with the example? If one takes into account the current status of the field and the level at which the subject is or might be taught, then an elementary textbook in astronomy might be one suitable for instruction at even the junior or the senior high school levels. At any rate, it is recognized that elementary textbooks in the sciences are the lowest level of textual material and have no necessary connection with elementary education.

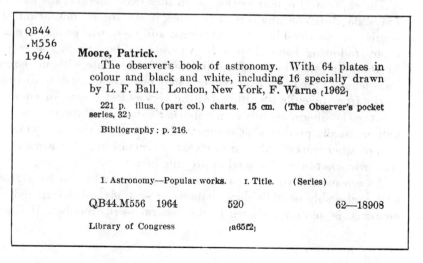

QB44
.M556
1964

Moore, Patrick.

The observer's book of astronomy. With 64 plates in colour and black and white, including 16 specially drawn by L. F. Ball. London, New York, F. Warne [1962]

221 p. illus. (part col.) charts. 15 cm. (The Observer's pocket series, 32)

Bibliography : p. 216.

1. Astronomy—Popular works.   I. Title.   (Series)

QB44.M556   1964   520   62—18908

Library of Congress   [a65f2]

Figure 3a

QB43
.W3
Wallenquist, Åke, 1904–
    Astronomi; den moderna astrofysikens resultat och forsk-
ningsmetoder. Stockholm, Svenska bokförlaget ₍1958₎

    308 p. illus. 23 cm. (Scandinavian university books)

    Includes bibliography.

    1. Astronomy.

                             Full name: Ake Anders Edvard Wallenquist.

    QB43.W3   62–25421 ‡

    Library of Congress   ₍3₎

QB43
.S3
Schatzman, Evry, *ed.*
    Astronomie. ₍Paris, Gallimard, 1962₎

    1834 p. illus. 18 cm. (Encyclopédie de la Pléiade, 13)

    Includes bibliography.

    1. Astronomy.

    QB43.S3   63–29678 ‡

    Library of Congress   ₍u63b1₎

The caption "Popular works" is, in the strict sciences, the easiest to associate
(Figs. 3a–3c). The language of the work is mature but not technical; all essential
words are explained but in adult terms; and there will probably not be a bibliography following each chapter but there may be one at the end of the book.
Furthermore, the illustrations will genuinely elucidate without requiring previous
knowledge of the field. These criteria may or may not serve to distinguish popular
works from juvenile literature (of the very oldest group, of course). If they do
not, the classifier must rely on a publisher's statement; the type of work which the
author usually produces, as determined either from the dust jacket or an inspec-
tion of other works in the card catalog; or inclusion of the work in a series which
has or has not been classified as juvenile literature.

An advanced textbook or treatise by a single author, or by a group of authors
with authorship of individual chapters or sections *not* designated in the table of
contents, is quickly assigned to the general works number. If the authorship is

shared and designated by section or chapter, a separation has to be made. The LC criterion is essentially this: If a work is systematically arranged so as to give coverage to an entire field but with the advantage of having a specialist contribute the various aspects, the work is still classed as a general work.

If the book on general astronomy is a collection of essays and lectures by one or several persons or, frequently, a collection of readings in the field, such as might be assigned as supplementary reading in a school course, it will be classed under "Essays, lectures, addresses, etc." (Figs. 4a–4c). If, on the other hand, the book deals with a collection of research reports, a collection of papers from a congress (and no congress number is provided in the schedule), or even the complete works of a single author, it would be classed in "Collections (nonserial)." In the science and technology schedules the caption "Collected works" without further qualification is interpreted as nonserial. Serial collections are classed in "Periodicals and societies" numbers. For purpose of classification,

QB51
.R2

Rapport, Samuel Berder, 1903–   *ed.*
  Astronomy, edited by Samuel Rapport and Helen Wright.
Academic editorial adviser: Serge A. Korff. ₍New York₎
New York University Press, 1964.

  xiii, 354 p. illus. 21 cm. (The New York University library of science)

  1. Astronomy—Addresses, essays, lectures.   I. Wright, Helen, 1914–   joint ed. II. Title.

QB51.R2   520.82   64–13609

Library of Congress   ₍5₎

Figure 4a

QB3
.S73
1961

Space Age Astronomy Symposium, *Pasadena, Calif., 1961.*
  Space age astronomy; an international symposium sponsored by Douglas Aircraft Company, inc., August 7–9, 1961, at the California Institute of Technology in conjunction with the xi General Assembly of the International Astronomical Union. Edited by Armin J Deutsch ₍and₎ Wolfgang B. Klemperer. New York, Academic Press, 1962.
  xxi, 531 p. illus., maps, diagrs., tables. 24 cm.
  Erratum slip inserted.
  Includes bibliographies.
  1. Astronomy — Congresses. 2. Outer space — Exploration — Congresses. I. Deutsch, Armin Joseph, 1918–   ed. II. Klemperer, Wolfgang Benjamin, 1893–   ed. III. Douglas Aircraft Company, inc. IV. California Institute of Technology, Pasadena, V. Title.

QB3.S73 1961   523   62—21142
Library of Congress   ₍63k10₎

Figure 4b

QB68
.P6

Portrait of the universe. With an introd. by Franklyn M.
Branley. ₍New York, Astro Murals, °1960₎

64, ₍1₎ p. illus. 16 cm.

Bibliography: p. ₍66₎

1. Astronomy—Pictorial works.

QB68.P6   523.084   61–34425

Library of Congress   ₍1₎

pictorial works must be picture books with the text serving as captions, not simply
highly illustrated works.

The caption "Elements" appears in QA and QC in juxtaposition to the caption
"Treatises," and this duality causes no difficulty since the works involved tend to
be either discursive and theoretical or concise and elucidative of basic principles
(Fig. 5). The same is true of BF's predilection for "Comprehensive" or "Treatises" as opposed to "Compends. Manuals." (Fig. 6). All the classes have their
idiosyncratic captions for specific purposes, such as "Atlases" in medicine and
"Handbooks and Tables" in engineering, but these require no specific interpretation.

Class S (Agriculture) Tables

The tables in the science classes present but few problems. For illustration,
Figure 7 shows the tables for Class S, which are excerpted here for ease of
manipulation.

Two examples follow (Figs. 8a and 8b) on forestry in the Soviet Union. The
number span in the Forestry excerpts (Fig. 7) indicates that for countries other
than the United States Table II is used, the table numbers being added to 144. As
shown in the excerpt of the Geographical Distribution Tables, Table II assigns to
Russia two numbers: 63 and 64. Immediately above this, instructions point out
that in the case of a 2-number assignment, the first is for general treatments and
the second is for local designations, Cuttered A–Z. The first book (Fig. 8a),
which is on the forests of European and Asiatic Russia, is certainly general
enough so 63 is added to 144 to obtain 207. The class number of the book is then
SD207, to which is added the author Cutter, in this case .U5. For the second
work, which deals with types of forests in the Ukraine (Fig. 8b), the second
number assigned for local subdivision is used. In this case 64 is added to 144 to
obtain 208. The class number then becomes SD208, to which is added a *local*
Cutter of .U4 for the Ukraine and then a second Cutter for the author, L3.

86

Dynamics.
    Cf. UF 820, Motion of projectiles (Ballistics).
845   Treatises.
846   Elements.

QC   PHYSICS   **QC**

EXPERIMENTAL MECHANICS

Analytic mechanics in QA 801–935.

General and solids.
122   History.
        General history of mechanics in QA 802.
123   Early works (to 1800).
125   Treatises, 1801–
127   Elements.

HEAT

251   Collections.
252   History and philosophy.
253   Early works (to 1800).
254   Treatises (Mathematical and general).
255   Elements.

NUCLEAR FISSION. ATOMIC ENERGY. RADIOACTIVITY

770   Periodicals, societies, congresses, etc.
771   Collected works (nonserial).
772   Dictionaries.
773   History.
        .A1 Development and projects leading to production of
             first atomic bombs.
774   Biography, A–Z.
        .A1 Collective.
        General works.
776   Treatises. *Elements.*
777   778   Popular works. Juvenile works.
780   Addresses, essays, lectures.

Figure 5

(0)	Early works (including Latin and Greek).
(1)	English.
(2)	French.
(3)	German.
(4)	Italian.
(5)	Spanish and Portuguese.
(6)	
(7)	
(8)	Other, A–Z.

When the class numbers ending 0–8 indicate early works (as in BF 550–558, BJ 1550–1558) use 0 for Latin or Greek and 1–8 for other languages as shown in the table.

Where six numbers have been assigned, figure 6=Other, A–Z (including Russian and other Slavic).

BF PSYCHOLOGY **BF**

	Early works to 1850.
110	Latin.
111–118	Other.*
	Later works, 1851–
121–128	Comprehensive.*
131–138	Compends. Manuals.*
139	Elementary textbooks.
	Mind and body.
150–158	Early works to 1850.*
161–168	Later works, 1851–*
171	Pamphlets.
173	**Pathological psychology. Abnormal psychology.**
	Psychoanalysis.
	Cf. BF 376, 423–437, 491, 687.S8; HV; QP; RC 343; etc.
	Psychoanalytical studies of individual persons with biography of person concerned.
	For psychoanalysis applied to childhood, *see* BF 721.
.A2	Periodicals. Societies.
175	General special.
	Physiological and experimental psychology.
	Cf. QP 351–499, Physiology.
181–188	Treatises.*
191–198	Compends.*
	Laboratory manuals, *see* BF 79.
620–628	**Freedom of the will.***
	Psychological treatises only. Prefer BJ 1460–1468, Ethics.

Figure 6

History of Forestry.   Forest conditions.

131	General.
139	America.
143	United States.
144	By region or state, A–W.

   e. g. .A117, Middle West; .A12, New England;
   .A13, Pacific Northwest; .A15, South; .A17,
   Tennessee Valley.

145–246	Other countries. Table II.

   Add number in the table to **144.**
   Under each:
      (1) General.
      (2) State, province, etc., A–Z.

VETERINARY MEDICINE AND SURGERY

SF

History.

615	General works.
621–723	By country. Table I.

   Add number in Table 1 to 600.

GEOGRAPHICAL DISTRIBUTION TABLES

In countries to which two numbers are assigned:
      (1) General.
      (2) Local, A–Z.

I	II	
85–86	63–64	Russia.
87–88	65–66	Spain.
89–90	67–68	Sweden.
91–92	69–70	Switzerland.
93–94	71–72	Turkey.
95	73	Other countries of Europe, A–Z.
99	75	Asia.
101–102	77–78	China.
103–104	79–80	India.
105–106	81–82	Japan.
107–108	83–84	Persia.
	85–86	Philippines.
109	87–88	Russia in Asia, Siberia.
110		Central Asia, Turkestan.

Figure 7

SD207
.U5
1918

U. S. *Forest Service.*
    The forests of European and Asiatic Russia; their extent,
utilization, and economic importance. ₍Washington₎ 1918.

    71 l. illus. 29 cm.

    1. Forests and forestry—Russia.

    SD207.U5   1918   52–59120 ‡

    Library of Congress   ₍₂₎

SD208
.U4L3

Lavrinenko, D   **D**
    Типы леса Украинской ССР.   Москва, Гослесбумиздат,
1954.

    90, ₍2₎ p.   maps.   22 cm.
    Bibliography : p. 89–₍91₎

    1. Forests and forestry—Ukraine.   I. Title.
                        Title transliterated: Tipy lesa Ukrainskoĭ SSR.

    SD208.U4L3   55–59820

    Library of Congress   ₍₂₎

Figure 8b

The third book (Fig. 9a), on the forests of Siberia and the Far East, shows an interesting development. The Soviet Union is a special case in that it is assigned *two* sets of double numbers in Table II, one pair for Europe, one pair for Asia. This is also true of Turkey.

For the work on the Siberian and Soviet Far Eastern forests (Fig. 9a), the classifier must go down to numbers 87 and 88 in Table II and select number 87 since the book is a general work on a large portion of Soviet Asia. When the computations are made, the number is SD231.K7, the .K7 being the author Cutter for Krylov. For the last work, that by Gudochkin on the forests of Kazakhstan, (Fig. 9b), the second or local number of the Asiatic pair is used, 88, and added to 144 to obtain SD232, the .K35 being the geographical Cutter for Kazakhstan and the G8 the author Cutter.

Under Table I, by contrast to Table II (Fig. 7), a book on veterinary medicine in Kazakhstan would have 1 number to be added to the base of 600 and would have been classed under SF710 (110 plus 600) without Cuttering for the local subdivision, since Table I has only 1 number which therefore includes general and local works.

Class T (Technology) Tables

The only table in Class T (Fig. 10) is essentially the same as Table I of the Class S schedule except that it has 6 numbers at the beginning assigned for historical divisions (historical divisions have to be written into the S schedule any time they are required). A further convenience of the tabular system in Class T is that the table slips neatly into place in the schedule and only the hundreds column has to be modified.

The subclass "Hydraulic Engineering," subsection "Harbors and coast protective engineering works" (Fig. 11), needs both a historical and a geographical

SD231
.K7

Krylov, Georgiĭ Vasil'evich.
    Леса Сибири и Дальнего Востока, их лесорастительное районирование.   Москва, Гослесбумиздат, 1960.

    155, [1] p. illus., maps. 22 cm.

    Bibliography : p. 154–[156]

    1. Forests and forestry—Siberia.   I. Title.
                    Title transliterated: Lesa Sibiri i Dal'nego Vostoka.

SD231.K7   62–35114

Library of Congress   [2]

Figure 9a

SD232
.K35G8

Gudochkin, Mikhail Vasil'evich.
    Леса Казахстана.   Алма-Ата, Казахское гос. изд-во, 1958.

    322 p. illus., maps (1 fold. in pocket) 23 cm.

    At head of title: М. В. Гудочкин, П. С. Чабан.
    Bibliography : p. 302–321.

    1. Forests and forestry—Kazakhstan.   I. Chaban, Pavel Sergee-
vich, joint author.   II. Title.   *Title transliterated:* Lesa Kazakhstana.

SD232.K35G8   59–36463

Library of Congress   [3]

Figure 9b

TABLE I

HISTORY AND COUNTRY DIVISIONS

History.

15	General.
16	Ancient.
17	Medieval.
18	Modern.
19	19th century.
20	20th century.

Special countries.

21	America.	
22	North America.	
23	United States.	
.1		Atlantic coast.
.15		New England.
.2		Appalachian region.
.3		Lake region.
.4		Mississippi Valley.
.5		South. Gulf states.
.6		West.
.7		Northwest.
.8		Pacific coast.
.9		Southwest.
24		States, A–W.
25		Cities (or other special), A–Z.
26	Canada and Newfoundland.	
27		Provinces (or other special), A–Z.
27.5	Latin America.	
28–29	Mexico.	
30	Central America.	
31		Special states, B–S.
32	West Indies.	
33		Special islands, A–Z.
34	South America.	
36–37		Argentine Republic.
38–39		Bolivia.

Figure 10

Harbors and coast protective engineering works.

203   Periodicals. Societies. Yearbooks.
204   Early works (to 1800).
205   General treatises (1801–).
209   Miscellaneous.
215–326   History and country divisions. Table I.
      Under each country except as otherwise specified:
        (1) General.
        (2) Special harbors (inlets, channels, etc.), A–Z.

TD   SANITARY AND MUNICIPAL ENGINEERING   TD

WATER-SUPPLY FOR INDUSTRIAL AND DOMESTIC PURPOSES

221–326   Country subdivisions. Table I.
      (Including all local or departmental reports.)
      Under each country (except as otherwise specified):
        (1) .A1, General; .A6–Z, States, provinces, etc.
        (2) Local (Cities, etc.), A–Z.

RAILROAD ENGINEERING AND OPERATION

For economic, social, and political aspects, *see* HE.

TF

History.
15   General.
16   Antiquities.
      (Including early curiosities of railroad development).
19   Nineteenth century.
20   Twentieth century.
21–126   Country divisions. Table I.
      Under each:
        (1) General.
        (2) Special railroads, A–Z.
        e. g. TF 25, Special roads, United States.
           TF 64, Special roads, Great Britain.
           TF 80, Special roads, Italy.
      Only technical works to be classed here.

Figure 11

TC224
.M4A45
1951

Massachusetts. *Special Commission to Study the Problem of Providing Better Protection Along the Coast Line of the Commonwealth Against Loss of Life and Property Caused by Storms.*

Report. Boston, Wright & Potter Print. Co., legislative printers, 1951.

17 p. 23 cm. (House. ₁Document₁ no. 2443)

1. Shore protection—Massachusetts.

TC224.M4A45 1951　　　　　627.5　　　　　51–62633

Library of Congress　　　₁1₁

TC227
.T5T6

Torrance, Archibald Allan.

... "New harbour works, Three Rivers, P. Q., Canada." By Archibald Allan Torrance ... London, The Institution, 1934.

17, ₁1₁ p. fold. pl. 21½ᶜᵐ. (The Institution of civil engineers. Selected engineering papers ... no. 152)

1. Three Rivers, Quebec—Harbor.　ɪ. Title.　　　　42–42947

Library of Congress　　　TC227.T5T6

——————— Copy 2.　　　TA1.I 68　no. 152

₁2₁

TC233
.M3A5

U. S. *Congress. House. Committee on rivers and harbors.*

Mayaguez harbor, Puerto Rico. Hearings before the Committee on rivers and harbors, House of representatives, Seventy-third Congress, first session, on the subject of the improvement of Mayaguez harbor, Puerto Rico. April 13, 1933. Washington, U. S. Govt. print. off., 1933.

ii, 19 p. 23ᶜᵐ.

Joseph J. Mansfield, chairman.

1. Mayaguez, P. R. (City)—Harbor.

　　　　　　　　　　　　　　　　44–21266

Library of Congress　　　TC233.M3A5　1933

　　　　　　　₁2₁　　　　627.2097295

approach, hence the reference to TC215–326, 215–326 being the entire span of Table I (15–126). To find the correct class number for any period or country, the number in the table is added to 200.

Figure 12a is a card for a book on shore protection in Massachusetts. Table I (Fig. 10) indicates that number 24 is reserved for States, A–W. For the class number of this book then, 24 is added to 200: TC224 plus .M4 for Massachusetts plus the added Cutter for author and date. (Figs. 12a and 12c as well as other examples in this chapter have "official" or "document" Cutters, which are explained in Chapter 8).

The second example (Fig. 12b) is a book by Torrance on the new harbor works of Three Rivers, Quebec. By consulting Figure 11 again, one will see in the note under "History and country divisions" that a second number whenever given in Table I means "Special harbors (inlets, channels, etc.), A–Z." According to Table I, Canada is given two numbers: 26, Canada and Newfoundland; 27, Provinces (or other special), A–Z. The Torrance book is "other special," namely harbors, inlets, channels, etc., so it will be classed in TC227 and Cuttered .T5 for Three Rivers and T6 for the author. In other words, the special instructions in the schedules take precedence over the general instructions in the table.

This can be demonstrated even more forcefully when one considers the work on harbor works at Mayaguez, Puerto Rico (Fig. 12c). The second number (33) under the West Indies in the table is labeled "Special islands, A–Z," but again the instructions in the schedule under TC215–236 designating special as harbors, inlets, channels, etc., takes precedence, and the class number becomes TC233, Cuttered, not for Puerto Rico, but directly for the harbor itself, .M3 for Mayaguez. This example stresses how extremely important are the specific instructions under the geographical number spread in the T schedule.

The second excerpt in Figure 11 deals with tabular references TD221–326 under "Water-Supply for Industrial and Domestic Purposes." The history numbers are omitted since they are already written into the schedule. Here, again, 200 is added to the table figures to get the proper number.

The water works of the State of Illinois are classed under TD224 since 24, as we have seen, is the number for the states, Cuttered A–W (Fig. 13a). An example of a work classed under GB705.I3 (Fig. 13b) has been included to show the distinction that works on the water-supply engineering of a place class in TD, but works on the potential water supply, with no engineering involved, class in GB under hydrology.

The third example (Fig. 13c) relates to the waterworks of the City of Chicago, which does not class under the State of Illinois but under TD225, the 25 representing the number of "Cities (or other special), A–Z" of the United States. The .C5 is the Cutter for Chicago, the A6 1933 the "official" Cutter.

Notice in TD (Fig. 11) the special instructions pointing out that with a 2-number spread the first stands not only for general, when Cuttered .A1, but for provinces and states when Cuttered .A6–Z. These instructions would take precedence over the general instructions in Table I so that a work on water-supply

```
TD224
.I3A5
1940
```

Illinois. *Division of Sanitary Engineering.*
   Data on Illinois public water supplies, April 1, 1940.
[Springfield, 1940]
   18 l. tables. 22 x 28 cm.
   Cover title.

   1. Water-supply—Illinois.

   TD224.I 3A5   1940   628.109773   40–28524 rev 2*

   Library of Congress   [r56e⅔]

```
GB705
.I3A25
```

Illinois. *Water Survey.*
   Circular.
   [Urbana]
        no. illus. 23–28 cm.
   Began publication in 1928.

   1. Water-supply—Illinois.

        GB705.I 3A25   57–28082 ‡

        Library of Congress

```
TD225
.C5A6
1933
```

Chicago. *Bureau of engineering.*
   A century of progress in water works. 1833. Chicago.
1933. Prepared by Bureau of engineering, Department of
public works, city of Chicago. [Chicago, The Fred J. Ring-
ley company, printers, 1933]
   47, [1] p. incl. illus., ports., maps, tables, diagrs. 23cm.

   1. Chicago—Water-supply.   I. Title.

                                                   34–11464
   Library of Congress   TD225.C5A6   1933
                                [2]   628.1097731

Figure 14a

TF23
.K3

Kalmbach, Albert Carpenter, 1910–

Railroad panorama, by A. C. Kalmbach ... Milwaukee, Wis., Kalmbach publishing co., 1944.

6 p. l., 228 p. plates. port. 23½cm.

1. Railroads--U. S. I. Title.

44-6180

Library of Congress TF23.K3

[4] 385

TF23
.6
.S73

Steinheimer, Richard.

Western trains, by Richard Steinheimer and Donald Sims. Contributing photographers: James L. Ehernberger [and others. San Marino, Calif., distributed by Golden West Books, 1965]

71 p. illus. 22 x 25 cm.

1. Railroads—The West. 2. Railroads—Pictorial works. I. Sims, Donald, joint author. II. Title.

TF23.6.S73 385.360978 65-28090

Library of Congress [3]

Figure 14b

TF25
.S16B3

Bain, William E

Frisco folks; stories and pictures of the great steam days of the Frisco Road (St. Louis-San Francisco Railway Company) Denver, Sage Books [1961]

272 p. illus. 23 cm.

1. St. Louis-San Francisco Railway Company. I. Title.

TF25.S16B3 385.0973 61-14372 ‡

Library of Congress [2]

Figure 14c

engineering in the Province of Manitoba would class, not in TD227 as the province note might suggest, but in TD226 with a local Cutter of .M3 followed by the author Cutter. The second number for Canada would be reserved for cities; so a work on the waterworks of Winnipeg, Manitoba, would class in TD227.W5.

In TF, "Railroad Engineering and Operation," only 4 of the 6 numbers reserved for the historical aspect are used, and they are adapted to the fact that there is no ancient or medieval history of railroading, as opposed to harbor or water-supply engineering which extends back to earliest history. Under TF also note the instruction for the application of the table; the special aspect is not geographical at all but reserved for special railroads. Note, too, that there is no base number, Table I numbers are accepted as is.

For Kalmbach's work on United States railroads the general number 23 is used, and the work classed under TF23.K3 (Fig. 14a). For Steinheimer's work on railroads of the West (Fig. 14b), the decimal for the particular region of the country involved under 23 in Table I is selected, and 23.6 is obtained, so the book is classed under TF23.6.S73.

Bain's work on a specific railroad (Fig. 14c) passes to number 25 since the special instructions indicated that TF25 is used for special roads in the United States. Thus Bain's work is classed under TF25 and Cuttered, first, .S16 for the St. Louis-San Francisco Railway Company, then B3 for Bain. This classification should indicate that the work is on the operation of the railroad and/or the history of its construction. A history of the St. Louis-San Francisco Railway Company as an enterprise that issued stocks, purchased lines, effected mergers or such actions would be classed in HE.

The real problems in cataloging science and technology are substantive. Substantive problems derive from concepts and situations beyond classifiers' control, and delineations are no sooner assimilated in one area than they arise in another. The chemical physicists and the physical chemists may indeed jest about which national congress they should attend, but the cataloger who tries to offer a book as physical chemistry to a scientist who rejects it as chemical physics cannot afford the uncertainty.

Subject Classification Choice

One category of problems centers about the stress of a work. Many subject concepts, after all, appear with good reason in several classes, and the cataloger must decide in which one a book on a given topic must be classed. An example of this stress and its problems for the cataloger would be hydrodynamics. A book on hydrodynamics can be shelved under four classes. If rigorously theoretical and mathematically expressed, it is analytical mechanics and classes in QA (Mathematics) (Fig. 15a); if experimental and/or descriptive in nature, it classes in QC (Physics) (Fig. 15b); a third book on hydrodynamics may concern itself with general engineering applications and be classed with engineering mechanics in TA (Civil Engineering) (Fig. 15c); while a fourth may be hydrodynamics as

Figure 15a

QA911
.K5

Kishore, Nand.
Advanced level examples in hydrodynamics. [1st ed.]
Allahabad, Central Book Depot, 1962.

349 p. illus. 23 cm.

1. Hydrodynamics. I. Title.

QA911 K5   S A 64–6335 ‡

Library of Congress   [2½]   PL 480 : I–E–192

QC151
.L453

Levich, Veniamin Grigor'evich.
Physicochemical hydrodynamics. Translated by Scripta
Technica, inc. Englewood Cliffs, N. J., Prentice-Hall, 1962.

700 p. illus. 24 cm. (Prentice-Hall international series in the
physical and chemical engineering sciences)

1. Hydrodynamics. 2. Chemistry, Physical and theoretical.
I. Title.

QC151.L453   532.5   62—20437 ‡

Library of Congress   [6715]

Figure 15b

TA350
.W16

Wagner, Paul.
Strömungsenergie und mechanische arbeit; beiträge
zur abstrakten dynamik und ihre anwendung auf schiffs-
propeller, schnelllaufende pumpen und turbinen, schiffs-
widerstand, schiffssegel, windturbinen, trag- und schlag-
flügel und luftwiderstand von geschossen, von Paul Wagner ... Mit 151 textfiguren. Berlin, J. Springer, 1914.

xi, 252 p. illus., diagrs. 24^{cm}. M. 10

1. Mechanics, Applied. 2. Hydrodynamics. I. Title.

14–3058

Library of Congress   TA350.W16

Copyright A—Foreign 9460

Figure 15c

TC171
.D4

Deemter, Jan Jozef van.
　　Theoretische en numerieke behandeling van ontwaterings-
en infiltratie-stromingsproblemen. 's-Gravenhage, 1950.

　　viii, 67 p. diagrs. 24 cm.

　　Proefschrift—Amsterdam.
　　Summary in English.
　　"Stellingen": ⟨2⟩ p. inserted.
　　Bibliography: p. 67.

　　1. Hydrodynamics. 2. Water, Underground. 3. Drainage.

TC171.D4　　　　　　　　　　　　　　53–24216

　　Library of Congress　　　　⟨⁴⟩

applied only to the hydraulics of waterworks and be classed in TC (Hydraulic
Engineering) (Fig. 15d). This is the type of sorting code a cataloger has
programmed in the back of his mind, but its performance is unfortunately not
always certain.

　　Much more easily separated are books entitled *Nutrition* (Figs. 16a–16c).
They may be placed in QP (Physiology), if they do in fact deal solely with the
physiology of nutrition (Fig. 16a); in TX if they treat of the food and nutrition
problem in general as a housewife or home economics major needs to know it
(Fig. 16b); and in RA (Public Health), subsection "Personal Hygiene," if they
deal with eating for health (Fig. 16c).

　　A clerk may hand the cataloger a book entitled *Chemistry of Vital Products*,
who must choose QD (Chemistry) if the subject matter is oriented around the
physical chemistry of these vital products and the reactions involved in their
synthesis and degradation. Otherwise, if he is dealing with both substances and
organisms, he has to distinguish between a place in QH (General Biology), if
dealing with both plant and animal material, or in QP (Physiology), if dealing
with animal alone. Yet at the same time a work on the chemistry of proteins
classes in QP (Physiology), even if it deals with both plant and animal material,
since QH (General Biology) does not have a breakdown for specific substances.
Of course, general plant substances or even plant proteins would class in the
chemistry section of Plant Physiology in QK (Botany). In this category of work
the table of contents is usually a reliable tool for the cataloger, but a table of
contents and certainly a title are never the whole answer.

　　A category of works in which the table of contents can conceal as well as reveal
is shown in Figures 17a–17b. Suppose the cataloger has a work on construction.
The table of contents, with entries for materials, forms, and processes, will not
necessarily tell him if the book is about engineering construction in general—
which would class it in TA—or if it is concerned exclusively with the construction
of buildings, in which case it falls into TH (Building).

QP141
.L175

Lang, Konrad.
    Biochemie der Ernährung. Darmstadt, D. Steinkopff,
1957.

    xv, 411 p. illus. 23 cm. (Beiträge zur Ernährungswissenschaft,
Bd. 1)

    Bibliography : p. ₍379₎-395.

    1. Nutrition.   ɪ. Title.   (Series)

QP141.L175

58–26002

Library of Congress   ₍8₎

TX551
.S537

Silver, Bernard E
    Fundamentals of nutrition. ₍Albany, University of the
State of New York, Bureau of Vocational Development and
Industrial Teacher Training, 1951₎

    232 p. illus. 26 cm.

    1. Nutrition. 2. Diet. 3. Deficiency diseases.   ɪ. New York
(State) University. Bureau of Vocational Curriculum Development
and Industrial Teacher Training. ɪɪ. Title.

TX551.S537   *641.1 612.39   52—62291 ‡

Library of Congress   ₍53d2₎

RA784
.F7
1964

Fredericks, Carlton.
    Nutrition: your key to good health. ₍Rev., enl. version₎
North Hollywood, Calif., London Press ₍1964₎

    271 p. 17 cm.

    Previous editions published under title: Eat, live and be merry.

    1. Nutrition. 2. Diet. 3. Hygiene.   ɪ. Title.

RA784.F7 1964   613.2   64–6545

Library of Congress   ₍1₎

TA404
.R9T6

Toropov, A   S
　　Новая техника и передовая технология в строительстве
и производстве строительных материалов и изделий. Москва, ВПШ, 1960.

51 p.　illus.　22 cm.

At head of title: Заочная высшая партийная школа при ЦК КПСС.
Кафедра промышленного производства и строительства.

1. Building materials.　2. Building.　I. Title.
　　　　　　　　　Title transliterated: Novaíà tekhnika i
　　　　　　　　　peredovaíà tekhnologiíà v stroitel'stve.

TA404.R9T6　　　　　　　　　　　　　　　　63–42465 ‡

Library of Congress　　　　[₂]

TH145
.G35
1958

Gay, Charles Merrick, 1871–1951.
　　Materials and methods of architectural construction [by]
Harry Parker, Charles Merrick Gay [and] John W. Mac-
Guire. 3d ed.　New York, Wiley [1958]

xi, 724 p.　illus.　24 cm.

In earlier editions Gay's name appeared first on t. p.

1. Building.　2. Building materials.　　I. Parker, Harry, 1887–
II. Title: Architectural construction.

TH145.G35　1958　　　　690　　　　　　　58–8213

Library of Congress　　　[20]

Figure 17b

In a work on gasoline engines chapters on ignition systems, carburetion, and so
on are not going to reveal whether this deals with gasoline engines in general or
only with those used in automotive vehicles. The decision must be made between
TJ (Mechanical Engineering) and TL (Automotive Engineering). In the case of
shipbuilding, a work might be classed under general shipbuilding, while if it were
examined, the work would turn out to be concerned only with iron and steel ships.

The category of recent and imprecise terminology causes classification problems. What does one do with a work appearing under such a term as "earth
sciences"? Is it simply physical geography, Class GB? Is it rather geology, Class
QE? Or is it usually best classed in QE, but under the section of geophysics, since
the work usually centers around dynamic and structural geology?

What are the criteria for classing a work dealing with the space sciences? The
space sciences are variously defined as the sciences needed for the exploration of
space, as well as the sciences which can be investigated through instruments

placed in space. A nice overlap exists, but not identity. LC classes them both in QB500 (Universe). Or is the book on space sciences really a work on astronautics and eligible for Class TL (Aerospace Engineering)? Consider the use of the term "space scientist" in the newspapers and how imprecise the term is.

Is the latest acquisition on cybernetics really on control systems in man and machine, including information theory? If so, it classes properly in the new section at the end of subclass Q (Science—General). But if it deals only with computers, it classes in QA if the mathematics of its programming is the point of interest, or in TK if the circuitry is the focal point—and probably in the latter if it deals with both. If it is a popular work on automatic control, it would go in TJ (Mechanical Engineering) or TK (Electronic Engineering). If the cataloger is working with several languages, the various interpretations of new terms invite an especially cautious examination of the scope of material presented.

The decision to choose one class over another does not always involve staying inside the science and technology area. Are not virtually all the technical fields represented as industries in the social sciences? A directory of manufactures by firm name, for instance, classes in H, but a similar directory arranged by product is classed in TS. The difference between the two approaches to the history of a railroad has been mentioned above.

There might even be a problem in distinguishing the technical from the historical classes in the case of such romantic fields as gold mining and windmills. The cataloger will also need to keep firmly in mind the instructions written into the schedules for distinguishing the proper classification of military history in D and E or the military classes of U and V.

In the LC classification system, as elsewhere, there are matters of precedence. A work on game conservation classes with SK (Hunting), but a work on the conservation of a particular species is classed in QL (Zoology). A work on the stratigraphic geology of Canada classes with the geographical number for Canada under the general geology section. A work on the Mesozoic *sediments* of Canada would class, on the contrary, with the number for the Mesozoic period under the stratigraphic breakdown. And what about the Mesozoic ammonites of Canadian sediments? Ordinarily the organism takes precedence over the strata or geographic location; in the case of the ammonites, which are used to establish zones within the Mesozoic, the cataloger has to decide in each case whether the stress is on the organism *per se* or on what stratigraphic information it provides. This latter situation argues for the inadvisability of writing too rigid orders of precedence into the schedules.

The biggest problem of all, certainly the most exciting, is that of expanding the schedules, and it encompasses all the aspects of the problems dealt with up till now: Where does a concept fit? What does it include? Should it be provided for in more than one class schedule?

In principle, LC will add a class as soon as it has a book requiring a new one; that is, LC has a "rule of one." Very commonly, however, the need for a new class becomes apparent only after the passage of time. New topics do not appear ordinarily all at once; they develop out of existing disciplines. Cybernetics is an example. It was defined by Wiener when he coined the term in his first book, but it could not be predicted how the concept would develop, particularly how the literature of the topic would emerge, and, therefore, the kind and extent of the provisions that would need to be made. The result is that, even with careful monitoring of the literature, the point at which there is sufficient stabilization to warrant the development in the schedule will find some of the literature already in other classes.

Another common case is the development of bodies of literature on the subtopics of a subject that had at first been treated generally. For example, at first there was a single number for the psychology of adolescence. Now there are provisions for such special topics as emotion, ethics, and so on. As the quarterly supplements of the *Additions and Changes* will testify, LC is constantly engaged in the search for optimal classification sites.

Discussion

Question: What is being done to keep subject headings in classes Q and T more closely related to current terminology and/or developments in technology and science?

Mr. Blume: This is a big problem in the field of science and technology and gets a lot of consideration, although the results may not always show it. To update terminology in a catalog the size of ours is quite a job. The amount of material is certainly a prime factor.

If there is an emormous body of material represented by cards in the catalog, we have to rely on updating the concepts by adding new *see* references to refer the user to the correct material. If there is a small body of material and we have what we might say is a retreatment of the subject (once in a while a subject dies cold, then somebody starts it again), we usually change the terminology.

Question: How did QM and QP get into Q rather than R?

Mr. Blume: These classes fit *our* concept of biology and not our concept of medicine; they could be put in medicine for a special library but not for ours. In the first place, QP is Animal Physiology, that is, it is not limited to human physiology but involves all animal physiology. QM, while labeled Human Anatomy, has a section on histology used for normal histology in the animal world, not only for man. Class R is used for Medicine as a field, including public aspects of medicine, education, and technical medicine. If we included QM (Anatomy) and QP (Physiology) in R, we would have to include BF (Psychology) with Psychiatry.

Question: Is anything being done to bring interdisciplinary areas of biological chemistry and/or physics, or topics such as quantum electronics and molecular biology, under any subclasses so as to put the entire subject areas together?

Mr. Blume: In general, no; such an arrangement creates as many problems as it solves. Most of these developments are, after all, linear developments. They are new approaches and new understandings. While one could justify setting up new subclasses for them, one would break the continuity of what is on the shelves in the shelflist. Cybernetics, for example, was attached to the end of subclass Q. It is the sort of thing that possibly could have its own subclass; it did not have to be there, but we used Q. I think I would have to say no, we are not, in general, trying to bring in new subclasses.

Question: When LC classes a monographic series of societies or institutions as a series rather than as separates, where does current policy class the series—in the number for societies or in collected works?

Mr. Blume: If it is a monographic series and if there is a number provided for serial collected works, we class it there; otherwise we use the societies and periodicals number.

Question: The field of conservation is growing and at present is scattered in the LC classification. Do you foresee its being consolidated as a new class eventually?

Mr. Blume: We thought we had made considerable progress recently in getting a general place for it, i.e., by placing conservation at the end of subclass S. No, as far as I know, we do not intend to make the field of conservation one for the same reason that I mentioned in relation to the interdisciplinary areas. It is already intertwined with material in other subclasses.

Question: How does LC make decisions on treating series as sets with or without analytics or as separates? This decision should also be reported in *New Serial Titles.*

Mr. Blume: Since we are discussing classification here, I assume the question means whether we will collect a series or break it down, in which case analytics, as subject problems, are really not in question.

What you do when you make a series decision is not so much make a choice as make an educated guess from the first number as to what the rest of the series will be like. In essence, with the mechanics that we have at LC, there is only one type of series in which you have a choice—this is a series in which each piece *could* be analyzed. You can choose to treat it as monographs or as a collection. Everything else is already predetermined. A numbered publisher's series is treated as monographs. Newspapers or magazines from the newsstand, and I am using series in the broadest sense, are already predesignated, i.e., collected, not analyzed.

If you have a series in which you suspect that you will have even one number that cannot be analyzed, the whole series has to be collected. At LC we would never put the analyzed parts of a series with their respective topic numbers and then put everything that was left over into one number for a series. Theoretically this could be done, but we do not do it.

Question: Is there any rule for assigning subject headings for alloys, for example, cadmium-zinc alloys, copper-magnesium? We already have magnesium-cadmium alloys.

Mr. Blume: The current practice is that the first time you have the combination, the alloy is established on the basis of the main components; since you have cadmium-zinc alloys, it would be established in this form. If you get zinc-cadmium alloys, you would still use the established subject because you should have *see* references from all the other combinations. This may not be satisfactory in a highly technical subject list, but for our purposes it is.

Chapter 6

Assignment of Author Numbers

Robert R. Holmes

The Library of Congress author or book notation has developed along with the classification schedules since the beginning of this century. If the Library were starting afresh today, there are some specific things which, in the light of the staff's present knowledge, would be done differently, but in general the concepts and principles which form the basis of present practice have proved their worth and merit over the years.

Derivation of Book and Author Notation

At the outset it should be very clear that the derivation of the author or book notation, which augments the class number into a definitive and unique call number, is in many respects an extension of the classification process. The purpose of the resulting call number is to bring the books on the shelves, and the cards which represent them in the shelflist, into an orderly and consistent subarrangement within the specific subject class numbers which the printed classification schedules provide. The most common of these subarrangements is alphabetical by author or other main entry—an arrangement with which both users of the library and the catalogers are familiar.

However, if the works lend themselves to another meaningful arrangement within the specific class, then such an arrangement is effected by the shelflister prior to the final subarrangement. This "meaningful arrangement" is the kind which places translations adjacent to and immediately following the original work, which places works about an author following the author's own works, and which places document publications ahead of other publications in the same class. The point which should be stressed is that in the derivation of the book notation the purpose is to arrange the works within the specific class numbers in the most orderly, consistent, usable, and simple manner.

Another point which merits constant awareness is that the author notation segment of each and every Library of Congress call number is derived from the Library of Congress Shelflist. Since this Shelflist is as unique as the shelflist in

AUTHOR NUMBERS

Library of Congress call numbers consist in general of two principal elements: class number and author number, to which are added as required symbols designating a particular work and a particular book. This statement offers a brief explanation of the Library's system of author numbers, or, more properly, of assigning the symbols by which names are designated and differentiated in call numbers.

Library of Congress author symbols are composed of initial letters followed by Arabic numbers. The numbers are used decimally and are assigned on the basis of the tables given below in a manner that preserves the alphabetical order of names within a class.

1. After the initial letter S
   for the second letter: a   ch   e   h   i   m o p t   u
   use number: 2   3   4   5   6   7–8   9

2. After other initial consonants
   for second letter: a   e   i   o   r   u
   use number: 3   4   5   6   7   8

3. After initial vowels
   for second letter: b   d   lm   n   p   r   st
   use number: 2   3   4   5   6   7   8

Letters not included in the foregoing tables are assigned the next higher or lower number as required by previous assignments in the particular class.

The following examples illustrate the application of these tables:

1. Names beginning with the letter S:

Sabine	.S15	Shank	.S45
Saint	.S2	Shipley	.S5
Schaefer	.S3	Smith	.S6
Schwedel	.S35	Steel	.S7
Scott	.S37	Storch	.S75
Seaton	.S4	Sturges	.S8
Sewell	.S43	Sullivan	.S9

2. Names beginning with other consonants:

Carter	.C3	Cox	.C65
Cecil	.C4	Crocket	.C7
Cinelli	.C5	Croft	.C73
Corbett	.C6	Cullen	.C8

3. Names beginning with vowels:

Abernathy	.A2	Appleby	.A6
Adams	.A3	Archer	.A7
Aldrich	.A4	Arundel	.A78
Allen	.A45	Atwater	.A87
Ames	.A5	Austin	.A9

Since the tables provide only a general framework for the assignment of author numbers, it should be noted that the symbol for a particular name is constant only within a single class.

L. C. card 49–238

Figure 1

every other library, the author notation which even an experienced and skilled shelflister selects will vary slightly, depending upon the particular library collection to which the work in hand is being added.

LC Author Numbers

The author notation is constructed for the Library of Congress Shelflist by using the Author Numbers sheet[1] as a guide (Fig. 1). Because the principles followed in using the author notation sheet are much the same throughout the classification schedules and the Shelflist, an understanding of and some practice in the use of this sheet are prerequisite. At the outset, several factors regarding this sheet and its use should be kept clearly in mind.

First, as the introductory paragraph of the Author Numbers sheet states, the sheet deals with the designation of names, that is, persons, titles, corporate bodies, countries, and topics. The kind of name makes little difference, for the principles of using the sheet remain the same.

Second, the sheet is an aid and nothing else; it is meant to be, and is at the Library of Congress, used flexibly. Thus, for a name beginning with the letter "S," the number "2" will not always be used when the second letter of the name is the letter "a." The choice depends on what names are already represented in the shelflist for the particular class.

Third, the numbers are used decimally. They are, therefore, indefinitely expandable and are selected to provide for an infinite number of later additions in such a way that a basic alphabetical subarrangement can be preserved and, at the same time, the call number kept as short as possible. Alphabetical subarrangement is used frequently in specific class numbers provided throughout the classification schedules. The alphabetical arrangement used is based upon the guidelines specified in *Filing Rules for the Dictionary Catalogs of the Library of Congress*,[2] where essentially the filing is done word by word, and letter by letter in each word, according to the order of the English alphabet.

A simple example will show how the system operates. (Since catalogers may be working with LC printed cards or from LC proof sheets, it will be helpful for them to get into the habit of reading the call number technically, and in order to do so the distinction between the class number and the author number is of prime importance.) Class Q (Science) contains subclass QL for "Zoology," and the specific number QL89 is provided for "Animal lore. Sea serpents, etc." In Brown's *Sea Serpents* (Fig. 2a), the call number QL89.B7 may be read by noting that the class number is QL89 and the author notation is .B7. The author number .B7 is built on the initial letter of the author's surname, and since the second letter following the initial consonant "B" is the letter "r," the Arabic numeral "7" is used as suggested on the Author Numbers sheet.

Burton's *More Animal Legends* is the next entry in the Shelflist (Fig. 2c). Again, the author notation is built on the initial consonant "B," and since the

Figure 2a

QL89
.B7

Brown, Charles Edward, 1872–1946.
    Sea serpents; Wisconsin occurrences of these weird water
monsters in the Four lakes, Rock, Red Cedar, Koshkonong,
Geneva, Elkhart, Michigan, and other lakes [by] Charles E.
Brown ... Madison, Wis., Wisconsin folklore society, 1942.

    cover-title, 10 p. 19 cm.

    1. Sea serpent.   I. Wisconsin folklore society.

QL89.B7   398.4   44—5754

Library of Congress   [a58c½]

QL89
.B79

Burton, Maurice, 1898–
    The elusive monster; an analysis of the evidence from
Loch Ness. London, Hart-Davis, 1961.

    176 p. illus. 23 cm.

    Includes bibliography.

    1. Sea-serpent. 2. Ness, Loch. I. Title.

QL89.B79   62–42445 ‡

Library of Congress   [1]

Figure 2b

QL89
.B8

Burton, Maurice, 1898–
    More animal legends. Illustrated by Jane Burton. London, F. Muller [1959]

    208 p. illus. 21 cm.

    1. Animal lore. I. Title. II. Title: Animal legends.

QL89.B8   591.508   59–65062 ‡

Library of Congress   [2]

Figure 2c

letter following is "u," the numeral "8" was selected from the Author Numbers sheet (Fig. 1).

Then in 1962 a shelflister received for processing *The Elusive Monster* (Fig. 2b) by the same Burton already represented in QL89. Since works in this class are arranged alphabetically by author, a subarrangement, alphabetically by title, must be introduced for works by the same author. In filing titles under an author's name, the initial article in the nominative case is disregarded in all languages (see *Filing Rules*),[3] and the shelflister therefore notes that the word "elusive" precedes the word "more" alphabetically. Thus, he selects a number which will cause the card representing *The Elusive Monster* to follow very close to, and immediately preceding, *More Animal Legends*. In this instance, he in fact selected the number .B79, expanding on the numeral "7," since the numeral "8" was already in use. The Library of Congress Shelflist for this small segment of Class QL89 actually reads as shown by Figures 2a–2c. In the literature classes different devices are used for indicating alphabetical subarrangement of works by the same author (see Chapter 7).

This particular example was selected for two reasons: first, to illustrate the development of author notation; second, to get reaction to the number used for Burton's *The Elusive Monster*. Most experienced catalogers working in their own libraries would probably have selected the number .B77 or .B78 for *The Elusive Monster* in order to allow room in this class for any additional works by Maurice Burton which would file between *The Elusive Monster* and *More Animal Legends*.

If Burton subsequently wrote a work entitled *Later Animal Legends,* also classed in QL89, the Library of Congress would have to use a three-digit author notation, perhaps .B795, to fit the new work into proper alphabetical order by title. If, however, the number .B77 had been used for *The Elusive Monster*, then .B78 could have been used for the more recent work, *Later Animal Legends*.

The use of these examples should give an idea of how the author notation sheet is to be used. The following points should be clear:

1. An attempt should always be made to keep the author notation as short and simple as possible.
2. The numbers should be selected with an eye to future insertions into the shelflist.
3. The number appearing on LC printed cards is based on the holdings of the Library of Congress as represented in its Shelflist.

A somewhat more populous class number will further illustrate the way in which the author notation is derived and will illustrate some additional points. Class H (Social Science) provides for "Economic History" in subclass HD, and the class number HD31 is used for general treatises in the English language on the organization of production, including general theory of management. In 1942 Schreiber's *Philosophy of Organization* was added to the Library (Fig. 3). From the Author Numbers sheet it can be seen how the .S34 was selected. *Guides to Management* by Schell was added to the same segment of the class in 1948 (Fig.

Figure 6

```
HD31
.S337
           Schmidt, Richard Nicholas, 1916–
               Executive control.  Buffalo, University Bookstore, °1956.
               266 p.  illus.  29 cm.




               1. Industrial management.    I. Title.

           HD31.S337                                          56–46279 ‡

           Library of Congress                 ₍₈₎
```

4), and was given the author notation .S33 to precede Schreiber's book alphabetically.

It became necessary in 1955 to insert a new work by Schleh between the two publications already mentioned (Fig. 5). Here the author notation is expanded to a three-digit number. In 1956 Schmidt's *Executive Control* was added to the collections (Fig. 6), and the author number .S337 was assigned. With a decimal system of notation, alphabetical order on the shelves and in the shelflist can be preserved with no difficulty.

These examples demonstrate how the decimal author notation is indefinitely expandable and how later works are inserted within existing limits, in this example between .S33, representing Schell, and .S34, representing Schreiber. The order resulting on the shelves and in the Shelflist by 1965 was as follows:

HD31   Schell, Erwin Haskell, 1889–
.S33   Guides to management operating policy . . .
HD31   Schleh, Edward C
.S335   Successful executive action . . .
HD31   Schmidt, Richard Nicholas, 1916–
.S337   Executive control . . .
HD31   Schreiber, Norman B   1905–
.S34   Philosophy of organization . . .

Corporate main entries are interfiled with personal author main entries, and the same principles of author notation are used. Further along in the HD31 Shelflist may be found four titles as shown in Figures 7a–7d. It is unlikely that LC will receive a work entered under title for incorporation into this particular class, but if it does, the work will be inserted alphabetically by entry and the author notation will be derived from the first word of the title which affects filing.

In addition to illustrating the point that corporate main entries are interfiled with personal author main entries, Figures 7a–7d also illustrate the style in which the call numbers are overprinted in the upper left corner of the cards filed in the LC catalogs.

113

When the shelflister has derived the author notation, he writes the completed call number on a temporary card which is immediately filed in the Shelflist to hold the number. He also writes the call number on the manuscript which is forwarded to the printer and on the verso of the title page of the book. The call number appears in the book in the same style as it appears on the overprinted cards filed in the LC catalogs, but the call number appears on the spine of the book in the style illustrated by the sample labels which show on the right-hand side of the cards in Figures 7a–7d.

The Library of Congress uses labels on which the symbols indicating the class or the subclass, one or two capital letters, are preprinted. As the books are readied for the shelves, a preparations assistant examines the call number as written on the verso of the title page of the book, selects an appropriate label preprinted with the one- or two-letter class symbol, and then hand-letters in India ink the remainder of the call number.

The single decimal digit "1" should be avoided unless one deliberately wishes to block further expansion. The illustration under the letter "S" on the Author Numbers sheet will serve as an example. If .S1 were chosen for the name *Sabine,* and a later work was received by an author called *Saab,* it would be difficult to provide a number which would fit the work by *Saab* into its proper alphabetical sequence without shifting *Sabine* from .S1 to .S15 or .S2. Therefore, the number .S15 is suggested for *Sabine* on the author notation sheet. As can be seen, there is plenty of room for decimal expansion prior to .S15. Similarly, the numeral "1" should be avoided as the final digit of the decimal. The sheet shows .C6 for *Corbett;* the number .C61 should not be used for *Costin* because the way would then be blocked for future insertion of the names *Cosby, Cosgrove, Costa,* etc. Rather, use .C63 or .C64 for *Costin,* and there is room for indefinite future expansion.

HD
31
.S65

HD31
.S65

Srivastava, V   L
    Industrial management and business administration ₁by₁
    V. L. Srivastava. Calcutta, Scientific Book Agency ₁1965₁

    xviii, 591 p.   illus.   23 cm.

    Bibliography: p. ₁583₁–586.

    1. Industrial management.   I. Title.

    HD31.S65   S A 65–9966

                                                           PL 480: I–E–4648

    Library of Congress   ₁2½₁

Figure 7a

Figure 7b

HD31
.S68

Stanford Research Institute. *International Development Center.*

    Managers for small industry, an international study ₍by₎ Joseph E. Stepanek, senior industries specialist. Introd. by V. T. Krishnamachari. Glencoe, Ill., Free Press, 1960.

    245 p. illus. 24 cm.

    At head of title: International Industrial Development Center, Stanford Research Institute.

    1. Small business. 2. Industrial management.   I. Stepanek, Joseph E. II. Title.

HD31.S68   658.9   60–16345 rev ‡

Library of Congress   ₍r61k4₎

HD
31
.S68

HD31
.S683

Stanford Research Institute. *Long Range Planning Service.*

    Planning, action, profits; highlights of a Long Range Planning Service management seminar. ₍Menlo Park, Calif., Stanford Research Institute, 1962₎

    16 p. illus. 28 cm.

    1. Industrial management. 2. Production control.   I. Title.

HD31.S683   64–2496

Library of Congress   ₍1₎

HD
31
.S683

Figure 7c

Figure 7d

HD31
.S69

Steiner, George Albert, 1912–   *ed.*

    Managerial long-range planning. Research seminar series conducted by the Graduate School of Business Administration, University of California, Los Angeles, sponsored by the McKinsey Foundation for Management Research, Inc. New York, McGraw-Hill ₍1963₎

    xii, 334 p. illus. 24 cm. (McGraw-Hill series in management)

    Bibliographical references included in footnotes.

    1. Industrial management—Case studies.   I. California. University. Graduate School of Business Administration. II. Title.

HD31.S69   658.082   63—19317

Library of Congress   ₍63f6₎

HD
31
.S69

Double Cutter Numbers

Library of Congress call numbers include double Cutter numbers when it is necessary and desirable to use them, but never do they include triple Cutter numbers. The double Cutter numbers occur in various situations. One of the most frequent uses of the first Cutter number is to indicate a subject, and when so used, the first Cutter number is properly part of the class number. At first illustratively and now for the most part exhaustively, such topical Cutter numbers are being printed in the classification schedules. They may be used for specific subjects; for example, in "Gas Industry," in TP761 (Other special kinds, A–Z), .B8 is used for "Butane gas," and .P4 is used for "Petroleum gas." Or, they may be used for specific literary authors, as .O46 is used for Jack London in PS3523. The feature which I wish to stress about the use of double Cutter numbers is that although the decimal point is placed only before the first Cutter number and is omitted before the second, *both* Cutter numbers may be expanded decimally. The books are arranged on the shelves and the cards are filed in the shelflist on the principle that the digits following each of the two letters are decimals.

Another point which merits inclusion in a general discussion of author notation is that the suggestions given on the author notation sheet are disregarded when tables printed in the classification schedules make other provisions. For example, Table IXa in Class PN–PZ specifies a .Z5–99 arrangement for biographical and critical works about authors who are explicitly provided for in the PN–PZ classification schedules. The class number PS3523.O46, which is reserved for works by and about Jack London, illustrates this provision. To the first Cutter .O46, a second Cutter number is added, selected in the range .Z5–99 so as to fit the biographical and critical works about London into the shelflist alphabetically by their own authors as in the examples in Figures 8a–8d. The .Z5–99 Cutter numbers may be expanded to three digits when necessary.

The above group of cards also illustrates the value of reading the call number technically. Observe that in these examples the author notation is .Z64, .Z67, .Z84, .Z87, and that the class number, which is provided in the printed PN–PZ schedule, is PS3523.O46, the number reserved for London as a twentieth-century individual author of American literature. In addition, London's number exemplifies the practice of deriving the Cutter number for the second letter of the name. In this instance, the whole number PS3523 is reserved for all authors whose surnames begin with the letter "L." Since, then, PS3523 means "L," the Cutter number is built on the *second* letter of the name, in this case the letter "o."

There are two other matters which should be mentioned briefly: the shelf arrangement of translations and the shelf arrangement of individual biography.

Translations Cuttering

Translations generally follow the original work in alphabetical order by language. They are distinguished from the original by the addition of digits to the

```
PS3523
.O46Z87
        Rentmeister, Heinrich.
           Das Weltbild Jack Londons, von Heinz Rentmeister.
        Halle (Saale) M. Niemeyer, 1960.

           256 p.   24 cm.

           Includes bibliography.




           1. London, Jack, 1876–1916.      I. Title.

        PS3523.O46Z87                                 61–34238 rev ↕

        Library of Congress              ₁r66b¼₁
```

Cutter number. To assign a Cutter number to a translation, the shelflist is first examined to see whether the original is already represented. If so, the translation number is added to the number for the original; if not, it must be determined what the number would be for the original and the translation number added to that number. If the number for a work in its original language is .L3, the numbers for translations would look like this:

.L3	Original work
.L313	English translation
.L314	French translation
.L315	German translation
.L316	Italian translation
.L317	Russian translation
.L318	Spanish translation

The languages most likely to be represented in American library collections are shown above. If a Bulgarian, Chinese, or Czech translation were to be inserted, .L312 would be used; a Hebrew translation would be added onto .L315; a Portuguese translation would be added onto .L316, and so on, according to what numbers had already been used.

Figures 9a–9b illustrate the use of this pattern: In this instance, obviously ".L314" would not be used for French translations since French is the language of the original work; ".L314" would be left open for later use for Finnish translations, or else German translations, Italian translations, etc., could be moved forward, if desirable, to provide an open three-digit number between Italian and Russian translations. In other words, the arrangement shown in the translation table is a general guide, but it is to be used flexibly depending on the language of the original work.

Note that the digit "1" is inserted between the number for the work in the original language (".L3" in Fig. 9a) and the number for the language of translation (3 = English, 4 = French, 5 = German, 6 = Italian, etc.). This is

SEE
p. 125

done to provide room for insertion of numbers for other works in the original language between book Cutters of ".L32" and ".L39."

A major exception to this practice is made when double Cutter numbers are used for authors and titles of individual works—a common practice in the literature classes. When the double Cutter number is employed, the digit "1" is omitted between the number for the work in the original language and the digit representing the language of translation. Mrs. Hines will cover this practice, but a brief example will prove useful. PS3525.A27 is the class number for the works of Archibald MacLeish, and his poem *Conquistador* was given the call number PS3525.A27C6. A Spanish translation of this work has the call number PS3525.A27C68 and thus stands on the shelves following the work in the original language. It is felt at LC that the call number can be safely shortened by omitting the digit "1" because, in instances like this, the class number PS3525.A27 is very specific. In other words, LC counts on the fact that MacLeish

---

DC239
.L3

Lachouque, Henry, 1883–
    Les derniers jours de l'Empire. ₍Paris₎ Arthaud ₍1965₎

    283 p. facsim., map, plates, ports. 21 cm. (Vies célèbres de l'histoire, 4)

    Bibliography : p. 279–₍280₎

    1. Napoléon ɪ—Elba and the Hundred Days, 1814–1815.   ɪ. Title.

DC239.L3   65–82180

Library of Congress   ₍2₎

Figure 9a

DC239
.L313

Lachouque, Henry, 1883–
    The last days of Napoleon's empire: from Waterloo to St. Helena ; translated ₍from the French₎ by Lovett F. Edwards. London, Allen & Unwin, 1966.

    3–299 p. front. (port.) 8 plates (incl. facsim.) 22½ cm. 42/–

    Bibliography : p. 292–293.   (B 67–2783)

    1. Napoléon ɪ, Emperor of the French, 1769–1821—Elba and the Hundred Days, 1814–1815.   ɪ. Title.

DC239.L313   940.2′7′0924   67–75412

Library of Congress   ₍3₎

Figure 9b

(or any other author similarly provided for in the classification schedules) will not write a great number of works whose titles begin with the letter "C," and that the numbers "C2" through "C5," and "C7" through "C9," will allow sufficient space for insertion of future titles beginning with the letter "C."

Biography Cuttering

For individual biography the following table has been found effective:

INDIVIDUAL BIOGRAPHY

.x	= Cutter number for the individual
.xA2	= Collected works
.xA3	= Autobiography, diary, etc.
.xA4	= Letters
.xA41–49	= Letters to particular individuals, A–Z, by correspondent
.xA5	= Speeches, etc.
.xA6–Z	= Works by other persons about the individual

Selections, excerpts, and the like may be put with .xA2, usually as .xA25–29, so that room for expansion of collected works is left between .xA2 and .xA24. Indexes, concordances, and the like are put in .xA6–Z. This table may be used with all schedules in classes which mean individual biography, except when other provisions are inserted in the schedule.

Discussion

Question: Will future editions of the LC *List of Subject Headings* reflect new class numbers if there have been changes in the numbers for certain subjects since the earlier editions?

Mr. Holmes: New class numbers are included in successive editions of the *List of Subject Headings.* They are also printed in the monthly *Supplements,* even if the only change in the heading is the addition or revision of a class number.

Notes

[1] The Author Numbers sheet reproduced as Figure 1 on p.108 is LC's "Cutter" table; the true Cutter-Sanborn tables are not used. The Author Numbers sheet is available free of charge, and has also been published in the *Cataloging Service Bulletin,* no.65, August 1964, p.5.

[2] U.S. Library of Congress, Processing Dept., *Filing Rules for the Dictionary Catalogs of the Library of Congress* (Washington: 1956). 187p.

[3] *Ibid.,* p.58.

Chapter 7

Subclassification and Book Numbers in Language and Literature

Prepared by Elizabeth Lockwood

Presented by Patricia S. Hines

In the area of philology and language there are no particular problems of subclassification, and the author notation is handled as described in the previous chapter by Mr. Holmes. It is in the area of the literature of each language that problems arise; this paper will show how the individual authors and their works are treated.

In each section of the P schedules for the literature of special languages or countries, there are classes within period subdivisions for individual authors and their works in all literary forms: fiction, poetry, drama, essays of a literary character (not dealing with a special subject), autobiographical works by writers, and biographies and criticism of writers. Tables are provided for the subdivision of these works of individual authors at the end of the PN, PR, PS, and PZ schedules, referred to as the PN–PZ schedule. Some of these tables are also printed at the end of other literature schedules; where no tables are provided, those in the PN–PZ schedule are used.

Individual Author Tables

Where the schedule has provided 98, 48, 18, or 8 classification numbers for a single author, the corresponding table (usually so indicated under the author) is used; for example, Robert Browning has been assigned Table II with 48 numbers, from PR4200 to PR4248. In most cases the authors are assigned a single number or a Cutter number to distinguish one author from another. Where single numbers are indicated, there is a choice of Tables VIII, VIIIa, or VIIIb; for authors with Cutter numbers, there is a choice of Tables IX, IXa, and IXb.

Tables VIII and IX

Tables VIII and IX are shown in Figure 1. These tables are rarely used for modern authors. They are most useful for authors, now dead, whose total output is known but about whom many biographies and criticisms have been written. In Tables VIII and IX, .A61–79 and .xA61–79 have been circled; only this small

TABLES OF SUBDIVISIONS FOR INDIVIDUAL AUTHORS

VIII (1 no.)	IX (Cutter no.)	Authors with one number or Cutter number In Table IX and variants, x=the Cutter number
		Collected works.
.A1	. x	By date.
.A11–19	. xA11–19	By editor (alphabetically).
		Translations (Collected).
.A2–29	. xA2–29	English. By translator.
.A3–39	. xA3–39	French. By translator.
.A5–59	. xA5–59	Other. By language (alphabetically).
.A6	. xA6	Selections.
.A61–79	. xA61–79	Separate works. By title.
.A8–Z	. xA8–Z	Biography and criticism.

Figure 1

space is reserved for separate works arranged by title. The more generous allowance has been reserved for biography and criticism: .A8–Z and .xA8–Z.

Figures 2a–2b are examples of Table IX. The first example (Fig. 2a) shows an author whose dates are 1770–1843. The author number as indicated in the schedule is .H2. The author's work *Hyperion* is given A7, which falls within the designated span of .xA61–79 for separate works by title. The second example (Fig. 2b) shows a criticism of the work. For this, the A7 has been expanded by adding two digits and becomes A723, because criticism of a single work classes with the work.

Tables VIIIb and IXb

Figure 3 shows Tables VIIIb and IXb. These tables were frequently used early in the century with Class PT (German literature) because they provided that translations, both collected and for separate works, be kept together by language, which may have been thought an advantage in open-shelf browsing. On the tables the span of numbers assigned to translations, subdivided by language, for collections and separate works has been outlined with a bracket.

However, present LC practice for all new authors and for most modern writers is to use Tables VIIIa and IXa as shown in Figure 4. These tables provide the greatest spread of numbers for separate works (in one instance, Table VIIIa, from .A7 to .Z4, and in the other instance, Table IXa, from .xA61 to Z49). Consequently, there has been less spread allowed for biography and criticism.

Tables VIIIa and IXa

Since these tables are the ones most used, perhaps a more detailed discussion is in order.

Figure 2a

```
PT2359
.H2A7
1947
```
Hölderlin, Friedrich, 1770–1843.
    Hyperion; oder, Der Eremit in Griechenland. Mit einem
Nachwort hrsg. von Erich Hock. Aschaffenburg, P. Patt-
loch, 1947.
    167 p. 22 cm.

    i. Title.
                  Full name: Johann Christian Friedrich Hölderlin.

    PT2359.H2A7 1947   51–31412

        Library of Congress   [₃]

```
PT2359
.H2A723
```
Wentzlaff-Eggebert, Friedrich Wilhelm, 1905–
    Opfer und Schicksal in Hölderlins "Hyperion" und
"Empedokles." Strassburg, Hünenburg-Verlag, 1943.
    24 p. 22 cm.

    "Als Vortrag gehalten am 26. Februar 1942 im Theater der Stadt
Strassburg bei einem Hölderlin-Abend, der gemeinsam veranstaltet
wurde von dem Theater der Stadt Strassburg und der Studentenschaft
der Reichsuniversität Strassburg."

    1. Hölderlin, Friedrich, 1770–1843. Hyperion. 2. Hölderlin, Fried-
rich, 1770–1843. Empedokles. i. Title.

    PT2359.H2A723   831.67   50–51681

    Library of Congress   [₃]

Figure 2b

Collected Works

    The first item "Collected works" is interpreted as meaning complete works, or a collection of whole works. Selections from various published volumes are classed as anthologies in the .A6 or .xA6 number, which has the caption "Selections." The date of imprint is added to the call number for the publication date of collected novels, essays, poems, plays in .A15, .A17, and .A19 and for selections in .A6.

    If an author is known primarily as a poet, such as Robert Frost, his collected poems are treated as collected works. There is no need to use the number for collected poems. With D. H. Lawrence, who wrote in many forms but who was best known for fiction, collected poetry is placed in .A17 and collected plays in .A19. Any collection of an author must be examined very carefully to see where it fits best and what other types of his works have already been shelflisted.

TABLES OF SUBDIVISIONS FOR INDIVIDUAL AUTHORS

VIII[b] (1 no.)	IX[b] (Cutter no.)	Authors with one number or Cutter number
		Collected works.
.A1	.x	By date.
.A11–14	.xA11–14	By editor.
.A15	.xA15	Collected novels.
.A16	.xA16	Collected essays, miscellanies, etc.
.A17	.xA17	Collected poems.
.A19	.xA19	Collected plays.
.A3–Z29	.xA3–Z29	Separate works.
		Translations.
.Z3–39	.xZ3–39	English.
.Z4–49	.xZ4–49	French.
.Z6–69	.xZ6–69	Other. By language (alphabetically).
.Z7	.xZ7	Selections.
.Z71–79	.xZ71–79	Adaptations, imitations, dramatizations, etc. (By title.)
.Z8–9	.xZ8–9	Biography and criticism.

Figure 3

TABLES OF SUBDIVISIONS FOR INDIVIDUAL AUTHORS

VIII[a] (1 no.)	IX[a] (Cutter no.)	Authors with one number or Cutter number
		Collected works.
.A1	.x	By date.
.A11–14	.xA11–14	By editor.
.A15	.xA15	Collected novels.
.A16	.xA16	Collected essays, miscellanies, etc.
.A17	.xA17	Collected poems.
.A19	.xA19	Collected plays.
		Translations (Collected).
.A2–29	.xA2–29	English. By translator.
.A3–39	.xA3–39	French. By translator.
.A5–59	.xA5–59	Other. By language (alphabetically).
.A6	.xA6	Selections.
.A7–Z4 .xA61	.xA7–Z49	Separate works.
.Z5A–Z	.xZ5–99	Biography and criticism.

Figure 4

An integral work brought out by an author is treated as a separate work, although it may be a collection. Volumes of poetry are common cases. Take, for instance, Edna St. Vincent Millay's *A Few Figs from Thistles*. This is an integral work (that is, not a collection in the special sense) and is treated as a single work, Cuttered .F4 for the title.

Translations

In the section of the tables on Translations are grouped not only collected works in translation but also selections from various works. Translations of collections in English appear in .A2–29, French .A3–39, and German .A4–49 and are arranged in alphabetical order *by translator*. However, in .A5–59 the arrangement is *by languages* other than the three above; for example, .A57 could be used for Russian, the 7 standing for *R*. Translations of individual works will follow the original work placed in .A7–Z4 or .xA61–Z49. This is accomplished by adding digits to the Cutter number for the title of the work in the original language. As examples, look at the two items in Figures 5a–5b.

In the first example (Fig. 5a) the book is a Spanish translation of MacLeish's *Conquistador*, PS3525.A27C68. The .A27 is the author number, the C6 is the number for the original work in English, and the digit 8 is added for the Spanish translation. In the second example the book is Hemingway's *Across the River and into the Trees* translated into French, PS3515.E37A74 being the number assigned this translation. .E37 is the author designation, the A7 is for the original title, and the 4 is added to denote a French translation (Fig. 5b).

(It should be understood that when a single Cutter number is used for the book number, LC follows the practice of inserting the numeral "1" between the book number for the work and the book number for the translation, as described in the previous chapter. However, when a double Cutter number is used for an author and title in a literature class or for biography, it is LC's usual practice to omit the numeral "1" between the number for the original and the number for the trans-

```
PS3525
.A27C68
        MacLeish, Archibald, 1892-
             Conquistador. Versión española por Francisco Alex-
        ander. Quito, Editorial Casa de la Cultura Ecuatoriana,
        1960 [°1932]

             137 p.  22 cm.

             Errata leaf inserted.




             1. Mexico—Hist.—Conquest, 1519-1540—Poetry.    I. Alexander,
        Francisco, tr.  II. Title.

        PS3525.A27C68                                    65—58069

             Library of Congress          [a66b1]
```

Figure 5a

Figure 5b

PS3515
.E37A74 **Hemingway, Ernest,** 1899–1961.
 Au-delà du fleuve et sous les arbres. Traduit de l'anglais par Paule de Beaumont. ₍Paris₎ Gallimard ₍1965₎

 253 p. 21 cm.

ɪ. Title.

PS3515.E37A74   65–73662

PR6045
.O72W37 **Collins, Robert G**
 Virginia Woolf's black arrows of sensation: The waves, by Robert G. Collins. Ilfracombe, Devon, A. H. Stockwell, 1962.

 47 p 23 cm. (The Modern novelist and the modern novel)

 1. Woolf, Virginia (Stephen) 1882–1941. The waves. ɪ. Title.

PR6045.O72W37   65–42114

Figure 6a

PS3507
.R55A83 **Schiffhorst, Gerald J**
 Barron's simplified approach to Theodore Dreiser's An American tragedy, by Gerald J. Schiffhorst. Woodbury, N. Y., Barron's Educational Series, inc. ₍1965₎

 viii, 108 p. port. 19 cm.

 On cover: Detailed analyses and summaries.
 Bibliography: p. 108.

 1. Dreiser, Theodore, 1871–1945. An American tragedy. ɪ. Title.

PS3507.R55A83   813.52   65–16320

Figure 6b

lation because in such instances it is felt that the call number can be safely shortened.)

Criticism of Separate Works

Criticisms of separate works follow translations and are arranged alphabetically by author. Figures 6a–6b show two examples. The first title (Fig. 6a) is a book by Robert Collins, *Virginia Woolf's Black Arrows of Sensation: The Waves*, classed in PR6045.O72W37. The number without the last digit 7 is the call number for Virginia Woolf's *The Waves*. The addition of the digit 7 denotes criticism and follows the work criticized. Any translations would appear between the W3 and the W37.

The second example (Fig. 6b) is a criticism of Theodore Dreiser's *An American Tragedy*. The first edition, assigned to the Rare Book Collection, is classed in PS3507.R55A7 rather than in PZ3. After the English-language edition came a series of translations: A72 for a Czech translation, A73 for a German, and A77 for a Russian. Further expansion for critical works was therefore switched over to the 8 digit, and A83 is assigned to this criticism by Schiffhorst.

Biography and Criticism

After separate works in Tables VIIIa and IXa follow numbers .Z5A–Z and .xZ5–99 for biography and criticism of the individual author and his literary

TABLES OF SUBDIVISIONS FOR INDIVIDUAL AUTHORS

X (1 no.)	X· (1 no.)	Separate works with one number Use X· for works after 1600
		Texts
.A1	.A1	By date
.A11–2	.A2A–Z	By editor
	.A3	School texts
	.A37	Adaptations, dramatizations, etc.
		Translations
.A21–29		Modern versions of medieval works
.A3–39		English
.A4–49	.A4–49	French
.A5–59	.A5–59	German
.A6–69	.A6–69	Other. By language (alphabetically)
.A7–Z	.A7–Z	Criticism
.5	.5	Special parts. By date

Figure 7

PQ1891
.A67

Racine, Jean Baptiste, 1639–1699.

Аѳалія; трагедія изъ Священнаго Писанія. Переводъ съ французскаго въ стихахъ. Москва, Въ Тип. П. Кузно-цова, 1820.

95 p. 25 cm.

ɪ. Title.   *Title transliterated:* Aѳalií̆a.

PQ1891.A67   54–48912

Library of Congress   [2]

PQ1891
.M6

Mongrédien, Georges, 1901–

Athalie de Racine. Paris, SFELT [1946]

175 p. 19 cm. (Les grands événements littéraires)

"Ouvrages consultés": p. [171]–175.

1. Racine, Jean Baptiste, 1639–1699. Athalie.   ɪ. Series.
PQ1891.M6   842.45   47–29202*
© 30Dec46; 1c 3Jun47; SFELT (Sté Fse d'éditions littéraires & techniques), Paris; AF3216.

Library of Congress   [1]

Figure 8b

work. There is no set pattern for the use of the numbers for biography and criticism in Table IXa, but the beginning numbers Z5, Z52, and Z53 are reserved for autobiography, letters in general, and letters to a particular person. After autobiography and the like, in both VIIIa and IXa, other books of criticism or biography are arranged in alphabetical sequence by author within the span provided.

Tables X and Xa

In some instances in the schedule a separate class number is assigned to an individual work, and Table X or Xa is used (see Fig. 7). Two examples are shown in Figures 8a–8b. The single number PQ1891 is assigned to *Athalie* by Racine. In Figure 7 it will be seen that .A1 and the date are used for the original text. Translations follow; Figure 8a is a Russian translation of *Athalie* and falls between .A6–69. Since the digit 7 is usually used for Russian, the number assigned to this book is .A67. In the second example (Fig. 8b), a criticism of the play as shown in Table X would fall in .A7–Z. The book by Mongrédien then is assigned .M6.

Table XI

If, instead of a whole number, a Cutter number is assigned to a work, editions of that work and criticism about it would be treated according to Table XI (Fig. 9). In Table XI, a 3-number spread is indicated. The first number includes editions of the text and translations, following a double Cuttering system; the second number is used for adaptations, dramatizations, and the like; and the third number is used for criticisms of the work. The use of this table is shown in the ten examples in Figures 10a–10j.

All of the sample cards are for *Madame Bovary*. An original text is classed in PQ2246.M2. The Cutter number for this work is .M2 plus date of imprint; two examples are shown: one with a 1930 imprint date (Fig. 10a), the other with a 1957 imprint date (Fig. 10b). For translations the .M2 is retained and the Cutter is doubled by language. Figure 10c is a Bulgarian translation showing this, .M2B8; then an English translation (Fig. 10d), .M2E5. (The English translation selected is a limited edition and was placed in the Rare Book Room, being classed in PQ instead of in PZ3 where it would normally class.) Figure 10e is a German translation in .M2G4; Figure 10f, a Norwegian translation in .M2N5; and the last (Fig. 10g) is a Turkish translation in .M2T8.

SUBDIVISIONS UNDER INDIVIDUAL AUTHORS

XI	Separate works with Cutter numbers
(1).x date	Texts
.xA–Z	Translations, by language
	.A3–39 Modern versions in same language
	.A4–Z Other languages
(2)	Adaptations, dramatizations, etc.
(3)	Criticism
	NOTE. In Table XI (1), (2), (3), .x represents successive Cutter numbers as, for example: .F6, .F7, .F8 or .F66 .F67, .F68
	In the case of works where division (2) is inapplicable the numbers may be modified by using two Cutter numbers only, as .F4, .F5 or .F4, .F41

Figure 9

PQ2246
.M2
1930

Flaubert, Gustave, 1821–1880.
    Madame Bovary, by Gustave Flaubert, with an introduction and notes by Christian Gauss ... New York, Chicago [etc.] C. Scribner's sons [ᶜ1930]

    xxxv, 415 p. 17 cm. (*Half-title:* The Modern students' library. [French series])

    "Bibliographical note" : p. xxxiv–xxxv.

    ɪ. Gauss, Christian Frederick, 1878–   ed. ɪɪ. Title.

    PQ2246.M2 1930   843.84   30—29775

    Library of Congress   [a61f1]

PQ2246
.M2
1957

Flaubert, Gustave, 1821–1880.
    Madame Bovary; [mœurs de province. Texte de l'édition originale, 1857. Paris, L. Mazenod, 1957]

    291 p. illus. 26 cm. (Collection Les Écrivains célèbres, œuvres, 6)

    At head of title : Le réalisme.

    ɪ. Title.

    PQ2246.M2 1957   58—29693 ‡

    Library of Congress   [62b½]

PQ2246
.M2B8

Flaubert, Gustave, 1821–1880.
    Мадам Бовари ; провинциални нрави. Преведе от оригинала Константин Константинов. [София] Народна книга [1949]

    398 p. 19 cm.

    ɪ. Title.   *Title transliterated:* Madam Bovari.

    PQ2246.M2B8   54—17653

    Library of Congress   [⅜]

PQ2246
.M2E5
1950

Flaubert, Gustave, 1821–1880.

    Madame Bovary. Translated by J. Lewis May, with an introd. by Jacques de Lacretelle and colour illus. by Pierre Brissaud engraved in wood by Théo Schmied. New York, Limited Editions Club, 1950.

    x, 348 p. col. illus. 28 cm.

    i. Brissaud, Pierre, 1885–   illus. ii. Title.

    PQ2246.M2E5 1950   843.84   50–13311

    Library of Congress   ₍3₎

PQ2246
.M2G4

Flaubert, Gustave, 1821–1880.

    Madame Bovary, Roman. Übertragung von René Schickelé; Nachwort von Guy de Maupassant. ₍Zürich₎ Manesse Verlag ₍1952₎

    590 p. 16 cm. (Manesse Bibliothek der Weltliteratur)

    i. Title.

    PQ2246.M2G4   843.84   53–15099

    Library of Congress   ₍3₎

PQ2246
.M2N5

Flaubert, Gustave, 1821–1880.

    ... Fru Bovary, roman fra det franske provinsliv; oversat af fru Johanne Vogt Lie med en indledning af Carl Nærup. ₍Kristiania₎ A. Cammermeyer ₍1898₎

    2 p. l., viii, 408 p. 17½ᶜᵐ.

    i. Lie, Johanne Eleonora (Vogt) 1870–   tr. ii. Title.

                                                    17–5024

    Library of Congress   PQ2246.M2N5

PQ2246
.M2T8

Flaubert, Gustave, 1821–1888.

... Madam Bovari (Madame Bovary) Taşra halkı âdet-
leri. Türkçeye çeviren: Ali Kâmi Akyüz. Madam Bovari
romanının bu ikinci basılışı aslının eksiksiz tam tercüme-
sidir. Eserin sonuna ayrıca avukat Senard'ın meşhur müda-
faanamesi ilâve edilmiştir. Kitabın içinde metin harici 5
resim vardır. İstanbul, Hilmi kitabevi, 1942.

xxi, ₁1₁ p., 1 l., 484 p., 1 l. front. (port.) plates. 21½ cm. (*On cover:*
Son dünya edebiyatı : 6)

"Gustave Flaubert, hayatı ve eserleri" signed: İbrahim Hilmi
Çığıraçan.

ı. Akyüz, Ali Kâmi, tr. ıı. Çığıraçan, İbrahim Hilmi. ııı. Title.

PQ2246.M2T8   49–38681

Library of Congress   ₁1₁

PQ2246
.M218B3

Baty, Gaston, 1885–

... Madame Bovary; vingt tableaux adaptés et mis en scène
d'après Gustave Flaubert. Paris, Coutan-Lambert ₁1936₁

2 p. l., 7–199, ₁1₁ p., 3 l. plates. 20ᶜᵐ. (*On cover:* Masques ; biblio-
thèque d'art dramatique)

ı. Flaubert, Gustave, 1821–1880. Madame Bovary. ıı. Title.

₁*Full name:* Jean Baptiste Marie Gaston Baty₁

37–2373

Library of Congress   PQ2246.M218B3

Copyright D pub. 46696   ₁2₁   [843.84] 842.91

PQ2246
.M3B6

Bopp, Léon, 1896–

Commentaire sur Madame Bovary. Neuchâtel, A la Ba-
connière ₁1951₁

550 p. 21 cm.

1. Flaubert, Gustave, 1821–1880. Madame Bovary.

PQ2246.M3B6   843.84   52–66127 ‡

Library of Congress   ₁65e½₁

```
PQ2246
.M3D8
```

Dumesnil, René, 1879–
    ... Flaubert et Madame Bovary, par René Dumesnil. Paris,
Société Les Belles lettres, 1944.

    2 p. l., 7–62 p., 1 l. incl. front., illus. (incl. ports., facsims.) fold. plan.
24½ᵐ. (Collection de documents des "Textes français," pub. sous le
patronage de l'Association Guillaume Budé)

    Illustrations: p. 12–62.

1. Flaubert, Gustave, 1821–1880. Madame Bovary.

PQ2246.M3D8   A F 47–259

New York. Public library
    for Library of Congress   ₍₄₎†

In the next example, a dramatic adaptation (Fig. 10h), .M2 changes to the
second number described in the table, in this case, .M218. This second number is
underlined in the table to make it clear that the book is an adaptation. The double
Cuttering is used again to indicate the author of this dramatic adaptation,
.M218B3, B3 for Baty.

The last two examples (Figs. 10i–10j) show critical works; the third number
described in the table is used, .M3. Again, double Cuttering shows the author of
the criticism: .B6 for Bopp, and .D8 for Dumesnil.

PZ Schedule

The last literature schedule is the PZ schedule. PZ1–PZ90 (Fiction and juvenile literature) have an entirely different plan of numbering. Since these classification numbers do not include translations, biography, or criticism, no tables are
used. A Cutter number is determined for each author following the Author
Number sheet, and the same Cutter is used for *all* of his works of fiction. The titles
are differentiated by the addition of the first *two* letters of the title to the Cutter
number, except that when the second letter is an "A," the first *three* letters of the
title are used. If these letters have been used for a previous title, other sequential
letters are used to preserve the alphabetical arrangement.

In 1961, Krasney's *Homicide West* was classed in PZ4 with a Cutter number of
.K897 for the author, plus the letters for the title: Ho. The card looked like this:

```
PZ4
.K897   Krasney, Samuel A.
Ho         Homicide West. 1961.
```

The author's next book, *Homicide Call*, was classed the following year. The
author notation of .K897 was retained, but since *Ho* had already been used on the
previous title *Homicide West*, other letters for the new title had to be selected in

133

order to keep it in alphabetical sequence; *Hn* was selected, although the letters **are** not according to the title. The card for *Homicide Call* looked like this:

> PZ4
> .K897   Krasney, Samuel A.
> Hn   Homicide call. 1962.

In the case of various editions of the same title in PZ3, PZ4, and PZ7–10.7, a fourth line is added to the call number in the form of numerals arbitrarily assigned, beginning with the numeral 3 for the second and subsequent editions added to the collection. The numeral 2 is reserved for a possible facsimile edition. No attempt is made in the PZ schedule to keep various editions of a work together if they appear under different titles; each title is given the letters for the title as it appears on the title page.

This discussion by no means gives the entire picture of the tables used with literature, but at least it may have answered some of the many questions that come up when to use Table VIII and Table IX and why there are Tables VIIIa and VIIIb.

Chapter 8

Subclassification and Book Numbers of Documents and Official Publications

Mary Catherine Arick

This chapter will try to explain the shelf arrangement that LC is trying to achieve for documents and official publications and how the book notation is derived to effect the desired shelf arrangement. By documents are meant official publications of any governing body of a country, state, city, etc., or any official publication of institutions, corporate bodies, and the like.

Document "A" Cutters

It is the practice at the Library of Congress to use the Cutter letter .A for document material. The purpose of using the letter .A is to place document material at the head of the class. (The practice of using the .A Cutter for documents in classes E, F, and Z was not followed until 1941. Since then, the Library of Congress is applying the Cuttering rules used in other classes as far as practical in the E, F, and Z classes.)

Not all documents are Cuttered under the letter .A. The question immediately arises: What determines whether a document is to be Cuttered under .A or merely alphabetically on the principles described by Mr. Holmes in Chapter 6?

First, the shelflister examines the meaning of the specific classification number given by the subject cataloger. If the publication is issued by a governing body of the country, province, state, or city for which the class or Cutter number stands, an .A Cutter is used; otherwise, the work is Cuttered from the author heading. Unless a special table is provided for documents, .A2–3 is used for serials and .A4–5 for monographs; this practice is flexible and may be decimally expanded in either direction, depending upon the quantity and type of material received in a specific class. The .A Cutter is used whether the item is cataloged under an official heading or by title.

Material is arranged alphabetically by the issuing body and title, and precedes any other author entries in the class. When the definition of the classification number in the schedule is for a country, province, city, etc., the Cutters .A1–5 are reserved for official publications of that country, province, city, etc., and regular

SF51
.18

Italy. *Comitato interministeriale per la ricostruzione.*
La genetica del bestiame negli Stati Uniti. ₁Rapporto della Missione nazionale di assistenza tecnica n. 45/18 sul viaggio effettuato nel 1950–51 negli Stati Uniti d'America₁ Rapporto pubblicato a cura del Comitato interministeriale per la ricostruzione e del Comitato nazionale della produttività. ₁Roma, Istituto poligrafico dello Stato, 1954₁

65 p. 26 cm.

1. Stock and stock-breeding—U. S. 2. Stock and stock-breeding—Research. I. Italy. Comitato nazionale per la produttività. II. Title.

SF51.I 8   60–23177

Library of Congress   ₁8₁

Figure 1b

SF51
.A5
1929   **U. S.** *Bureau of agricultural economics.*
... Regional changes of farm animal production in relation to land utilization. A preliminary report. Washington, D. C., 1929.

1 p. l., 47 p. incl. tab. maps, diagrs. 26¼ᶜᵐ.

At head of title: United States Department of agriculture. Bureau of agricultural economics.
Autographed from type-written copy.
"By O. E. Baker, senior agricultural economist, Division of land economics."—p. ₁1₁

1. Stock and stock-breeding—U. S. I. Baker, Oliver Edwin, 1883–II. Title.

                                                     30—23121

Library of Congress   SF51.A5 1929
——— ——— Copy 2.   ₁38c1₁   636.0973

SF55
.R95A5
1932   **Russia** *(1923–   U. S. S. R.)* *Tˢentral'noe upravlenie narodno-khozĭaĭstvennogo ucheta.*
Животноводство СССР в цифрах. Составил В. П. Нифонтов. Москва, Гос. соц.-экон. изд-во, 1932.

xi, 351 p. 23 cm.

Errata slip inserted.

1. Animal industry—Russia—Stat. I. Nifontov, V. P.
          Title transliterated: Zhivotnovodstvo SSSR v tsifrakh.

SF55.R95A5 1932   50–45820

Library of Congress   ₁3₁

```
SF55
.R95U53
        U. S.  Dept. of Agriculture.
              Livestock in the Soviet Union.  ₍Prepared by Ralph E.
        Hodgson and others.  Washington₎ Agricultural Research
        Service, U. S. Dept. of Agriculture ₍1961₎

           84 p.  illus., map.  26 cm.

           Cover title.
           Report of a departmental technical study group.
           Bibliographical footnotes.



           1. Stock and stock-breeding—Russia.  ₍1. U. S. S. R.—Domestic
        animals₎  I. Hodgson, Ralph Edward, 1906–     II. Title.

        SF55.R95U53                                    Agr 61–401

        U. S. Dept. of Agr.  Libr.      A40Ag8
        for Library of Congress         ₍5°₎†
```

author notations in these classes start with .A6. That is, any publication not considered a document in a specific class and having an author starting with the initial letter "A" will be Cuttered from .A6 to .A9. A book by Adam, which would ordinarily receive an .A3 notation, must be Cuttered from .A6 on. A publication, normally Cuttered as .A7, must be Cuttered as .A8+ or .A9+ to leave room in the class for publications by Acton, Adams, Ames, etc.

If a class is defined as limited to one country, then the .A Cutter is used only for the documents on the topic issued by that country. In the following examples, since SF51 stands for "Animal culture. History. United States," the Italian government publication receives a regular author Cutter and the U.S. publication the official Cutter .A (Figs. 1a–1b).

Another example would be SF55, "Animal culture. History. By country. Other countries, A–Z." Thus SF55.R95 means Russia. In SF55, "Other countries, A–Z," official U.S. publications are not considered documents for Cuttering purposes. Therefore, the Russian document (Fig. 2a) receives the .A Cutter, and the U.S. document (Fig. 2b) receives a regular Cutter.

When a class number means "By city, A–Z," official publications of the city precede official publications about the city issued by the state. In Figures 3a–3c, the class number HD5726 stands for "Labor market. By country. United States. Local, A–Z"; .C4 stands for "Chicago." State publications in class number HD5726 (Fig. 3c) take the .A Cutter, but *follow* the publications of the city for which the first Cutter specifically stands (Figs. 3a–3b).

In addition to the use of the .A Cutter for documents (government publications), the .A Cutter is used in the same manner if the class or Cutter number is established for a certain agency, organization, etc. All material for that body should be Cuttered as document material. An example of this is shown in Figure 4, with the number for the International Atomic Energy Agency established as HD9698.5.

HD5726
.C4A4

Chicago. *Mayor's commission on unemployment.*

Report of the Mayor's commission on unemployment. Chicago [Cameron, Amberg & co., printers] 1914.

175, [1] p. 23^{cm}.

Charles R. Crane, chairman. Charles Richmond Henderson, secretary.
Appendix: I. Bureaus of employment (labor exchanges) in Europe, by the secretary.—II. Unemployment insurance, by the secretary.—III. Unemployment and public employment agencies, by E. H. Sutherland.

1. Unemployed—Chicago. 2. Insurance, Unemployment. 3. Labor exchanges. I. Crane, Charles Richard, 1858– II. Henderson, Charles Richmond, 1848–1915. III. Sutherland, Edwin Hardin. IV. Title.

14–18204

Library of Congress   HD5726.C4A4

HD5726
.C4A5

Chicago. *Municipal markets commission.*

Report to the mayor and aldermen, by the Chicago Municipal markets commission, on a practical plan for relieving destitution and unemployment in the city of Chicago. Chicago [H. G. Adair, printer] 1914.

69 p. 23^{cm}.
Alderman James H. Lawley, chairman.
Dated Dec. 28, 1914.
Appended are a report by Miss Amelia Sears, director of the Bureau of public welfare of Cook County, on the problem of unemployment and possible destitution, and letters from Eugene T. Lies, general superintendent of the United charities of Chicago, submitting plans for dealing with unemployment and poverty.
1. Unemployed—Chicago. 2. Chicago—Poor. I. Lawley, James H. II. Sears, Amelia. III. Lies, Eugene Theodore, 1876– IV. Title.

15–9356

Library of Congress   HD5726.C4A5

HD5726
.C4A56

Illinois. *State Employment Service.*

Survey of worker commuting patterns in the Chicago metropolitan area, prepared by Illinois State Employment Service, Research and Statistics Section. Chicago, 1959.

10 l. illus. 22 x 36 cm.

1. Commuting. 2. Labor supply—Chicago. I. Title.

HD5726.C4A56   A 60—9262

Illinois. Univ. Library
for Library of Congress   [a64b1]†

Figure 4

HD9698
.5
.A23   **International Atomic Energy Agency.**
            Gen/pub. no. 1–
            Vienna, 1958–

            v. 21 cm.

            Title varies: no. 1, G/publ.

            1. Atomic energy—Societies, etc.

        HD9698.5.A23   63–4356 ‡

        Library of Congress   [2]

HC107
.C2A6
1913   **California.** *Dept. of public instruction.*

        ... Conservation of natural resources ...   Issued by the
        superintendent of public instruction. [Sacramento] Cali-
        fornia state printing office [1913?]

            111, [1] p. illus. 22½ᶜᵐ.

            At head of title: Second edition.
            1st ed., 1909.
            Includes extracts from letters, addresses, newspaper and magazine arti-
        cles, etc., etc.

            1. Natural resources. 2. California—Econ. condit.   ɪ. Title.

                                                                14–31157

        Library of Congress   HC107.C2A6 1913

Figure 5a

HC107
.C2A6
1918   **California.** *Development board.*

            Agricultural and soil survey of San Diego County, Cali-
        fornia. Made by the California Development board co-
        operating with the San Diego County Board of super-
        visors and the San Diego Chamber of commerce. [San
        Diego, Press of Frye & Smith, 1918]

            93, [2] p. incl. map, tables. 25ᶜᵐ.

            1. Agriculture—California—San Diego Co. 2. San Diego Co., Calif.—
        Econ. condit.   ɪ. San Diego Co., Calif. Board of supervisors. ɪɪ. San
        Diego, Calif. Chamber of commerce. ɪɪɪ. Title.

                                                        21–7787

            Library of Congress   HC107.C2A6 1918
                                        [2]

Figure 5b

139

Figure 5c

HC107
.C2A6
1940

California. *Dept. of education.*
    ... California's natural wealth. A conservation guide for secondary schools. Sacramento, California state Department of education ₍1940₎

cover-title, xi, ₍1₎, 124 p. incl. illus. (incl. double map) tables, diagrs. 23ᶜᵐ. (*Its* Bulletin of the California state Department of education, vol. IX, no. 4. December, 1940)

Includes bibliographies.

1. Natural resources. 2. California—Econ. condit.   I. Title. II. Title: A conservation guide for secondary schools.

41–52384

Library of Congress   L124.B62   1940   vol. 9, no. 4

    ₍3₎   (370.61794)   339.0712794

HD7096
.U5A5
1938

U. S. *Congress. Senate. Committee on finance.*
    Amending the Social security act—providing for an investigation of the Tennessee unemployment compensation division of the Social security board. Hearing before a subcommittee of the Committee on finance, United States Senate, Seventy-fifth Congress, third session, on S. Res. 226, a resolution providing for an investigation of the Tennessee unemployment compensation division of the Social security board; S. 3235, a bill to amend the Social security act so as to provide for the selection on a merit basis of certain personnel for whose

compensation appropriations are made by the federal government; S. 3370, a bill to amend the Social security act to provide for the establishment and maintenance of certain personnel standards on a merit basis, and for other purposes. February 15, 1938 ... Washington, U. S. Govt. print. off., 1938.
    ii, 31 p. 23ᶜᵐ.
    Printed for the use of the Committee on finance.
    David I. Walsh, chairman of subcommittee.

1. U. S. Social security board. 2. Insurance, State and compulsory—U. S.   I. Title.

38–20449

Library of Congress   HD7096.U5A5   1938

    ₍4₎   331.25440973

Figure 6a

Document Monographs

For many years the Library of Congress assigned .A4 and date to *all* document monographs in the same class. This practice necessitated the addition of a, b, c, d, etc. to the date as a means of identifying individual entries which carried the same date. Sometimes .A5 or .A6 was used. In this system, headings and titles were disregarded, and the date alone distinguished each title. Some examples follow in Figures 5a–5c, 6a–6d, and 7a–7c.

In Class HC (Economic history), HC107 stands for "United States. By region or state, A–W," and California is assigned the Cutter .C2. In Figures 5a–5c, .A6 was used as the second Cutter number for document monographs issued by the state. The date used is that of imprint. *Conservation of Natural Resources* (Fig. 5a) received the number .C2A6 1913; *Agricultural and Soil Survey of San Diego County* (Fig. 5b) received the number .C2A6 1918; and *California's Natural Wealth* (Fig. 5c) received the number .C2A6 1940.

Under "Unemployment," HD7096 stands for works "By country, A–Z"; the United States has the Cutter .U5. In Figures 6a–6d, four documents were shelf-listed: the first classed (Fig. 6a) received the number .U5A5 and the date 1938. Figures 5b–5d show the numbers assigned to the next three documents classed, all

---

HD7096
.U5A5
1938b **U. S.** *Social security board.*
... A directory of state agencies administering unemploy-ment compensation laws, May 1, 1938. Social security board. Washington, D. C. ₍1938₎

1 p. l., 14 numb. l. 27ᶜᵐ.

At head of title : Bureau of unemployment compensation.
Mimeographed.

1. Insurance, Unemployment—U. S.   I. Title.

                                                  38-26543

Library of Congress   HD7096.U5A5   1938 b
——— ——— Copy 2.   ₍5₎   331.254440973

Figure 6b

HD7096
.U5A5
1938c **U. S.** *Congress. House. Committee on appropriations.*
Supplemental appropriations, fiscal year 1938, grants to states for administration of state unemployment compensa-tion acts, Social security board. Hearings before the subcom-mittee of the Committee on appropriations, House of repre-sentatives, Seventy-fifth Congress, third session, on H. J. Res. 678, making an additional appropriation for grants to states for unemployment compensation administration, Social secur-ity board, for the fiscal year ending June 30, 1938 ... Wash-ington, U. S. Govt. print. off., 1938.
ii, 46 p. incl. tables. 23ᶜᵐ.
Printed for the use of the Committee on appropriations.
Edward T. Taylor,   chairman.
1. U. S. Social security   board—Appropriations and expenditures. 2. Insurance, Un-   employment—U. S.   I. Title.
Library of Congress   HD7096.U5A5   1938 c   38-35239
                              ₍n44f1₎   331.254440973

Figure 6c

HD7096
.U5A5
1938d **U. S.** *Congress. Senate. Committee on appropriations.*
        Social security board administration expenses. Hearings
before the Committee on appropriations, United States Senate, Seventy-fifth Congress, third session, on H. J. Res. 678 ...
Washington, U. S. Govt. print. off., 1938.

ii, 16 p. incl. tables. 23^{cm}.

Printed for the use of the Committee on appropriations.
Carter Glass, chairman.

1. U. S. Social security board—Appropriations and expenditures.
2. Unemployed—U. S.   I. Title.
                                    38–37571

Library of Congress   HD7096.U5A5 1938 d

———— ———— Copy 2.   [5]   331.254440973

HD9106
.A4
1919c **U. S.** *Congress. Senate. Committee on agriculture and
        forestry.*
          ... Sugar shortage ... Report. ⟨To accompany S.
3284⟩ ... [Washington, Govt. print. off., 1919]

4, 3 p. incl. tab. 24^{cm}. (66th Cong., 1st sess. Senate. Rept. 286)

Calendar no. 242.
Submitted by Mr. McNary. Ordered printed November 3, 1919.
"Views of the minority" (3 p.) submitted by Mr. Ransdell. Ordered
printed November 3, 1919.

1. Sugar trade—U. S.   I. McNary, Charles Linza, 1874–   II. Ransdell, Joseph Eugene, 1858–   III. Title.

                                    19–26896

Library of Congress   HD9106.A4 1919 c

———— ———— Copy 2.   [5]

HD9106
.A4
1919e **U. S.** *Congress. House. Committee on interstate and for-
        eign commerce.*
          Investigation of the scarcity of sugar. Hearing before the
Committee on interstate and foreign commerce of the House of
representatives, Sixty-sixth Congress, first session, on H. Res.
150. July 14, 1919. Washington, Govt. print. off., 1919.

12 p. 23½^{cm}.

John J. Esch, chairman.

1. Sugar trade—U. S.

                                    44–21306

Library of Congress   HD9106.A4 1919 e

                            [2]

Figure 7c

```
HD9106
.A4
1919f
```

U. S. *Congress. House. Committee on agriculture.*

... Continuing the sugar equalization board ... Report. ⟨To accompany S. 3284⟩ ... ₍Washington, Govt. print. off., 1919₎

6 p. 23ᶜᵐ. (66th Cong., 2d sess. House. Rept. 506)

Submitted by Mr. Haugen. Referred to the House calendar and ordered printed December 16, 1919.

1. United States sugar equalization board. 2. Sugar. 3. Sugar trade—U. S.   I. Haugen, Gilbert Nelson, 1859–1933.   II. Title.

19—25902

Library of Congress   HD9106.A4   1919 f

———— ———— Copy 2.   ₍a37d1₎

with the same date of imprint but differentiated by the addition of letters to the date.

Economic policy of the United States in regard to sugar classes in the single number HD9106. Figures 7a–7c show three titles classed as .A4 with the dates and letters. It should be obvious that the three examples were the third, fifth, and sixth 1919 documents classed in HD9106.

In later years an expansion of the .A Cutter was used in anticipation of simplifying the servicing of document material by the attendants, which had a tendency to make the .A Cutter too long in some classes. For example, in Class VC263 "Naval maintenance. Supplies and stores (General and personal) United States," it became necessary to build on .A57. Some of the long Cutter numbers which resulted are illustrated in Figures 8a–8c:

```
VC263
.A57213
1945
```

U. S. *Bureau of Naval Personnel.*

Storekeeper 3c and 2c, prepared by Standards and Curriculum Division, Training, Bureau of Naval Personnel. Washington, U. S. Govt. Print. Off., 1945.

166 p. illus. 20 cm. (*Its* Navy training courses)

1. U. S. Navy—Supplies and stores. 2. Stores or stock-room keeping.   I. Title.

VC263.A57213   1945   359.8   56—15702 ‡

Library of Congress   ₍3₎

Figure 8a

143

```
VC263
.A57215
          U. S. Bureau of Supplies and Accounts (Navy Dept.)
              The Navy supply system, 1951. ₍Washington₎ 1951.

              1 v. (unpaged)  illus.  20 x 27 cm.

              "Navsanda publication 256."




              1. U. S.  Navy—Supplies and stores.

              VC263.A57215              359.8              53–63384

              Library of Congress            ₍1₎
```

```
VC263
.A5723
1951
          U. S.  Congress.  House.  Committee on Armed Services.
              Investigation of paint purchases by Navy Department,
          January 1951 (need for and utilization of)  Report of the
          Procurement Subcommittee of the Committee on Armed
          Services, United States House of Representatives, under the
          authority of H. Res. 38, 82d Congress.  Washington, U. S.
          Govt. Print. Off., 1951.

              ii, 8 p.  24 cm.

              1. U. S.  Navy Dept.  2. Paint.  3. Public contracts—U. S.
              VC263.A5723  1951              359.8              52–61855



              Library of Congress            ₍2₎
```

```
VC263
.A57
1959
          U. S.  General Accounting Office.
              Examination of administration of major subcontracts
          under Department of the Navy, contract NOa(s) 56–719–f
          with Philco Corporation, Philadelphia, Pennsylvania; re-
          port to the Congress of the United States by the Comp-
          troller General of the United States.  Wash₍ington₎ 1959.

              21 l.  27 cm.


              1. U. S.  Bureau of Ordnance (Navy Dept.)  2. U. S.  Bureau of
          Aeronautics (Navy Dept.)  3. Philco Corporation.  4. Subcontract-
          ing—Price policy—U. S.

              VC263.A57  1959                            60–61765

              Library of Congress            ₍1₎
```

144

VC263
.A57
1959a   **U. S.** *General Accounting Office.*
        Examination of selected Department of the Navy contracts and subcontracts; report to the Congress of the United States by the Comptroller General of the United States. ₍Washington₎ 1959.

        46 l.   27 cm.

        1. U. S.   Navy—Procurement.   2. Defense contracts—Price policy—U. S.   .

VC263.A57   1959   359.62   60–61763

Library of Congress   ₍2₎

VC263
.A57
1959b   **U. S.** *General Accounting Office.*
        Examination of the military assistance program administered by the Department of the Navy; report to the Congress of the United States by the Comptroller General of the United States. Wash₍ington₎ 1959.

        28 l.   27 cm.

        1. Military assistance, American.   2. U. S. Navy.   Supplies and stores.

VC263.A57   1959b   60–61758

Library of Congress   ₍2₎

VC263
.A57
1960   **U. S.** *General Accounting Office.*
        Review of the use of contractor-furnished drawings for procurement purposes, Department of the Navy; report to the Congress of the United States by the Comptroller General of the United States. ₍Washington₎ 1960.

        21 l.   27 cm.

        1. U. S.   Navy Dept.—Procurement.   2. Engineering drawings.

VC263.A57   1960   60–61779

Library of Congress   ₍1₎

```
VC263
.A57
1965d       U. S.  General Accounting Office.
                Failure to obtain and consider cost data in the procure-
            ment of HY80 steel plate used in the construction of nuclear
            submarines, Department of the Navy; report to the Con-
            gress of the United States by the Comptroller General of
            the United States.  [Washington] 1965.

                3 l., 39 p.   27 cm.

                Cover title.


                1. U. S.  Navy—Procurement.  2. United States Steel Corporation.
            3. Lukens Steel Company.   4. Ship-building—Supplies.    I. Title.


                VC263.A57   1965d                              65–61950

                Library of Congress              [1]
```

The present practice in the Library of Congress is a compromise between .A4, .A5, or .A6 for all document monographs, and expansion of the .A Cutter. In Class VC263, which is a typical example, each government agency is assigned a Cutter number. The date is added to give a distinctive book number for all publications of the agency.

The accompanying table for the VC263 class is for the guidance of the assistants as entries are received or cards reprinted. If a publication of an agency not provided for is received, a Cutter number will be assigned in as nearly an alphabetical order as is practical.

VC263	Naval Maintenance
	Supplies and stores
	By country
	United States
.A45+date	U.S. Navy Dept.
.A47+date	U.S. Bureau of Construction and Repair
.A477+date	U.S. Bureau of Naval Personnel
.A48+date	U.S. Bureau of Ships
.A52+date	U.S. Bureau of Supplies and Accounts (Navy Dept.)
.A55+date	U.S. Congress (Both houses—all committees)
.A57+date	U.S. General Accounting Office
.A576+date	U.S. Naval Supply Center, Oakland, Calif.
.A58+date	U.S. Office of Naval Material

As entries are recataloged, the call numbers of the examples shown in Figures 8a–8c will be changed:

.A57213 to .A477+date
.A57215 to .A52+date
.A5723 to .A55+date

With the use of the table, some typical entries would appear as in Figures 9a–9e.

Document Serials

There was a period in the Library of Congress when document serials were Cuttered chronologically, that is, the Cutter .A3 was expanded according to the date of the first number cataloged. This Cuttering for serials seemed a logical plan and could have continued had the Library of Congress been able to Cutter by the first year of publication, not by the first number received or cataloged. As document serials appeared in classes where there had been no document serials before, the basic plan of an alphabetical arrangement was used for Cuttering. If a class previously started by chronological arrangement is consistent, that is, if the first issue of a serial determined the Cutter, then the plan is continued as far as practical. Because the name of the government agency is likely to change or be replaced by another agency, the practice of using a title entry for cataloging document serials having a distinctive title is becoming more extensive.

Figure 10 shows the treatment given a recataloged document serial. The

```
S339
.A6
        Bulletin agricole du Congo belge et du Ruanda-Urundi.
           Landbouwtijdschrift voor Belgisch-Congo en Ruanda-
           Urundi. v. 1–          nov. 1910–
           Bruxelles.
              v. in        illus. 25 cm.
              Four no. a year, Nov. 1910–1952; 6 no. a year, 1953–
              Vol. 18, no. 1 and v. 19, no. 1–2 are photocopies (negative)
              Title in French only, 1910–38.
              Title varies slightly.
              Issued Nov. 1910–          by the Direction de l'agriculture, des
           forêts et de l'élevage (Nov. 1910–1953 under earlier and variant
           names) of the Ministère des affaires africaines (called in Nov. 1910–
           Aug. 1958, Ministère des colonies; Oct. 1958–          Ministère du
           Congo belge et du Ruanda-Urundi.
              Published in London, Sept. 1914–Mar./Dec. 1918.


              "Comptes rendus de la Conférence africaine des sols, 1948": v. 40.
              Vol. 43, no.          include Bulletin d'information of the Institut
           national pour l'étude agronomique du Congo belge, v. 1, no.
              Separately paged supplements accompany some numbers.
           INDEXES:
              Vols. 1–26, 1910–35, in v. 26.
              Vols. 1–36, 1910–45, with v. 36.
              Vols. 1–50, 1910–59. 1 v.


              1. Agriculture—Congo, Belgian.          I. Belgium. Ministère des
           affaires africaines. Direction de l'agriculture, des forêts et de
           l'élevage.


           S339.A6                                    13–8224 rev 2*‡

           Library of Congress          [161d1]
```

Figure 10

original entry for the example was: Belgium. *Ministère des colonies. Direction de l'agriculture de l'élevage et de la colonisation.* Bulletin agricole du Congo belge. Bibliographical notes on the card in Figure 10 indicate that this publication is published by agencies of the Belgian government. In addition, the descriptive catalogers have provided an added entry for the government agency. This title remained under documents Cuttering (.A6) to keep the official material issued by the ministry involved together.

In the case of new serial title entries published by official government agencies, the Cuttering will be as for a document. If, however, the serial entry is published *jointly* by a government agency and an unofficial body, the entry will be Cuttered from the title. If the serial is published by more than one government agency, the Cutter number should represent the first added entry showing the name of the agency.

Double Cuttering

Although triple Cuttering is never done, double Cuttering is; certain parts of the schedules provide for double Cutters. Under "Electrical engineering" of the HD subclass "Mechanical industries," there is a caption for "Machinery. Supplies. Apparatus" with the class number HD9695. According to directions in the HD schedule, the following table is to be used with single numbers such as this:

    .A1   Collections.
    .A2   General works.
    .A3   Law and legislation. By country, A–Z.
    .A4–Z   By country.
                Under each:
                    (1) Collections.
                    (2) General works.
                    (3) Local, A–Z.
                    (4) Firms, etc., A–Z.

Under Cutters .A1 and .A2, the shelflister provides the second Cutter by regularly prescribed Cuttering rules. Under .A3, a second Cutter is provided by the schedule: "By country, A–Z." However, this Cutter .A3 is no longer used at LC. Material formerly classed here will be incorporated into the K schedule as it is developed.

Under .A4–Z "By country," 4 numbers are provided for each country. Their use is illustrated in the following example. (At the time these 4 numbers were assigned to Germany, 9 was not used as a terminal digit; 1 is still not so used. That is why, in the example, .G38 jumps to .G4.)

.G38   Germany. Collections, A–Z. Document serials would precede document monographs on the regular "A" Cutter (i.e., .G38A3–4 for document serials and A4–5 for document monographs). Other monographs and serials are arranged alphabetically by author.

.G4   Germany. General, A–Z. (Cuttering done as for .G38.)
.G42   Local, A–Z, e.g., .G42B4, Berlin.
.G43   Firms, etc., A–Z, e.g., .G43S5, Siemens und Halske.

In .G42 and .G43, no attempt is made to place documents and serials at the head of the class. To avoid triple Cuttering, the second Cutters are developed decimally.

General Serials

"General serials" means periodicals such as the *Ladies Home Journal* or monographic series of an unofficial nature. In classes which are not reserved for collections alone, provisions are frequently made in the schedules or the shelflist, itself, for the segregation of bulky general serials at the beginning of a class instead of intermingling it alphabetically with the single works. Such an arrange-

Figure 11a

HD1694
.A137

Interstate Conference on Water Problems.
Summary of proceedings ₍of the₎ annual meeting.

Chicago, Council of State Governments.

v.   28 cm.

1. Water resources development—U. S.—Congresses.   ɪ. Council of State Governments.

HD1694.A137   61–63043 ‡

Library of Congress   ₍1₎

Figure 11b

HD1694
.A14

Montana. State University, *Missoula. School of Law.*
Proceedings of the annual water resources conference.
1st–   1956–
₍Missoula₎

v. illus. 24 cm. (Montana State University studies in law)
Each vol. has also a distinctive title: 1956, Is a preference among distributors of Federal power justified?

1. Water resources development—U. S.—Congresses.   ɪ. Title: Water resources conference.

HD1694.A14   333.91   57–63362

Library of Congress   ₍1₎

ment for periodicals is made possible by the reservation of groups of numbers, such as .A1A–Z, .A1–19, and .A1–5, with an alphabetical arrangement by heading within the number group. Periodicals may be intermingled alphabetically with the monographs in very specific classes. When there are identical periodical titles, arrangement is alphabetical by place of imprint; and if the places are also identical, arrangement is made chronologically by date of imprint of the earliest volume.

Expansion of Cutter Numbers in Tables

Inquiries are frequently made about development of book numbers in the H schedule. The H subclasses have been provided with numerous tables in the schedule proper, as well as the tables at the end of the schedule; however, there are areas in the subclass tables where it becomes necessary for the Classification Record Unit assistant to provide guide cards in the LC Shelflist in order to maintain a logical sequence.

A few examples concerning "Water rights" in HD1694 may be helpful in showing how tables are developed. The table printed in the H schedule under "Water rights" is as follows:

HD	ECONOMIC HISTORY
	Utilization and culture of special classes of lands
	Water rights . . .
1694–1698	By country.
	United States.
1694.A1–15	Collections.
	International questions. By date.
.A17	General.
.A2	United States and Canada.
.A3	United States and Mexico.
	Conservation of water resources.
.A4	Documents. By date.
.A45–47	Federal Power Commission.
.A5A–Z	General works. Monographs.
.A51–59	General special. By date.
.A6–W	States.

Figures 11a and 11b show two cards for collections of works on United States water resources in general (the .A1–15 Cutter).

Following "Collections" in the table is the caption "International questions. By date." Works treating of United States–Canadian relations are Cuttered under .A2. Originally the Cutter .A2 was sufficient for works classed here, but with the development of the St. Lawrence Seaway Project and the large amount of material written on it, .A2 became overcrowded. Another problem is that serials cannot be given a Cutter number and date. In order to keep subject material together, regardless of format, the following table was inserted into the Shelflist:

.A25–254	St. Lawrence River Project
.A25–2519	Serials alphabetically
.A252–254	Monographs
.A252	U.S. headings by date
.A253	Canada headings by date
.A254A–Z	Other

The phrasing under .A252 means official publications of the United States, as indicated by Figures 12b and 12c.

Figures 12a–12e show examples based on the table inserted in the Shelflist; in particular, note Figure 12a for a serial publication, and Figure 12e "Other" for nonofficial works on the Seaway. By the development and insertion into the Shelflist of this type of guide card on the Seaway, all material relating to the

---

HD1694
.A2515 **Power authority of the state of New York.**
Annual report.

Albany, 1932–

v. 23 cm.

First report covers the period from May 6, 1931 to December 31, 1931.

1. St. Lawrence river—Power utilization. 2. St. Lawrence river—Navigation. 3. St. Lawrence river—Comm.

HD1694.A2515   627.1097   32—27669

Library of Congress   ₁a59e¼₁

Figure 12a

HD1694
.A252
1933   U. S. *Congress. House. Committee on interstate and foreign commerce.*

... St. Lawrence river ... Report. ⟨To accompany H. J. Res. 157⟩ ... ₁Washington, U. S. Govt. print. off., 1933₁

3 p. 24ᶜᵐ. (73d Cong., 1st sess. House. Rept. 49)

Submitted by Mr. Rayburn. Committed to the Committee of the whole House on the state of the Union and ordered printed April 20, 1933.

1. St. Lawrence river.   ɪ. Rayburn, Sam Taliaferro, 1882–

Library of Congress   TC427.S3U5   1933 b   33—26277

—— —— Copy 2.   ₁3₁   627.1097

Figure 12b

HD1694
.A252
1934

U. S. *President, 1933–*   (*Franklin D. Roosevelt*)
   ... St. Lawrence waterway. Message from the President of
the United States requesting the consideration of ratification
by the Senate of the so-called "St. Lawrence treaty with Canada", and transmitting a summary of data prepared by the Interdepartmental board on the Great lakes-St. Lawrence project
... Washington, U. S. Govt. print. off., 1934.
   v, 21 p. maps (2 fold.) diagr. 23½ᶜᵐ. (73d Cong., 2d sess. Senate.
Doc. 110)
   Read; ordered to lie on the table and be printed with illustrations,
January 10, 1934.
   1. St. Lawrence river. 2. Great lakes. 3. Inland navigation—U. S.
4. Inland navigation—Canada.   ɪ. U. S. Interdepartmental board on
the Great lakes-St. Law-   rence project. ɪɪ. Title.

                                                          33—26953

   Library of Congress   TC427.S3U5 1934
   ———— Copy 2.   ₍36f5₎   627.1097

HD1694
.A253
1928b

Canada. *Parliament. Senate. Special committee on development and improvement of the St. Lawrence River.*
   ... Proceedings of the Special committee appointed to in-
quire into the development and improvement of the St. Law-
rence River with prefatory digest of the evidence adduced and
documents fyled ... Ottawa, F. A. Acland, printer, 1928.
   lxx, 338 p. incl. tables. fold. maps (in pocket) 24½ᶜᵐ.
   At head of title: The Senate of Canada.
   Chas. E. Tanner, chairman.
   "Documents submitted but not included in the printed record": p. iv.
   "Report of the committee": p. vi.
   "A quarter century of international negotiation." By Mr. George W.
Yates: p. vii–xv.
   1. St. Lawrence River.   ɪ. Tanner, Charles Elliott, 1857–
ɪɪ. Yates, George Wash-   ington, 1872–   ɪɪɪ. Title. ɪᴠ.
Title: A quarter century   of international negotiation.
                                                          29—11086

   Library of Congress   TC427.S3A5 1928 b
   ———— Copy 2.   ₍8₎

HD1694
.A254J8

Judson, Clara (Ingram) 1879–
   St. Lawrence Seaway. Drawings by Lorence F. Bjork-
lund. Illustrated with photos. of the seaway. Chicago, Fol-
lett Pub. Co. ₍1959₎
   160 p. illus. 24 cm.

   1. St. Lawrence Seaway.

   HD1694.A254J8   627.12   59—8989 ‡

   Library of Congress   ₍62r591³31₎

Seaway can be kept together in the specific class number, and will not be mixed in with other works relating to United States–Canadian water resources which is also classed in HD1694.A2.

Congresses and Conferences

Congresses, conferences, and their like are generally arranged alphabetically by name and then chronologically by year of session. In this way all publications of a particular congress are kept together. Should the proceedings or reports of a number of years be combined in one catalog entry, this entry is arranged ahead of the single session on a different Cutter number.

Over a period of many years, the Library of Congress has formulated a plan for the arrangement of conference material. A Cutter number is derived from the name of the conference, to which is added the date on which the conference was held. A lower-case letter or letters is added to the date, each letter or combination of letters representing a category of material.

Some examples follow:

Q101 .P3 1929f	Pacific Science Congress. *4th, Djakarta and Bandung, 1929.* Excursion guides. Bandoeng, Vorkink [1929]
Q101 .P3 1929z	Pacific Science Congress. *4th, Djakarta and Bandung, 1929.* Miscellaneous printed matter . . .
Q101 .P3 1933f	Pacific Science Congress. *5th, Victoria and Vancouver,* *B.C., 1933.* Excursions. Guide book [n.p., 1933]
Q101 .P3 1961c	Pacific Science Congress. *10th, Honolulu, 1961.* [Papers, proceedings, and reports. v.p., 1961–64]

Q101
.R68
1948a
	Royal Society of London. *Scientific Information*
	     Conference, 1948.
	     Report and papers submitted. London, Royal Society,
	1948.

This plan is likely to be added to or adjusted for each congress. As new types of material appear for a specific congress, a new combination of letters is added. Accordingly it is unlikely that any two congresses in the Library of Congress carry the identical combination of letters.

For this reason it was thought advisable to prepare a similar but **simplified** table for the use of other libraries and as a general indication of the **manner in** which LC book numbers are assigned for congress and conference publications. The table follows:

SUGGESTED TABLE FOR USE WITH CONGRESSES AND CONFERENCES

Date   – Proceedings
Date a – Papers read
Date b – Abstracts of papers read
Date c – Reports (Including official bulletin)
Date d – Committee discussions
Date e – Resolutions (Including opening and closing speeches)
Date f – Statutes (Including handbooks and directives)
Date g – Expositions
Date h – Bulletins (general)
Date i – List of members
Date j – Biography of members
Date l – Reports of delegations alphabetically
Date m – Technical reports
Date n – Circulars
Date q – Charts
Date r – Final acts
Date z – Miscellaneous printed matter

Societies and Institutions

Publications of societies, institutions, and corporate bodies may be arranged in a logical sequence according to the relative importance of the publications rather than adhering to an alphabetical arrangement. Official publications of a society are arranged in a logical sequence beginning with the most comprehensive work and ending with the material of minor significance.

Tables of Subdivisions under Individual Societies and Institutions (Fig. 13) is printed at the end of subclass AS (Academies and Learned Societies). Although printed in AS, the tables may be used wherever applicable throughout the classification.

There are several ways in which the tables may be developed. An example would be the Inter-American Press Association which classes in PN4712 (Journalism. Societies). The material concerning this society could be arranged according to the 9 numbers of Table I of Figure 13 by Cuttering .I5–59. Annual reports would be Cuttered under .I54, directories under .I57, and so on. Or Table II (3 numbers) could be used in two ways. The first would be by assigning three Cutters—.I5–53:

.I5   Serial publications.
.I52   Constitution, by-laws, etc.
.I53A–Z Other, by author, i.e., History, etc.

It should be remembered that .I51 does not exist, since no Cutters end in the numeral 1.

The second way of using Table II would be by using a single Cutter:

> .I5A1–4   Serial publications.
> .I5A5–7   Constitution, by-laws, etc.
> .I5A72–Z   Other, by author, i.e. History, etc.

TABLES OF SUBDIVISIONS UNDER INDIVIDUAL SOCIETIES AND INSTITUTIONS

The headings and order of publications as indicated are merely suggestive and may be modified to meet the requirements of special cases (for variations, *see* Shelflist).

The numbers (1), (2), (3), etc., prefixed to the headings are not part of the notation, but may be used for that purpose in combination with other numbers (Cutter numbers, etc.) when convenient. They are given to facilitate reference.

I

(1)   Proceedings and transactions.
(2)   Collections: Bulletins, contributions, memoirs, etc.
(3)   Periodicals. Yearbooks.
(4)   Annual reports.
(4.5)   Other reports (nonserial).
(5)   Congresses and conferences. Expositions.
(6)   Constitution and by-laws.
(7)   Directories. Lists of members.
(8)   History and biography. Handbooks.
        Handbooks issued annually in (2), (3), (4), or (7), as the case may be.
(9)   Addresses, lectures, essays.
(9.9)   Miscellaneous printed matter: Announcements, programs, etc.

II

(1)   Serial publications.
(2)   Constitution and by-laws, lists of members, etc.
(3)   Other.

Figure 13

Figure 14 shows the development of a book number in which the society and the subject are both involved. QD71 is the class number for "Analytical Chemistry. Periodicals, societies, etc." The subject heading assigned to Figure 14 is "Chemistry, Analytic—Congresses," and the first added entry is for the Society for Analytical Chemistry. The Cutters .S6–619 provide a 9-number table for the Society based on Table I of Figure 13. The fifth number on Table I provides for congresses, hence the Cutter .S615 on the card in Figure 14. Congresses cataloged as monographs are given a date to prevent too long an expansion of the numbers and to identify a particular congress more clearly.

A final example (Figs. 15a–15h) will show that a breakdown by other than alphabetical order—i.e., by author, then by title—is sometimes advisable in order to prevent the Cutter number from becoming cumbersome and to place the material in its logical place on the shelf. Under S401, "Agriculture. Documents and other collections. Congresses. International," a table was developed for the Food and Agriculture Organization of the United Nations. The FAO was assigned Cutter numbers .U6–63. The table reads:

.U6	Official documents.
.U6A1–5	Serials (alphabetically)
.U6A6–Z	Monographs (by title)
.U62(A–Z)	Committees, all subdivisions, etc.
.U63(A–Z)	Individual authors (including official publications of preliminary conference and of various countries)

Figures 15a through 15c are examples of serial Cuttering for the FAO. Figure 15a was Cuttered for the first two numbers of the *FAO Development Paper*, which were called *Agricultural Development Paper*. Figure 15b was originally Cuttered for *Annual Report*; when the entry was recataloged to *Work of FAO*, the original Cutter was retained. There was no point in changing the Cutters of these two entries because the titles could change again and again; by retaining the original Cutters the serials are at least kept together.

```
QD71
.S615
1965      Shallis, P      W        ed.
               Proceedings of the SAC Conference, Nottingham, 1965:
          a conference on analytical chemistry organised by the So-
          ciety for Analytical Chemistry and held at the University
          of Nottingham, 19–23 July 1965; edited for the society by
          P. W. Shallis.  Cambridge, Published for the Society for
          Analytical Chemistry by Heffer [1966, ᵉ1965]

             xii, 611 p.  illus., tables, diagrs.  25 cm.  £6/6/-
                                                                 (B 66–8008)
          Bibliography:

          1. Chemistry, Analytic—Congresses.      I. Society for Analytical
          Chemistry.  II. Nottingham, Eng.  University.  III. Title: SAC Con-
          ference.

          QD71.S615   1965            543.008              66–71593
          Library of Congress              [5]
```

                                                                 Figure 14

Figure 15a

S401
.U6A13

Food and Agriculture Organization of the United Nations.
FAO agricultural development paper. no. 1–

Rome [etc.] 1949–

    no. in   v. illus. 24–29 cm.

    Title varies: no. 1–2, Agricultural development paper.—no. 3–44, FAO development paper, agriculture (no.   –17, FAO development paper, agriculture and forestry)

    1. Agriculture—Collected works.   i. Title.

    S401.U6A13   51–6978 rev 2 ‡

    Library of Congress   [r57d⅜]

S401
.U6A15

Food and Agriculture Organization of the United Nations.
    The work of FAO; report of the Director-General. 1945/
46–
Rome.

    v. 23–34 cm. illus.

    Reports for 1955/57–   issued as Documents of the organization's Conference (S401.U6A215)
    Annual, 1945/46–1954/55; biennial, 1955/57–
    Reports for 1945/46–1946/47 called 1st–2d.
    Title varies: 1945/46–1946/47, Report of the Director-General to the FAO Conference.

    Subtitle varies.
    Report for 1952/53 has also a distinctive title: Growing food for a growing world.
    Reports for 1945/46–1949/50 published in Washington.

    i. Food and Agriculture Organization of the United Nations. Report of the Director-General. ii. Title. iii. Title: Growing food for a growing world.   (Series: Food and Agriculture Organization of the United Nations. Doc[ument])

    S401.U6A15   47–17137 rev 2*

    Library of Congress   [r65g½]

Figure 15b

Figure 15d shows an example where the work was originally Cuttered under the United Nations document number in JX; subsequently the work was reclassed to fit in with other FAO materials in S401. The Cutter .U62(A–Z) on the above table reads "Committees, all subdivisions, etc."; Figure 15e is an example of a subdivision Cuttered I5 for Information Division. The last Cutter on the table is .U63(A–Z) and is used for "Individual authors." Figure 15f is Cuttered A8 for Australia, and Figure 15g B4 for Belgium, both for official publications of those countries, while Figure 15h is Cuttered D6 for the author of a monograph, Dodd.

S401
.U6A24

Food and Agriculture Organization of the United Nations.
Journal. v. 1–
Oct. 16, 1945–
₁Quebec, etc.₁

v. in 29 cm.

S401.U6A24 338.10631 48–17805*

Library of Congress ₁1₁

S401
.U6A32

Food and Agriculture Organization of the United Nations.
Report. 1946/47–
₁Lake Success₁

v. 32 cm. (United Nations. ₁Document₁ E/597 ₁etc.₁)

At head of title: United Nations. Economic and Social Council.
Some reports accompanied by Addenda.
Supplements issued for some reports, with title: Supplementary
report.

ɪ. United Nations. Economic and Social Council. (Series)
JX1977.A2 E/597, etc. 338.10611 48–11134*‡
—— ———— 2d set. S401.U6A32

Library of Congress ₁3₁

S401
.U62I5

Food and Agriculture Organization of the United Nations.
Secretariat. Information Division.
Documentos. t. 1–
mayo 20, 1946–
₁Washington₁

v. 27 cm.

Issued May 20, 1946– . under the
division's earlier name: Information Service.

1. Food. 2. Agriculture.

S401.U62 I 5 338.10611 48–23475 rev*

Library of Congress ₁r52b1₁

S401
.U63A8

Australia. *Delegation to the Food and Agriculture Organization of the United Nations, Quebec, 1945.*

United Nations Food and Agriculture Organization. Report by Australian delegation of conference held at Quebec, Canada, October–November, 1945. Canberra, L. F. Johnston, commonwealth govt. printer ₁1946₎

23 p. 34 cm.

At head of title: 1945–46. The Parliament of the Commonwealth of Australia.

1. Food and Agriculture Organization of the United Nations.

S401.U63A8   338.10611   47–26178*

Library of Congress   ₁2₎

S401
.U63B4

Food and Agriculture Organization of the United Nations.
Delegation from Belgium.

Rapport de la Belgique à la ₁₁ᵐᵉ conférence annuelle, Copenhague, septembre 1946. ₁Bruxelles, 1946₎

56 p. 21 cm.

S401.U63B4   338.10611   50–27408
Library of Congress   ₁1₎

S401
.U63D6

Dodd, Norris E   1879–

The world talks over its food and agricultural problems. ₁Washington, Division of Publications, Office of Public Affairs, 1947₎

7 p. 26 cm. (₁U. S.₎ Dept. of State. Publication 3002. Conference series 105)

Caption title.

1. Food and Agriculture Organization of the United Nations.   I. U. S. Dept. of State. Office of Public Affairs. II. Series: U. S. Dept. of State. Publication 3002. III. Series: U. S. Dept. of State. Conference series, 105.

S401.U63D6   338.10611   48–45744 rev*

Library of Congress   ₁r48n10₎

Discussion

Question: Is .A1 automatically used for all periodicals classed in nonperiodical classes?

Mrs. Arick: No, it is not. Years ago the use of .A1 for periodicals was quite automatic, but it was found not to be necessary. Presently, .A1 is being incorporated into the classification in places where the subject catalogers want periodical material at the head of a class.

Question: Is .A2 for general works in some classes always expanded decimally?

Mrs. Arick: Not necessarily. As a matter of fact, the .A2 Cutter should be subdivided A–Z even though not so specified in the schedule. Under "Egypt. History. By period. Roman rule," DT93 is the number for "General works." Under this caption is found .A2 "To 1800" and .A3–Z "1800–   ." The .A2 should be automatically subdivided A–Z. The .A2 *could* be expanded decimally, but in some classes the .A2–29 would become overcrowded. Three titles in .A2–29 is no problem, but fifty, a hundred, or more would certainly be. The A–Z breakdown would solve the problem.

Question: Would you explain the Cuttering under More's *Utopia* in HX? Is the use of the Cutter by author or by date?

Mrs. Arick: Thomas More's *Utopia*, classed in HX811, is arranged by date. The first edition, in Latin, was published in 1516, and the letter "A" is used, plus the last three figures of the date for various editions. The first edition would then be HX811.1516.A516; the Latin edition of 1663 would be HX811.1516.A663.

Translations of the *Utopia* are arranged by date alphabetically: HX811.1516.E551 is the number for the 1551 English translation; HX811.1516.H946 is the number for the 1946 Hebrew translation; and HX811.1516.R947 is the number for the 1947 Russian translation. Criticism is provided for in HX811.Z5A–Z.

As you recall, Cutters never end in the numeral 1; the above use is a date, so is not a true Cutter. The use of the "A" Cutter for the original work *Utopia* follows general principles used in the literature classes.

Question: How does one know what abbreviations to use in call numbers?

Mrs. Arick: There is a list for internal use at LC. Naturally we like to use what is actually in the volume in hand: "Teacher's manual," "Index," "Supplement," and the like. Some abbreviations are already well known from LC cards, such as "suppl" for "supplement," and "appx" for "appendix."

Question: Please define the statement which sometimes is found in schedules, "Use successive Cutters."

Mrs. Arick: This means decimal expansion, described earlier in this chapter. For an author such as Brown, given a Cutter of .B7, other works would be expanded .B7, .B72, .B73, and so on.

Question: Sometimes .A19+ is found in the schedules. What does it mean?

Mrs. Arick: It means that .A19 is expanded decimally. When a notation like .A2± is found, as it is in the JS "Local government" tables, it means that

Cuttering starts with .A2 and is expanded decimally; if necessary, expansion may be done *before* .A2 (i.e., .A195).

Question: When a date is called for in a call number, which is used: copyright date or imprint date?

Mrs. Arick: The imprint date is used in the call number.

Question: Under F124, Nevins' book on Herbert Lehman is Cuttered .L532, but Chesman's book on Theodore Roosevelt as governor is Cuttered .C46. Was the latter Cuttering an error or done on purpose?

Mrs. Arick: F124 is the class number for "New York. History. 1865–1950," which includes biography of the period. In some of the older classes, specifically E and F, biography was Cuttered successively rather than according to present practice of double Cuttering. In F124 the Cuttering for Nevins' book on Lehman is correct; that for Chesman's book is incorrect since Roosevelt should be .R+. It is probable that the error has been found at LC and the call number changed; the printed cards for sale have not reflected the change as yet.

Question: When a date is called for immediately after the class number, followed by a Cutter number (say, JL65.1936.C8), and another edition of the work so classed is received with the date 1942, is the 1936 replaced with 1942 when classing the later edition?

Mrs. Arick: Certainly not. The first edition was classed as JL65.1936.C8. When the 1942 edition is received, it becomes necessary to expand the book number. The date 1936 in the call number represents a period or era, which is important in the classification. At one time, a second date was added under the call number for later editions, so the above number would have been JL65.1936.C8 1942. However, for various and practical reasons, the Cutter numbers are being expanded, so that the call number for the example would be JL65.1936.C812 or JL65.1936.C82.

Chapter 9

The Organization of Materials in Academic Libraries Changing to the Library of Congress Classification

Carl R. Cox

This chapter is concerned with the organization of materials in academic libraries changing to the LC classification, with particular regard to procedures, problems, and possible adjustments. The inclusion of the word "problems" allows for considerable leeway, since everything about reclassification from the decision to do it through the actual accomplishment presents a problem from one point of view or another.

I must warn the reader at the outset that I am a completely biased evangelist. Although I am going to attempt impartiality in presenting alternative ways of facing basic problems, I shall probably not be successful, since I hold some strong convictions as to how these problems should be met. If I forget to label my viewpoint as I go along, it may be picked up from what I have to say about the reclassification procedures at the University of Maryland, for inevitably I will be drawing a goodly number of my procedural descriptions from the system with which I have had the most experience. Although the planning for that reclassification is now almost six years in the past, Mr. William Connors, who directed the project at Maryland, has brought me up to date by allowing me to use material from his paper on that system which is now being readied for publication.

Basic Problems

To get into the subject in an orderly fashion, one must realize that the first problem to be faced, and probably the most difficult of all, is that of making the decision to adopt the LC classification. Since Chapter 13 will discuss the general advantages and disadvantages of using the classification, I will not go into these basic considerations beyond noting that it is vitally important in any reclassification effort that the library staff be convinced of the advantages if the change is to be effected with any degree of efficiency at all. For the administrator it is even more important if he is to face a group of budget officers and ask for a hefty appropriation just to change one set of incomprehensible numbers on the back of a book to another equally incomprehensible set.

For the academic library which is fast growing, the decision is probably easier to reach than it is in public and small libraries, since there has been general acceptance of the fact that the LC classification is more suited to the large research collection than to the small, popular, reading type of collection. Although I have used this argument myself where it might be effective, I personally believe that the present or future size of a collection is probably one of the least dependable and least significant criteria for selecting a classification in today's rapidly changing library picture. I cannot tell you all the reasons which have led so many libraries to decide upon the plunge into reclassification to LC, but I do know the primary factors which have influenced two library systems with which I have been connected, and I suspect something very like that reasoning has occurred in almost every case of change.

In 1961 the University of Maryland library was reaching middle-sized academic library status, with a collection of just over 300,000 volumes classified in Dewey and the addition of an average of 20,000 volumes per year. The book budget was increasing in giant steps, however, which made it apparent that the collection would double by 1967 and probably reach the millionth volume by 1970. It was obvious that the library could not keep up with such rapid expansion without both additional equipment and personnel, and even if systems could be devised and the necessary equipment acquired to mechanize operations, it would still be faced with the problem of an ever expanding cataloging staff combined with a shortage of professional librarians.

From the use of LC cards over the years the Catalog department knew that from 60 to 80 percent of new titles had LC coverage and that it was already following LC entries and subject headings. With adequate revision, well-trained library assistants could be utilized to handle these books if the LC classification system was adopted as well. It was realized also that the point had been reached where a further delay in a final decision on reclassification was, in effect, making the decision *not* to reclassify, since the expanded size and consequent added cost might make the change almost impossible later. It was decided, therefore, that the time had come to investigate the situation thoroughly and to settle the problem one way or another.

As a closer look was taken at the collection, it was found that many of the books already had six numerals following the decimal point in the Dewey classification—some few actually had nine—and this confusing notation could only become worse as the library continued to purchase more specialized material. Due in part to the lack of a proper number in Dewey and in part to local interpretation, the library over the years had diverged from the Dewey scheme in so many places that only a professional cataloger trained in the ways of the library could assign the classification, even though the recommended Dewey number was included on the LC card for the book. Revised editions of the Dewey classification had further contributed to inexactness by the split of older and newer material on the same subject.

Moreover, the University of Maryland library, like most libraries using Dewey, had developed its Cuttering to a fine art of special schemes in order to make the

Dewey number serve the collection more adequately. Capital "A" was used for bibliography, "Y" for criticism, "W" for biography, and so on. A biography of Adler written in German by Adenauer and translated into English by Brecht would be Cuttered Ad73WadEb, for example, while selections from Adler's works, translated into English by this same Brecht, would be Ad73E.B.

Not only did this proliferation of peculiarities make Cuttering and shelflisting by a professional librarian necessary, it also made the open-stack system a nightmare for both user and shelver. This long, hard look at the usefulness of what had been carefully created over some forty years of intellectual ingenuity pretty well decided Maryland that it had everything to gain by adopting LC. The carrot of being able to free professional catalogers for more challenging work than editing LC card copy, combined with the stick of increasing workloads, provided the necessary impetus for making the decision to reclassify.

The State University of New York, with some 4 million volumes in 58 campus libraries, followed much this same reasoning in deciding in June, 1966, to convert the entire system to the LC classification. An added argument in this case, however, was the desire to establish a standardized system which could (1) simplify centralized processing, and (2) be utilized in the automated library network being planned.

Total versus Partial Reclassification

Once the decision to reclassify has been accepted, the next general decision is one of extent of reclassification. Whether or not a library decides to reclass its entire collection depends upon a great many local factors. The size of the collection combined with the availability of staff has pushed most libraries in one direction or another. The smaller the collection, the more the likelihood exists that the decision will go to total reclassification. Even in large collections, however, many librarians have found it intolerable to live with two classifications, given the combination of open stacks and a vocal faculty.

A closed-stack situation, where pages service the collection, provides the ideal opportunity to start the new classification without changing any of the older works, and a few libraries have tried this. The sad fact of the matter is, unfortunately, that no college or university library really has closed stacks. Even when the library considers itself as such, in actual practice all faculty members, and usually graduate students as well, have access to the closed stacks and expect to find their material by browsing in the appropriate section of the classification. Consequently, no established academic library has been able to adopt LC without doing some reclassification in response to demand. It is a fact that most academic libraries which have begun with the premise that partial reclassification would suffice have been forced over the years to go on to virtually total reclassification. Moreover, the advent of more library automation nationwide will probably increase the trend to total reclassification; it may, on the plus side, also provide a less laborious means of accomplishing the job.

One of the more interesting approaches to the reclassification, rather than the new book, part of the problem is what may be considered as the random method. Based on the theory that roughly 20 percent of the library's titles account for 80 percent of the total circulation, this method of operation relies upon reclassifying the titles as they return from circulation, with the hope that those titles no longer in great demand will never have to be reclassified. No one has had a sufficiently lengthy experience with this method to prove or disprove its validity, but the organizational problems it presents may well be greater than the potential gain.

One of the steps that should be done in any total reclassification approach is to set up arrangements for weeding older volumes and outdated multiple copies. In the academic library, unfortunately, this is more often talked about than done. In addition to the perfectly correct assumption that college and university libraries have a historical repository function to perform, the library field's reliance upon volume count as a measure of excellence makes administrators most reluctant to reduce the size of the collection in any way.

The third major decision affecting the organization of the reclassification project is the amount of recataloging to be done. Here, again, there are no ground rules, and the decision must be tailored to local needs. The older, established universities making the change have generally felt impelled to make some fairly extensive catalog renovations a part of the reclassification effort. It is this decision that has led to the great projects which have still not been completed after many years. Make no mistake; there is always some recataloging to be done to adapt to the new classification, particularly in the area of serials treatment. The trick is to find a means of keeping this to a minimum. Some intensive study of the card catalog prior to beginning the project is a necessary step if any intelligent decision is to be made as to what is essential and what would be desirable given the time and the staff.

Maryland was fortunate enough to have a card catalog in good condition, since it had been following LC entries and using LC subject headings religiously for many years. A random sampling of trays in one catalog disclosed that more than 80 percent of the cards were LC printed cards, and of the remaining 20 percent all but the very early cards were based on LC copy. It was quickly decided, therefore, that recataloging was not needed and was to be actively discouraged. The problem thus became one of remarking volumes with LC numbers and changing the call numbers on the catalog cards. Once this conclusion was reached, it was realized that the change could be accomplished with mostly clerical assistance, provided the LC classification could be accepted without major changes and local adaptations.

Total Acceptance of LC and Local Variations

There are at least three major areas of LC classification policy which are likely to differ from Dewey classification practice in the academic library; the treatment of biography, of bibliography, and of fiction in English. Biography under Dewey most often is classed together in the .920's, whereas LC classifies by the subject interest of the biographee. Bibliography is treated in LC with what seems at times a blithe disregard of any established policy, but most often is placed in the Z(Bibliography) classification rather than with the subject. What really distresses many librarians and faculty, however, is LC's reliance upon PZ3 and PZ4 for fiction in English rather than upon the marvelously detailed national literature numbers (the P schedules). It is safe to say that most academic libraries deciding to adopt the LC scheme up to the present time have refused to accept one or more of these LC classification policies.

As at other libraries, this dilemma was faced at Maryland; a very close look was taken at the advantages to be expected from making the change of classification before selecting the course of action. In addition to the closer classification of material in the stacks, which would benefit the reference personnel by reducing the amount of patron assistance necessary, and the greater ease of shelving which would benefit the circulation department, the following major advantages were to be expected for the cataloging area:

1. New titles for which LC card copy was available could be handled by trained library assistants, and only in cases of shelflist conflict would the title need to be referred to a cataloger. This advantage would eventually apply to about 60 percent of new material, thus freeing the professional staff to concentrate on purely original cataloging.
2. In original cataloging, or on books for which LC had not supplied a class number, the task of fitting the title into the classification would be much quicker because of the fullness of the LC classification breakdowns and because the LC subject heading list gives the preferred classification number to correspond with the heading.
3. Author Cuttering could be done by clerical personnel, impossible with Dewey because in Dewey the Cuttering is so much more important in differentiating the greater mass of titles in one class number. Thus the job of assigning the class numbers would be cut in half for the cataloger.

Against these advantages which were to be gained if the classification was accepted as LC interpreted it, pleas for special adaptations were weighed. Although the LC classification in all its aspects could not be defended in terms of logic, the adaptations suggested were based for the most part on special interest and, as such, would displease as many people as they would please. For example, zoologists still insisted that animal behavior be classed in zoology, while psychologists believed just as firmly that it should be classed with books in their field. If adaptation was accepted, the new classification would diverge from the basic scheme over the years to come as much as the Dewey had in the past, with classification being done not so much on the basis of subject as by anticipated use or, more bluntly, by the interest of the academic department recommending that particular book for purchase. The library would, in effect, be right back where it was with the Dewey classification and would have failed to release the time of the professional catalogers to do the truly necessary original work. It was felt that this was too high a price to pay over the years for the dubious advantage of local adaptation, and decided to accept the LC classification number as given by the Library of Congress without deviation.

Without deviation, including the LC book number. For some reason the break with the Cutter tables causes more disorientation in some quarters than any other facet of the LC changeover. It does take a mental adjustment for most librarians to accept an author number which is not tied in some way to a printed list and which is not constant in meaning from class to class. Many libraries have balked completely at this concept and have either continued the use of the Cutter tables in conjunction with the LC class numbers or adopted the LC book number system but with some specific guidelines for its use locally—developing, as a result, a sort of abbreviated Cutter table. In either case, much of the advantage of following the LC classification is lost since each book must be adjusted individually.

The fear is, of course, that titles done as original cataloging locally will be assigned numbers which LC later uses for another title, and this will inevitably happen. What is forgotten under the pressure of this fear is the basic reason why such an imprecise shelving device works at all—the degree of expansion in the LC classification which, except for PZ3 and PZ4, makes for very few books in any one classification number. Although, at the beginning, statistics were not specifically kept on this aspect, the magnitude of the problem, as nearly as could be determined, was in the ratio of 175 titles needing adjustment out of approximately 30,000 original titles done over a three-year period—a bit more than one half of 1 percent of the titles locally classified, which seemed to be a very minor irritant. Titles classed locally were changed to avoid conflict with LC numbers, rather than altering LC numbers on printed cards.

Law Materials

What should be done with titles LC classes in its Law collection must also be decided before the project gets under way. Although there are law classification schemes that work very well, if it is necessary to integrate this material into the newly adopted LC classification there are only two basic choices: use the letter K, or use the word "Law" on the spine of the book and shelve the book by author or assigned Cutter number. Some libraries have done this. Most, however, have dodged the problem in the way Maryland did, by continuing to add law titles to the Dewey 340's in the hope that sometime before the end of the library's reclassification effort LC may have issued the Class K schedule. Either solution means reclassing these titles, naturally, but the latter solution of keeping the 340's has the virtue of being familiar to the patron through long usage.

Series Classification

One other major determination should be made, at least in principle, before the routine is set—how closely to follow LC in the classification of works in series. The mechanics of following are not difficult when LC classes a series together, or when each piece is classed as a separate, but the abandon with which a series will be treated both ways, depending upon the volume in hand, will cause grave problems to the reclassification crew unless some guidelines are established. Since series make up such an important segment of a scholarly library, a great deal of time was spent at Maryland trying, first, to interpret LC's classification policy and, secondly, to decide upon local policy. It was decided eventually to follow LC wherever possible, the series classification being preferred whenever there was a doubt or a choice. This brought up the immediate problem of what to do with the monographic volume purchased for subject content but which LC had classified in the series number. It was still put in the series number, with its proper volume marking, since it could be found through the card catalog, and on the supposition that other volumes of the series would probably be added later. On the rare occasions when the local rule was broken and the piece was treated as a separate, no entry for series was made in the card catalog. A series treatment authority file was set up so that consistency could be ensured.

These primary decisions have been dwelt upon, not only because they define the organization of material under the new classification, but also because at many points they determine the procedures and the staff needed to make the changeover. As a side benefit, a thorough knowledge of the extent of the problem may give the administrator the ammunition to annihilate the budget officer when the latter informs him that some other library accomplished its reclassification at a much lower cost. Even more important than this benefit is the opportunity to reexamine and straighten out some of the kinks in procedure that entangle well-established systems. Perhaps the library does not really need to record each periodical issue in five different places, perhaps ownership stamping can be abandoned on a special page, perhaps typewritten spine labels will serve as well as hand-lettering, and perhaps subject headings on cards need not be in red caps. This is the time to decide to break with those practices which may be outmoded or unnecessary.

Having made all the decisions, the library is ready to outline the procedures to be followed in the switch, to make time studies to determine the number and level of additional staff needed, to investigate equipment and supplies, to lay out the working space and an orderly work flow, and to prepare a private plan of operation to go into effect if the budget is less than the amount necessary. Listed in the aggregate this way, the undertaking sounds formidable, but if decisions have been firm, much of the operational pattern becomes obvious.

For the few libraries which have decided not to reclass the older material, the problem appears to be reduced to applying the new classification to new books only, and in theory this can be handled in the time-honored way. In actual practice, particularly in the large academic library which is most prone to take this approach, it almost always means reclassing all reference works in scattered reading rooms or departmental libraries, reclassing long runs of serials to keep from splitting the title, and reclassing copies and sometimes older editions. As noted before, this decision generally leads to total reclassification over the years, and since one of the bases for the decision is to avoid asking for additional staff for the reclassification, these libraries soon find themselves in trouble unless they have made the corollary decision to accept the LC number as printed and thus have released staff time to handle more extensive reclassification.

For most college and university libraries in the past few years, procedures have been set up at the beginning for reclassification of the full collection, although in the larger systems there has been established, also, a pattern for phasing-in certain segments of the older collection according to some local priority criteria. To belabor the obvious, working out such a procedure really boils down to amending the cards in the catalogs and renumbering the books, with, hopefully, some timely coordination between the two. For the library deciding upon recataloging, the task is one of beginning anew with every book. For the library which accepts the LC notation but insists upon local adaptation, the job is shorter but still demands that a professional cataloger examine each book and decide upon the suitability of the classification, and usually other elements as well. For the library which can bring itself to accept the LC card *in toto* the procedure becomes largely clerical, and the goal becomes one of creating as close an approximation of assembly-line production as possible.

Changing Books and Cards

Although there are some difficulties inherent in changing the numbers on the physical books the biggest problems come with the conversion of the entire card catalog. Reduced to the simplest of alternatives this means either changing the call numbers on the existing cards or making new cards to replace them. The amount of catalog revision should determine the approach used, while a time study of the mechanics should pinpoint the method. Methods vary from erasing and typing new call numbers on each card or pasting labels over the old call numbers on each card, through reproducing a new unit set from an existing main entry or ordering a new set of LC cards. No one has arrived at a strictly empirical "best" way of doing this job divorced from local requirements.

The quickest conversion known to the author, and one which may indicate the shape of things to come, was accomplished by the State University of New York at Albany in changing approximately 150,000 volumes from Dewey to LC on a crash program in less than six months. Utilizing temporary student help over the course of a summer the staff worked from the shelflist to fill out brief information forms which included the author's last name and brief title, accession number for the volume, LC call number as printed on the LC card, and the number of labels needed to amend all catalog cards and volumes. This information was keypunched and sent in numbered batches to the local computer center. The center used an IBM 1401 computer programmed to sort each batch into accession number order and to print both labels and new book cards for circulation. While the batch was at the computer center, the full set of cards was pulled from the catalog and filed behind the shelflist in accession number order and the books assembled from the shelves in the same order. When the batch of new labels and book cards was returned to the library, a quick matching and pasting operation finished the changeover, catalog cards were refiled, and books shelved in their new location. As can well be understood, this operation depended upon timing, to a large extent.

General Procedures Based on Total Acceptance

The Maryland procedure may be gone through very briefly as an example of a procedure based on full acceptance of the LC call number. It was found very shortly after beginning operations that both timing and proceeding in the shelflist order, rather than skipping around to round up copies and older editions, was essential to production. New books were handled by the regular staff, and additional staff was hired for the reclassification of the existing collection. In outline, then, the procedure has the following steps.

Books are removed in classified order from the stacks at the rate of about one book truckful each day and brought to the work area near the shelflist, where the shelflist cards are pulled. Shelf cards for which there are no books available— whether the books are lost, misshelved, or in circulation—are ignored at this time, and the cards left in the Dewey shelflist. As each decimal segment of the reclassification is finished, books which have been returned to the shelves in the meantime are caught and the circulation desk is alerted that the segment is done, so that any book bearing that Dewey classification number thereafter is automatically sent to the reclass unit upon return from circulation. A temporary slip is prepared from the shelflist card noting author, title, date of publication, and indicating that the book is being reclassified. This slip is filed in the public catalog, replacing the main entry for the title which is pulled as the next step.

This preliminary work is performed by student assistants, and at this point, with book, shelflist, and main entry matched, 70–80 percent of the titles are ready for reclassification—in other words, those which have as main entry an LC printed card with call number thereon. These go to a reclassifier (a clerical position), who revises the matching and watches for any discrepancies which may have to be referred to a cataloger for adjustment. The reclassifier then makes out a work order instructing the typist to change the call number on the main entry, to make new labels for the book, and to order the proper number of new cards reproduced on the Xerox 914. For the roughly 20 percent of the titles not having an LC printed card as main entry in the catalog, a student assistant searches the printed *National Union Catalog* and reproduces the LC entry on a 3M model 107 dry photocopier, at which point these books also go to the reclassifier. The approximately 3 percent of the titles for which LC entries are not located, are routed to a professional cataloger for original classification before being sent to the typist.

The typist uses a commercial white correction fluid to cover the old call number on the main entry and types the LC number over it, or types a single main entry for those titles not having LC printed cards. The main entry and attached work slip are sent to the Xerox operator, who produces the unit set of cards by Xeroxing the main entry directly on card stock and returns the new set to the typist the same day. The typist then adds the subject headings and added entries to each card and makes a new shelflist for filing. Completed cards and book labels (typed on a bulletin-size typewriter) are matched with the books, old numbers on the books eradicated by an opaque ink marker, labels affixed, and cards and books revised and released. Books are shelved in their new locations, and secondary entries from the original set of cards are discarded as the replacement cards are filed. The old Dewey shelflist is destroyed if all copies of the title were located; otherwise, the copies changed are lined through on the old card, and it is refiled in the Dewey shelflist to be pulled finally as the missing copies are found or withdrawn. Further complications are avoided by assigning copy numbers in the LC classification independently of the copy number assigned the same volumes under the Dewey classification.

Maryland started with a month-long moratorium on cataloging, except for rush books, while catalogers were trained and campus-wide publicity was disseminated. In the meantime the old Dewey collection was close-shelved to make room in the stacks for the new LC. As the first reclassification areas to be done it was decided that possible confusion in the classification had to be cleared up by redoing the old Dewey F (for fiction) class, B(for bibliography) group, and the like. It was also decided not to reclass the reference works first, and the project proceeded in shelflist order according to the local priority scheme, actually beginning with the science classes.

Reclassification is not an easy task, and anyone would be well advised to take a long, hard look at present procedures and the real, rather than the fancied, necessity for local adaptation, before building old elements into the new system. With the pressures for faster access to material building up throughout the university community, the only hope for the academic library to serve its clientele as that clientele needs to be served is to accept what has been done in a standard fashion by LC and devote the time released to doing what has not been done.

Discussion

Question: What policy about the use of *older* LC numbers should be adopted when reclassing? Should they be accepted as given on the cards, or checked to see if they need to be updated? How much updating was done?

Question: How does one reconcile the need to keep costs down by accepting the LC classification as given on printed cards with the stated need to check occasionally for updated classification numbers in schedules?

Mr. Cox: Classification numbers were accepted as they appeared on the cards, without attempting to find out whether they had changed over the years. If at a later time it was discovered that a particular title was causing difficulty due to the assignment of the older class number, then that title was changed, but I can remember no instance of this happening.

I know of no absolutely foolproof way of keeping up with LC's own reclassification unless one is ordering a new set of cards from LC for a particular title, when the revised card will be sent. Revisions do not appear in LC's printed catalog as a general rule, although if extensive recataloging has been done along with reclassification, the new card may be printed. In the case of a title with several editions, if a later edition is found to be classified differently from the earlier ones, one may assume that the earlier editions have been reclassified at LC to shelve with the latest. Other than those instances, however, about all that can be done is to keep up to date on the additions and changes to the class schedules themselves, and where wholesale expansion of the schedules by LC occurs, alert the reviser to refer titles falling within those areas to a cataloger for decision.

Question: How do you organize the work connected with changes LC makes in subject headings and in classification schedules?

Mr. Cox: In theory we thought it desirable to make the subject-heading changes, but in practice the extent and currency of the changes became, as it does in most large libraries, a function of the personnel time available to make those changes. We maintained a copy of the LC printed list of subject headings as our authority file, and this book was annotated and brought up to date regularly as the LC list of *Additions and Changes* appeared. The high-level clerk in charge of this official copy was also responsible for seeing to it that all cross references were made for the card catalog and for notifying the catalogers in the respective subject fields of the changes. Where a new heading appeared on an LC card before its listing in the *Additions and Changes,* a special note was made of this fact so that when it appeared on the list and our subject-heading authority was annotated, we could add the check mark which indicated we had used the heading and make all necessary references at that time. Where a new heading was a split-off from an older heading and not merely an updating of terminology, the cataloger in that subject field was responsible for determining what cards should shift from the older to the newer heading.

Since the acceptance of the LC call number in our reclassification brought about more released time for the catalogers, we were able to devote more professional time to card catalog investigation and planning the subject-heading changes. But we were still hampered by the lack of sufficient clerical time to make the physical changes, so that backlogs of work still accumulated in this area. Classification changes were annotated in the schedules as the LC list of *Additions and Changes* appeared, but no systematic attempt was made to go back and change books classified prior to the changes.

Question: What was your statement about copy numbers in reclassifying at Maryland?

Mr. Cox: We renumbered copies in the order in which they were reclassified. In other words, if we had five copies of a title and only copies 2, 3, and 5 were located at the time that title was reclassified, those three copies became copies 1,

2, and 3 of the title in the LC shelflist. If the other two copies were located subsequently, they were assigned copy numbers 4 and 5; but if they were withdrawn, we were not left with copy number gaps in the new classification.

Question: Should not compact storage be considered for little-used and outdated material in lieu of reclassification?

Mr. Cox: Yes, I think it should be considered, and it can reduce the size of the reclassification problem. It is always difficult to predict with any certainty just what titles will be used infrequently, but if the library has material that it thinks can be handled in this way, by all means try.

Question: Would you discuss in more detail how you allocated Cuttering? Who did the Cuttering (professional, clerical, etc.), and what training was involved?

Mr. Cox: Our plan was to follow the procedure that LC itself uses in its Subject Cataloging Division, where the cataloger assigns the class number and a clerical working with the Shelflist adds the Cutter for that specific book. Training of the clerical shelflister consists of a thorough explanation of the LC Cuttering system, aided by general guideline sheets of the type used by LC, and a period of revision by someone familiar with the system. Our biggest training obstacle stemmed from our long use of Cutter tables with Dewey, which made it difficult to convince these people that a number as abbreviated as .B6, for example, would place the book in its proper position on the shelf. This became less of a problem as the LC shelflist became more extensive and the new shelflister could see more clearly the lack of conflict, even with many books, in a specific classification number.

Question: Did a temporary slip in the card catalog have the LC number and was a temporary slip filed in the LC shelflist?

Mr. Cox: The temporary slip in the card catalog did not have the LC call number on it, even though in most cases we knew what that number would be at the time the slip was written. We left the number off deliberately to keep the patron from making a trip to the stacks to find a book which was still in processing. We did file a temporary slip under the new number in the LC shelflist —since this was not a public record—to hold the number should there be any undue delay in clearing the reclassed book through processing. The two temporaries were made at the same time, but only the carbon for the shelflist had the call number penciled on it.

Question: What do you mean by partial reclassification?

Mr. Cox: I meant the phrase "partial reclassification" to be taken in its most literal sense, referring to any plan of classification conversion which is based on the premise of redoing only a portion of the back collection rather than all. A large library facing reclassification quite naturally looks for ways to reduce the size of the job, and frequently makes the decision to start classing the new material in LC but to reclass only the volumes in the older collection which must be redone to keep material together. Or the decision may be made to reclass a departmental science library which is separated physically from the general collection, or, conversely, to reclass the main collection but leave certain departmental collections in the former classification or on special schemes.

Question: In a university library using LC classification with Cutter-Sanborn tables for author numbers, would you continue using this system, or would you adopt LC's Cutter numbers in full?

Mr. Cox: I personally cannot think of any valid reason why a library which accepts the LC classification number cannot accept the author notation which was developed to accompany that number.

Question: Does the University of Maryland use PZ3 and 4?

Mr. Cox: In accordance with the policy of accepting the LC classification without deviation, Maryland does use PZ3 and 4. The decision to use these classes was made only after much deliberation and forethought, for, like our colleagues in universities everywhere, we wished that LC had used the national literature classes for fiction in English and had not presented us with the necessity for this decision. We knew that we stood to gain a great deal in processing time if we could accept PZ and route this large segment of material through a clerical routine to the shelves; whereas if we changed LC's classification from PZ to literature numbers, all those books would have to be handled individually by a cataloger. As against this loss of time, what would we be gaining by adopting the literature numbers?

Our first thought was that we would be gaining a classification rather than a catch-all location device. Looked at as such, we failed to see where the literature classification served the student any better than the PZ location, since he was generally looking for a specific book on his reading list and not just any nineteenth-century novel written by an American; nor could we see where the professor needed such help since he already knew his authors and literature periods and could find the works he wanted in the single alphabet of PZ as easily as in the multiple alphabets of the literature classes.

We turned next to the argument that the literature classes would keep all the works of the author together. This was a very promising prospect indeed, until we realized that neither Maryland's library nor any other library ever could promise that. We would not take our rare edition of *Moby Dick* out of the rare book room to shelve with the majority of Melville's works in the stacks; the many pieces Steinbeck contributed to anthologies would still be in another location from his separately published works; the microcard and microfilm copies we had in the collection would still be in special collections and not in the stacks with the author's other novels; we still would put juvenile editions of the author's fiction with the juvenile collection. So, even at best, we would be providing only a partial answer to this problem.

Lastly, we turned to the theoretical faculty revolt at having fiction and translations separated from the poetry and the original-language text. Here we had an advantage over most libraries in that for years we had had the opportunity to observe a faculty which used interchangeably our library under Dewey and the Library of Congress itself only eight miles away, noting over this period of time no marked symptoms of schizophrenia which were attributable to the differences in book location and classification treatment. We found that the professor had no difficulty at all when he could understand the library policy and when that policy was followed consistently. The number on the book did not matter to him at all as long as he knew where to find the book. What did cause some heat was a situation which was completely understandable to the librarian but not very clear-cut for the professor—such a situation as that faced by the professor teaching a course in abnormal psychology, who never knew whether the book he wanted would be classed in B with psychology or in R with psychiatry. With the proliferation of subject reading rooms and departmental libraries, most professors in the large university today are overjoyed to find all the books they want in one building, much less on one floor or in one stack area. Considered in this way, you must admit that the rule that all fiction in English will be found alphabetically by author in PZ3 is not difficult to understand and sell.

This was the reasoning process we followed, and thus adopted PZ3 and 4 with the conviction that, as a location device, it was in the long run no worse than the literature schedules, and that adopting it would save us hours and hours of time which would otherwise be spent looking up and assigning new numbers to, for the most part, minor material, which would be creating more and more potential future classification conflicts for ourselves.

Question: In accepting the classification for Q and T on old cards, does this not separate current material on these subjects, especially works shelved in open stacks?

Mr. Cox: Yes, I am sure it does. This is the same problem that many of us have had over the years with the expansions in later editions of Dewey, where we could not go back and change all the earlier works classified under the previous Dewey editions. Had a situation arisen where this spread was causing problems, we would probably have made an effort to bring that particular area into complete currency, but the problem did not occur. The preference of most patrons for the most recent book, of course, helps to keep the problem minor. One of the more interesting side effects of reclassification is that the patrons start using the newer classification as they would a new book list, going to the LC classified shelves as their first approach and ignoring what they consider the old books. Circulation of the LC classified books goes up very rapidly, with a corresponding drop in the Dewey.

Chapter 10

The Organization of Materials in Public Libraries Changing to the Library of Congress Classification

Marian Sanner

The organization of materials in the Enoch Pratt Free Library involves a complex series of operations. There are nine central library departments, each with its own card catalog; twenty-three branches with separate adult and juvenile catalogs in each; and two full dictionary catalogs of the complete holdings of the system, one in the catalog department and one in the central hall. Several factors are causing unusual complexities in our operations at the present time: (1) six of the central subject departments were recently reorganized into three; (2) the book collection is presently classified under three systems; (3) the library is preparing to issue its first book catalog in September, 1966; (4) a new major branch is to open in January of 1967 with a collection of 40,000–45,000 volumes; (5) the budget year, along with that of the City of Baltimore of which the library is a department, recently changed from a calendar year to a July-to-June fiscal year, necessitating changes in all statistics and operating procedures which have relationship to the budget.

In its early days the Pratt Library had a classification system which was called a "block classification." Letters were assigned to broad subject areas, and within each letter blocks of numbers were set aside for various categories of books. As books were cataloged, they were given consecutive numbers in the blocks to which they belonged. As long as the collection remained small, this was a satisfactory arrangement; as the library's holdings increased, the "block classification" became inadequate.

Pratt adopted the LC classification in 1920, but with modifications. The first modification was to substitute the letters from Pratt's "block classification" for LC's letters, except for the Political Science schedule which retained the J. More than a mere substitution of letters was involved in this change; in some cases one letter was assigned to two LC classes, for example, the letter H was assigned to LC's E and F schedules. In order to prevent a duplication of numbers in the two schedules, 1000 was added to all numbers in the F schedule, so that F1 became H1001 in Pratt's classification. Additional problems were created by the lifting of small blocks of numbers from one schedule, adding two or more thousand numbers to them, and fitting them into other schedules; for example, the topics in LC's G schedule were divided among six classes in Pratt's system.

One further modification made was to eliminate decimals from the LC system and substitute whole numbers for them. This was done by going through the schedules, lining out the decimals, and inserting consecutive whole numbers. As a result, there were many places where Pratt's numbers were entirely different from LC's numbers. The most serious aspect of this change was the scarcity of numbers left in some sections of the schedules for expansion of old subjects and for insertion of new ones.

When the Library of Congress issued a revised schedule, years elapsed before Pratt could use it because of all the costly and time-consuming alterations which had to be written into the schedule. Another aspect of Pratt's classification policy was the practice of consulting heads of subject departments as to the classification of specific titles. These consultations frequently resulted in the assigning of an incorrect class number for a book in order to place it in one department in preference to another. As the years passed, this policy of "custom classification" was producing chaos in the system, and with the increasing staff turnover of recent years, indoctrination of new catalogers was becoming more time-consuming and less effective.

This brief description of Pratt's classification system indicates what a costly and difficult system it was to apply. The expense and complications were mounting as acquisitions increased and as the disciplines became less sharply defined, thereby requiring more time to be spent on the classification of many titles. In addition, subject headings did not always conform to those in LC's list. If the head of a subject department did not like an LC subject heading, another was used instead, or, in some cases, a heading was made up. If an inverted heading was preferred, it was inverted even though LC did not. So that, even in the case of subject headings, changes in a new edition of the list had to be made before it could be used.

In the summer of 1964, Dr. Maurice Tauber was called in as a consultant on matters pertaining to the proposed book catalog. During the course of the discussions, he became so concerned over the Pratt classification system that he recommended it be abandoned immediately and the LC classification, unmodified, be adopted. This step was not taken lightly; much thought and study preceded the decision to change. The recommendation was in the fall, and the final decision was not made until spring of the following year. It was felt that with the expansion of knowledge and the tremendous growth in publishing, the classification system would break down completely within the next few years. Also, it was becoming increasingly necessary that Pratt be in a position to make more use of LC's cataloging than it had been able to do in the past. It was decided that Pratt Library's future would be best served by changing to the Library of Congress classification, and the change was made May 1, 1965. Since that date all new titles and new editions added to the library have been given LC classification numbers.

It was decided at the outset that no changes in the numbers in the LC schedules would be made and that no new numbers would be created. The following deviations from LC were accepted, but these will not disturb the structure of the LC schedules:

1. Pratt is a departmentalized library, and it was felt that the bibliography of a subject would be more useful with the subject. The bibliographies which LC classifies in Z5051–7999 are being scattered throughout the subject classes, being put in the "general works" numbers and Cuttered .A1. Reference books have an X prefixed to the call number so that within each department, or branch, the reference books are shelved together; the .A1 Cutter numbers are easy to spot on the shelves.

2. Personal bibliography is being classed with individual biography, and Cuttered .A1.

3. Law of a subject is being classed with the subject. This also goes in the "general works" number, and is Cuttered .A2. With a Cuttering device for bibliography and law they can be separated from other materials on the subject without altering LC's schedules or the meaning of their numbers. This is not something which has to be written into the schedules because all concerned know that it applies throughout the classification.

4. It was necessary to make some provision immediately for general law not connected with a subject field. It was decided to retain the law classification in use, a simple schedule but adequate for the amount and types of general legal materials acquired. The class letter has been changed to K so that there will not be a letter conflict with LC's system.

5. Pratt has never classified fiction, and this policy was retained. Fiction is shelved alphabetically by author, and the catalog cards carry the abbreviation "FICT." in call number position.

6. Periodicals have not been classified, although fully cataloged. Periodicals are located in the subject departments arranged according to catalog entry, which is usually the title.

7. Phonograph records are fully cataloged and classified. Nonmusic records have been, and are, classified with the subject. Pratt had a special classification for music records but is now putting music phonorecords in MP—a class that LC does not use—so that music and music records will be in the same class letter.

8. Some provision had to be made for the juvenile collection. The nonfiction is classified in the same numbers as adult nonfiction, with a small "j" prefixed to the number. Juvenile fiction is not classified, but a small "j" is used on books and catalog entries to distinguish it from adult fiction. PZ6 is used for foreign-language books, PZ7 for picture books, and PZ8 for fairy tales; these numbers are all prefixed by a small "j."

After a year with the Library of Congress classification Pratt feels that the foregoing deviations were wise decisions; it does not contemplate any others. The practice of "custom classification" has now become a thing of the past, because general agreement was secured at the beginning of the new program that LC's classification would be followed, with those exceptions previously noted.

One thing which has not been mentioned is the book number, and since there has been much discussion recently about the great economies to be achieved in adopting LC straight across the board, including book numbers, a few remarks should be addressed to this topic. Pratt is not using LC's book numbers; LC's author number table is being used, but the numbers are being assigned locally. In the first place, if a quantity of LC's book numbers are examined, it will be seen that there is some variance from the table, due to LC's internal shelflisting. Since Pratt is unlikely to have as many titles in any classification as LC has, it will be able to keep book numbers shorter by assigning them locally. Secondly, there are the great numbers of titles for which there is no LC classification, and for these the library must assign classification and book numbers. Pratt would run into conflicts at once if it was trying to use LC's book numbers, and would be changing them continuously.

A temporary card is filed in the shelflist before the book is released, and it takes less than half a minute to assign the book number at that time. In a public library, where the same title may be going into twenty-five or more agencies at the same time, it would be a major catastrophe if a number conflict were discovered later and all copies of the book had to be located and recalled from circulation for remarking.

When the "block classification" was abandoned in 1920, a reclassification section was set up and titles were reclassified on a priority basis; however, the project was discontinued before the entire collection was completed. Some titles have been reclassed over the intervening years, but about 30,000 or more titles still remain in the original classification.

Some libraries which have changed classification systems have used the new classification for new titles and have allowed the older collection to remain in the previous classification. This possibility was discussed at Pratt, but it was decided that the best interests of staff and readers would be served if the library reclassified the entire collection, including those titles in the original classification. Pratt's classification looks, of course, like the LC classification, but the letters have entirely different meanings. They are being distinguished at present by a yellow stripe on the spine of each book in the LC classification, but this practice will not be continued throughout the library's future. The problems of shelving and retrieving books are many when the call numbers look alike yet belong in different departments, depending upon whether they are old or new class. Even in a branch, where the collection is shelved in one large room, the readers have difficulty using the two collections. Separate drawers in the catalog cases are being used, but it would be difficult to maintain the distinction between the two classifications in a book catalog.

Pratt considers the book catalog basic to either of its two reclassification programs. It must get out of the business of reproducing catalog cards in order to have staff and space for the reclassification. The first book catalog is due in

October (1966) and another near the end of the year; these will contain all the classified or reclassified titles cataloged since May 1, 1965, in the LC classification. Only titles which have been classified or reclassified by the LC system will go into the book catalog. Until the book catalog is in a regular production schedule, supplements containing new titles will be issued intermittently. Shelflist cards and main entry cards will be made for all agencies receiving new titles; this will give staff and readers some access to them during the interim periods between book catalog supplements. The book catalog will contain all necessary cataloging information, including notes. Some of the information will be abbreviated slightly, and everything following the main entry will be printed in one paragraph, with the tracings forming a second paragraph.

The original plan for reclassification called for a ten-year program to complete the entire collection of some 350,000 titles and almost 2 million volumes. Under this plan, the catalog department would work with only one copy of each title. Clerical assistants, working from the shelflist cards, would get from departments and stacks one copy of each title, and would withdraw the corresponding main entry and branch holdings cards from the official catalog. They would search these entries through the LC printed catalogs and the *National Union Catalog,* noting LC's class number and any variations between LC's and Pratt's cataloging. The clerical assistants would then type temporary cards for the shelflist and would turn over their work and the book to the catalogers. The catalogers would check the class number to be sure it was still an active number and that it had not been subdivided, and they would check subject headings to bring them into line with the current list of LC subject headings. Main and added entries would be verified and descriptive cataloging altered to conform to policies for the book catalog. Catalogers would assign the book numbers and file temporary cards in the shelflist.

The cards and book would then move on to the clerical assistants, who would prepare new book cards and pockets for all accession numbers on the shelflist, and type copy for the book catalog, the official main entry card, and a new shelflist card. All active accession numbers would be transferred to the new shelflist card, and the new number would be typed at the top of the old shelflist card. The new shelflist would be filed, and the old one, along with the book cards and pockets, would be sent to the preparations and binding department. This department would be responsible for searching for the additional copies from the old shelflist, for inserting the book cards and pockets in the located volumes, and for the remarking. It would also have the responsibility to continue the search for missing books. Those copies which could not be located after a specified lapse of time would be removed from the shelflist cards; in effect, the reclassification would serve also as an inventory of the collection. After a title had been reclassified, catalog cards would be withdrawn from the card catalogs, and the entry would appear in the next supplement to the book catalog.

During one of the hearings on the budget requests for the reclassification and book catalog, the city's budget director asked if this job could be completed in less time if the money needed for it would be available in a lump sum; if so, he suggested that Pratt apply for a loan in the amount required. The program was replanned and the costs refigured, and the library applied for a loan in the amount of $1,700,000 to reclassify the collection in a period of from two to four years. This loan was placed on the November ballot and was accepted by the voters.

If the loan had been defeated, Pratt would have proceeded with the ten-year program; since the voters approved it, Pratt will embark on a different type of program. It will increase the staff of catalogers and senior clerical assistants and will set up an assembly-line operation. Clerical assistants will proceed as in the plan just described except that they will not send for any books. The staff assigned to this project to perform the cataloging operations would consist of college graduates, trained on the job. They would go through all the necessary steps for those titles for which LC classification is available. Any titles for which LC classification is not available, or which involve complex cataloging problems, will be turned over to professionally trained catalogers, who will send for the books and proceed with the reclassification.

Under this plan, no cards will be withdrawn from the card catalogs, and the entries will not go into the book catalog until the reclassification of the central collection is completed. Until the books are remarked, there will be access to them through the card catalogs. When the remarking begins, access to them will be almost nonexistent until the titles appear in the book catalog. This will be a difficult period for staff and public, but the merit in this alternate program is that the collection will be reclassified in a much shorter period of time and there will be fewer years to live with three classifications.

All the titles in the new branch will be in the LC classification, and there will be separate adult and juvenile book catalogs of the collection. The catalogers are working on these titles now in addition to cataloging new titles for the system. The titles being reclassified for the new branch are remaining, for the present, in the old classification in central and the other branches. As soon as the catalogers have completed their work on the collection for the new branch, they will proceed to reclassify all other titles which are in any branch collection. A new shelflist card will be made for every title in every branch, and one new book card and pocket will be made for each title in every branch. These will be taken to the branches by teams of about eight people in each team from the catalog and the preparations and binding departments. The new shelflist cards will contain the old number in the upper, righthand corner so that the remarking teams will be able to locate the old shelflists. They will transfer accession numbers to the new shelflists, make additional book cards and pockets for those titles of which a branch has more than one copy, and locate and remark the books. There is no master branch shelflist in the main library so it is not known how many copies of a title a branch has. The teams will remain in a branch until all located books have been remarked.

While the remarking is in progress, copy for the reclassified titles will be sent to the book catalog contractor so that a book catalog can be issued containing all reclassified titles in branch collections. This catalog and the current new title catalog and supplements will make possible the elimination of all card catalogs in the branch system. Central copies of these titles will be remarked along with other reclassified titles as the books in each department are remarked.

The next priority consists of books in those groups of numbers which were lifted from one schedule and inserted in another by the process of adding several thousands to the class numbers. These present difficulties in use now, since new books on these subjects are going into different central departments because of the assigning of certain LC class letters to each of the subject departments. The last order of priority to be reclassified will be any earlier editions of titles which have been given LC classification since May 1, 1965.

Catalogers will proceed with the reclassification of the major part of the collection, working through all the old class letters in one department before moving on to the next department. When everything in Pratt's old modified LC classification has been reclassed the books in the old "block classification" will be done.

There is one other large collection which has not been mentioned. This year the trustees of the Enoch Pratt Free library and the Peabody Institute Library have agreed that Pratt should take over the Peabody Library, operating it as a special branch library and merging the major part of the Peabody collection—some 280,000 volumes—with Pratt's collection. The Peabody books are in the Dewey Decimal Classification, so they must be reclassified before the merger of the collections can take place. The Peabody building will be set up and operated as a student center, and funds have been included in the budget to purchase 30,000–50,000 volumes to be used in this center. These volumes, too, must go into the LC classification.

Whatever the program or method used, reclassification is a formidable job, and the staff at Pratt would not recommend it unless the classification system used by a library had become intolerable or was showing evidence of future collapse.

Chapter 11

Orientation of Staff and Clientele into the Library of Congress Classification

Mary Darrah Herrick

The LC classification is large and complex, and there is no reason to expect librarians without experience in its practice to be able to carry out a reclassification program (including requirements for original classification) unless they are allowed some time to have a review of its policies and practices. As the writer reflected on the topic, "Orientation of Staff and Clientele," the only clientele that she could envision as needing a formal orientation into LC was a university's faculty. In public libraries large enough to warrant changing to LC, the stacks are closed, the public does not have access to them, and in general what classification the library uses is of no moment to the public. In open-stack rooms and branches, the materials are usually in some form of "reader's interest" sectioning.

In academic libraries with open-shelf collections for students, the pamphlet *Outline of the Library of Congress Classification* might be made available, with a list of LC subject classes posted in a prominent place. There is perhaps no necessity to go any further than this. Of paramount importance to students is the location of the books they want, not methodology or organization. In this paper, therefore, clientele is going to be equated with academic faculty, and to some extent whatever is said of their orientation may apply to the general library staff or to the staff of special libraries within a system.

The LC classification is certainly the best publicized of currently used systems, with its distribution of printed cards and the publicity of the printed catalog. But LC is also guilty of a shyness that is unequaled in putting into print any manuals or policy statements. Therefore, in any institution planning to adopt LC, unless there is personnel experienced in its use, orientation should be given.

Faculty Orientation and Preplanning

Some of these four circumstances have probably arisen:

1. The organization of the sciences may be out of date.

2. The humanities staff may have long disliked the location of biography, and the separation of description and travel in countries from the history of those countries.

3. The extensive notation that recent Dewey revisions have required may have been a minor annoyance.

4. Departments in literature may have deplored the form separation of literary works of individual authors.

One or any of these situations creates a climate of dissatisfaction among the faculty. If this dissatisfaction is strong enough, they will be willing to accept a change. The faculty's paramount concern will not be for the costs involved—these are headaches for the administration—but they will be concerned to know what will happen in their own fields of knowledge while a reorganization of materials is going on. Questions that they may ask, and that the librarian should be prepared to answer, will be such as these:

1. What will be the disposition of my field in the new system?
2. Will any material be taken from it?
3. Will the new classification make any major location changes in the materials that I am accustomed to use?
4. When are you going to start with my area?
5. How many of the books and records will be unavailable at any one time?
6. What are you going to do about discards? How may I be sure nothing is discarded that may yet be of value?
7. Will it be possible to shelve the newly classified books in my field near the older area until the two are totally merged?
8. What is going to happen to the material [although they may not phrase it this way] that has been classified as courses are taught? Is that going to be dispersed?

Most faculty are, through experience, aware that no one book classification is perfect or equally efficient in all areas. It should not be difficult to convince them that a system already tried out in the largest library in this country will be adequate in scope for any institution. If this argument is not strong enough, recent figures may be quoted to show the large number of libraries that have adopted LC. The fact that this system also provides for printed cards with classification numbers already assigned that may be used for a considerable part of the materials, is an economic factor that is of importance, especially if it is stressed that this may mean the release of some professional staff to process arrearages that are keeping useful materials virtually inaccessible and unknown. It may be wise to state honestly that certain aspects of the LC classification leave much to be desired, or that in parts of the schedules it may even appear that access to materials is much more complicated than in the Dewey classification. To put it another way, the specificity of LC breaks down fields into minutiae, and this may not always seem necessary to individual faculty members.

In all probability, early in the discussions suggestions will be made for some adaptations in LC. This is to be avoided. There is little or no record of any successful precedent for the adoption of a classification and then the making of local revisions in it, and there is a large body of evidence and experience showing that most revisions are unnecessary, ill-achieved, and, except in the rarest cases, to be absolutely forbidden.

This admonition cannot be stressed too strongly. The validity of a proposal for a reclassification program cannot be substantiated if, at the same time the plan is proposed, it is also decided to build into the new system local decisions that would require extra labor costs indefinitely. Even a few local adaptations mean that the LC numbers cannot be accepted as received without checking, because they may be in the very area that local adaptations have been inserted. One cannot depend on human memory to recall these. If LC numbers on cards are accepted, the need for *some* editorial work arises, but there is no justification for permitting or condoning unnecessary costs. In the Winter, 1966, issue of *Library Resources & Technical Services*, Eric Moon expressed a similar opinion, saying of local peculiarities in cataloging and classification that " 'rugged individualism' in cataloging practices is now only rugged stupidity. If we could ever afford it the day when we could do so has long gone."[1] So, if adaptations are asked for, the librarian must exercise his responsibility by denying them, and the faculty must respect his professional judgment.

The time and method of faculty orientation may be decided according to the size and nature of the institution. A campus-centered faculty may well be met as a group for the first presentation, with a follow-up later by departmental meetings. The same format could be used in a university, if necessary, with the first presentation to the university senate or other joint faculty group, followed by department meetings or meetings with individual college faculties. The program may be designed with a view toward how much the faculties may be interested or may wish to be involved. In some cases it will not be necessary to go through as elaborate a procedure as outlined above. However the faculty is approached, the first announcement should be backed with the highest administrative and academic authority.

Policy Decisions

A few policy decisions must be made before the staff orientation begins. One of these is what will be done with legal materials. There are provisions under many subjects for legal treatises or studies, with the exception of places for civil law codes and the other large collections which will have to be placed in K. Using the existing provisions within schedules is a very practical and workable solution for an institution that does not have, nor wishes to have, a special law collection.

Some libraries have thought that they must also make some local adaptations for bibliography (the Z schedule), rearranging it by subject fields into the separate schedules. While LC's provision for bibliography does appall the logical mind, in practical use it does not cause undue hardships in the general reference collection, and it is possible to shelve sections of bibliography into special collections areas by using locator devices, though the results are less than perfect. There is no real justification, however, for any tampering here, as the costs and labor involved would be considerable.

Another decision has to be made before the actual orientation work begins, and this involves LC book notation. Some libraries which are now reclassifying into the LC classification have decided that they will accept the complete notation as it is given on the cards, in order that the full benefit of the work done at the Library of Congress be realized, and this seems to me the logical decision to make.

Staff Orientation

Staff orientation may have to begin with a general review of the situation that has necessitated the change and what it is hoped will be accomplished, thus creating a climate of understanding and cooperative willingness among all personnel. The orientation can be done at several levels. The first may be when the consultant (if used) meets with the staff to discuss with them some of the general problems involved. Sometimes this meeting is limited to the department or division heads and is concerned only with administrative problems that will arise in the reorganization.

One institution with which the writer is familiar, after using a consultant's services, then called upon a nearby library school to have one of its faculty lecture to the staff about the philosophical concepts and the development of the LC classification, comparing it with Dewey and drawing attention to what patterns of thinking might need to be changed as the new system was adopted. The guidelines for a staff to follow so as to become familiar with the working of the LC system can, of course, best be given by someone who has had considerable experience in the use of that classification. A combined lecture-workshop type of program often works well.

General Aspects of LC

One of the first things to be done is to go over the whole series of LC schedules, pointing out the general characteristics that apply throughout the classification and mentioning some of the general trends and biases that one may expect to find. Among the points that might be mentioned are some that may be already known and understood, such as the bias of LC in its presentation of the American Indian material and material on the American Negro. Another general characteristic is the widespread use LC makes of tables by placing them within the schedules to expand specific areas, and by appending them to a specific schedule, thus providing that the tables may be used under a wide variety of topics. Reference might also be made to the use of general form divisions in almost every section of each schedule, corresponding to the Dewey form numbers with which the staff has already become familiar.

There are other general practices that may, or may not, be known to a staff relatively unacquainted with LC. Among these are:

1. The provision made in almost every schedule in the general form divisions at the beginning of a subject for separate numbers for treatises, minor works, general, popular, and juvenile works

2. The propensity of LC to divide geographically, not only under general aspects of a topic, such as "Labor," but also under specific aspects of it, such as "Hours of Labor"

3. The implicit permission to use the regional U.S. tables from HC107 whenever a geographical division by state or region is required and no table is assigned

4. The designation of periodicals by form number .A1 that may be done practically anywhere in the classification when no provision for periodicals is provided under a topic

5. The custom of indicating autobiography or letters of a man by the form number .A3 appended to a subject number, even when no table or direction to do so is given

6. The policy of omitting the numeral "1" in a number range when it is provided for in a special table, such as Table C in the H schedules, and in other areas of the classification

7. The distinction between the placement of biography in a part of the C schedule, and the more commonly found placement throughout all schedules

8. The fact that although the individual works of an author are brought together under his name in both literature and philosophy, yet when one of his works is on a specific subject, the subject takes precedence, and that work is classified elsewhere

9. The distinction made in the classification of the works of an individual classical philosopher in the original language and in translation, the former being assigned to PA and the latter placed in B

10. And, finally, the use of a number and the term "general special" to provide, not only for the general subject in a special situation, but also for a new aspect of a subject until that aspect is recognized by a distinctive number. As this term "general special" is not always understood, it helps in explaining it to draw on the excellent examples to be found in the H schedules. These, when examined as a unit, do much to clarify the way LC uses this subject device, and show how one may interpret it in other areas. Examples from the schedule can be selected to show the use of the term without any definition, the places where a brief definition is given, and then a range of numbers with specifically defined aspects of "general special" allocated to each number in the range.

Introducing New Subjects

A knowledge of the ways that LC provides for the development of new subjects is also an important part of the introduction to the classification. Some of these are by:

1. The insertion of new numbers or ranges of numbers
2. The insertion of decimal numbers
3. The activation of a parenthesis number
4. The narrowing-in of the subject designation for a number by giving a part of that subject to a new number
5. The application of a table to an already established subject field. (This has been done recently in the DT schedules for Africa where the small countries heretofore having only one number, or a decimal or Cutter number, are now all assigned to one of three tables that give each a ten-number range)
6. And, finally, the redefining or addition of a more modern term to an already established subject, such as that represented by JC319 which was first defined as "Geographic works. Nation and territory" under Political Theory, and by the addition of the term "Geopolitics" has its concept brought up to date.

Cutter Numbers

Inasmuch as Cutter numbers appear within the classification in many places, it is well to draw attention to the various ways they are to be used, such as to express minor aspects of a topic and to indicate geographical and form divisions. In the literature and philosophy sections, they are used to designate separate works of an author and to express a specific theme in an author's works. A book number involving the use of a double Cutter number, then, may be expressing classification through the first Cutter number and piece identification after that, or both Cutter numbers *may* be a part of the classification.

Dates

The presence of dates as parts of the classification numbers should also be explained, citing some examples, such as their use to distinguish individual naval battles in English history, DA87.5, or their use in the HD schedules to designate labor strikes by the year of the strike.

Book Notation

If a decision to accept LC notation is made, during the staff orientation time there should be an examination of examples to show how much of a number is a part of the classification, what part belongs to the book numbering system as mentioned above, and how LC designates additions, copies, and variants. It is usually understood that LC uses an author numbering system to arrange its books under topic alphabetically by author, distinguishing titles when necessary either by successive Cutter numbers or by lower-case letters, and editions by date. However, the fact that LC often uses .A1–.A5 for book numbers for documents or governmental publications must also be noted. These book numbers are form numbers, having no relevance to the author entry as far as getting it placed alphabetically on the shelves is concerned. In some instances the pattern of book numbering is difficult to interpret because nothing on it has appeared in print. There is one explanation of how Cutter numbers are assigned in the *Cataloging Service Bulletin*, no. 65, August 1964, but it is brief and incomplete for an understanding of general notation practices.

The quarterly *LC Classification—Additions and Changes* is used in close conjunction with the schedules and subject headings. One fact should be noted immediately. Subject headings and class numbers will appear on proof slips before they are received in the *Additions*. There may be up to a year's delay, though usually the new terms and numbers appear in the *Additions* after a reasonable period. Sometimes, however, they never appear, and then it can be assumed that the assignment was incorrect and was caught by the editors at LC and canceled.

At whatever point in time an institution decides to adopt LC, there may be a discrepancy between a classification number printed on a card and the number assigned to the same subject in the schedules. This occurs when the classification of a field is revised or changed after the cards were printed for a book in that particular subject area. For example, in 1952 there was a substantial revision in the RC schedule, so naturally cards issued prior to that date for books in that field do not reflect these changes. In 1965 the area of "Commercial Aviation" was moved en bloc from the TL section to HE; and just this year there has been an insertion of numbers in the H tables to provide for a separate place for Latin America. All these represent areas where editing of numbers on cards might be necessary. As an alternate, some institutions may choose to disregard all changes, accepting numbers as given, and relying on the subject catalog to bring the materials together. However, constant attention to the *Additions and Changes* is important, if the total potential of a living classification is to be realized. Ideally, all additions and changes should be acted upon as they are received, but this is not feasible; some compromise should be made so that at least significant changes may be noted.

Indexes to LC

The extent to which the LC subject-headings list can serve as a relative index to the classification should be defined and its limitations clearly understood. The recent trend of adding relative indexing to the topical indexes at the end of schedules is important, as this increases the usefulness of the indexes and draws together references to related areas in other classes. To a limited extent this is satisfying the crying need for a complete relative index to the LC classification. The experience at Boston University where a relative index to LC has been made has enabled the staff to speed up its work considerably.

Individual Schedules

In whatever way the many facets of LC classification are presented, at some time in the orientation attention must turn to a study of the individual schedules.

The H schedule is often taken first in any training program because of the difficulty of the application of tables.

The "Philosophy" classification is also one that warrants some practice in the application of its tables for individual philosophers with Cutter numbers. Formerly, Table V with a range of 4 Cutter numbers was used for all these writers. In the last *Additions* three new tables have been given, now providing for ranges from 2 to 5 numbers, without any designation when they are to be used. The assumption is that the more important writers may be assigned the larger tables, and the smaller tables kept for less prolific authors, though this still leaves two tables in each category to be considered.

The writer also recommends selecting a subject, such as "Romanticism," to show how it is treated as a literary theme in PN, and is represented in all national literatures under period when relevant, under form of writing, and then also under certain authors. The PN–PS sections all should have some practice sessions that include applications of their extensive tables for individual authors. Examination of the J schedule at the same time as D and E helps to illustrate the relationships in the treatment of the history and the political administration of a country. In conducting this detailed study of individual schedules, theoretical problems may be assigned to illustrate significant points, and preselected collections of actual materials compared.

Termination of Orientation

The period of orientation should be long enough to allow the staff to do some original classification, and long enough for questions on the trial work to be discussed. A limitation, however, should be put on the practice sessions, and as soon as possible regular work assignments should begin.

The consultant's part in the work is then over, and the learning process becomes a part of the day's assignment. It is now the responsibility of the head of cataloging to determine to what extent any further group discussions will be held; whether or not LC numbers will be accepted exactly as received; and if consultation of the schedules shall be limited to materials requiring original classification.

Frequent mention has been made of the phrase "assembly-line procedure" as being a necessary and recommended practice to institute in a library program. Of course it has to be instituted, but all administrators who are contemplating adopting LC should use this term with caution. High output is related not only to efficient methods of procedure but also to the level of morale of the staff members. It is far better to stress the freeing of professional staff time for difficult original classification than it is to allow highly intelligent and sensitive workers to think they are being put into a program in which they as individuals matter very little.

Expertise in the new classification may well take six months to a year, depending on the extent of the subject areas assigned to the individual staff member. Problems will arise as they would in whatever classification were adopted. But in the end there will be a collection organized into a usable and satisfactory system that is economical to maintain; up to date; logically reflective of the development of past knowledge; and adequately aware of, and providing for, new knowledge as it becomes recorded.

Discussion

Question: Wouldn't one way of acquiring proficiency in the LC classification be to start the catalogers off with books with LC cards?

Miss Herrick: This is a most sensible thing to do, of course.

Question: How can you keep up staff morale when so much of the work in the beginning period is practically copying LC?

Miss Herrick: In the beginning period you can keep your own spirits up just by the excitement of learning and meeting the challenge of a very great classification and trying to see what it is saying to you about the book so that you can reproduce the same kind of thinking in the original classification you will have to do.

Question: How do you, at Boston University, keep any classification schedule up to date? Do you do it at all?

Miss Herrick: Yes, we do. We have one official schedule in which all additions and changes are put. This has been necessary for us because of our use of a classified catalog, but it is an excellent way of becoming sensitive to the way LC is developing. If you can afford to do it, it will help you a great deal in your own original classification because you know when new fields are developing and how a new topic, such as electronic data processing, is being treated in its applications in various disciplines.

Question: What book notation system do you use? Isn't it different from LC?

Miss Herrick: We use Biscoe time numbers. These are given in the literature tables of the LC schedules and are a combination of letters and numbers. An initial letter stands for the century, and that is followed by the last two digits of the date. The first letter used, "A," indicates the fifteenth century, "B" the sixteenth, and so on, so that 1966 would be written as "F66." We use no alphabetical book notation. And what effect has this had on our reclassification program? It has speeded it up tremendously.

Question: Would it be possible for a staff to begin reclassification without an orientation procedure and the use of a consultant?

Miss Herrick: Of course it would. All the times I ever started LC, no one helped me, but I made mistakes and some of them the libraries have had to pay for.

Notes

[1] Eric Moon, "RTSD and the Big Wide World," *Library Resources & Technical Services*, 10:10 (Winter, 1966).

Chapter 12

Cost Estimates and Time Schedules in Reclassification

Jennette E. Hitchcock

There is an old saying: If we had some ham, we could have some ham and eggs—if we had some eggs. If conditions and decisions among libraries were the same, we could have cost estimates based on the costs of other libraries —if other libraries had cost figures. Published figures on the costs of cataloging are hard to find; when found, they seem to be not quite what fits the local picture.

Perhaps these introductory remarks are too simple and too bleak. Some libraries do have cost figures, at least a few. Some conditions are the same, or similar. Certain it is that, for any decision as important and far reaching as a change in classification systems, one should search the literature and ask advice of friends and experts. But certain it is also that cost figures from other institutions should be used with discretion.

In particular, the cost figures presented in this paper should be treated with due consideration of their nature. In some instances they are semihypothetical, derived from data contributed by kind and cooperative colleagues or taken from published material, tailored for purposes of illustration with simple arithmetic. But even when figures are cited specifically, the very persons who cooperatively made educated guesses, pulled data out of past files, or have bravely written for publication in the past, are the ones who realize the perils of quoting out of context or of jumping at conclusions.

In any proposal for a change of classification, the experience and costs of other libraries may prove valuable supporting documentation; ultimately, however, the rationale of justification and the details of planning and cost estimates should be developed locally. This does not have to be done as a do-it-yourself job. It can be done with a consultant, but the consultant would have to work on the local scene.

Presumably the planning will progress in stages: general estimates for policy decisions; the development of procedures and specific estimates; and implementation activities, with or without a pilot test of procedures for further refined estimates. Perhaps the proposal will never progress beyond the first stage. The policy decision may be *not* to change classification, or *not* to reclass. Possibly, specific estimates never will be made. This paper touches on all stages.

192

General Estimates

What Kind of a Cost Figure Is Wanted?

For policy discussions prior to decision on a recommendation to change classification schemes there may or may not be a need for detailed cost estimates. Possibly general ideas on reclassification costs may be sufficient: a rough estimate of unit cost per volume or title, an understanding of the problems involved, some concept of the length of time and extra staff which might be required. The kind of a cost estimate needed will depend on the reasons for considering a change.

The proposal may be subsidiary to a new method of processing: conversion to computer techniques; participation in a regional, centralized cataloging system; prospective adoption of a book catalog. The cost of changing classification in such a situation could be relatively incidental to the total costs or benefits. A rough estimation might be sufficient. There may be an upsurge in acquisition rate, so that custom-tailored classification is viewed as a luxury, even though well liked by everyone concerned. It would seem that greater speed in cataloging could be obtained by adopting the Library of Congress classification system. If this proposition is not accepted at face value, some rather close estimation of savings versus costs may be required to justify the proposal in dollars and cents. If the catalog is in a "grown like Topsy" state and has not yet been converted to the use of LC cards and American Library Association cataloging rules, the change may be merely part of a program of total recataloging.

This paper does not deal with the cost of computer techniques, book catalogs, or general recataloging; in a more isolated fashion, it concerns itself with costs directly related to changing the classification system. It is further restricted in scope because many costs are intangible and cannot be reduced to cost figures. This is particularly true of the implications for public departments of the library and of the impact on the library patrons. The pros and cons can be visualized in policy discussions, and they can be verbalized in a proposal to reclassify; rarely can they be reduced to concrete budget items. Inevitably, then, the cost data in this paper are preponderantly the costs of reclassification, with related data for the estimation of savings potentially to be achieved by changing to the LC classification. This is in contrast to discussions on a proposal to change, wherein arguments over the ramifications of a change may extend to many more hours than would a succinct statement of costs.

Because of the necessity for verbalizing the many intangibles of the advantages and disadvantages, and the necessity for an understanding of the problems, a search in library literature for costs should not exclude classic discussions of the fundamental questions in reclassification and recataloging programs. Minimal reading would be the Bentz and Cavender article in *Library Trends*, October, 1953,[1] and one, several, or many of the writings by Tauber.[2] The recent bibliography on reclassification by McGaw[3] lists thirty-nine items including the above. The *Library Trends* issue of October, 1953, which has the Bentz and Cavender article, is doubly valuable as first reading because it contains also an article on "The Costs of Cataloging" by Reichmann.[4]

What Cost per Volume and per Title Can Be Found from Work in Other Libraries?

Articles have been published on three large-scale projects, written after completion of the projects. These have been in the journal literature for years. They are noteworthy for their comprehensive reporting of policy decisions, procedural details, *and* costs. These articles should be read, even to the exclusion of the articles previously mentioned if time is too limited for reading all. The three projects took place at the University of Rochester,[5] the University of South Carolina,[6] and the State University of Iowa.[7] Excerpted for presentation here are the unit costs per volume and title, together with the years of the projects, the number of titles and volumes, and the unit costs updated to the 1960's.[8]

TABLE I

Excerpts from Three Project Reports

Item	Rochester	South Carolina	Iowa
Years of the project	1927–31	1946–53	1950–51
Volumes reclassed	86,644	56,113	66,207
Titles reclassed	41,616	32,035	24,364
Cost per volume	$0.26	$1.69	$0.45
Cost per title	$0.54	$3.07	——
Costs updated to 1960's:			
Per volume	($0.90)	($3.20)	($0.85)
Per title	($1.80)	($5.80)	——

Rochester changed from "home-made" schedules to LC; South Carolina from Cutter Expansive to Dewey; Iowa from Dewey to LC. The projects are not comparable in many important respects, e.g., in the extent of recataloging and the inclusion versus exclusion of recataloging costs. The articles should be read and studied carefully. They contain a wealth of information useful in preparing cost estimates.

As information for this Institute,[9] Columbia University provided a copy of a cost summary of the reclassification of reference and reserve books in its science departmental libraries in 1965. The cost per title was $2.31, excluding filing costs. The University of Colorado sent reclassification figures for periodicals and serials, during the first six months of a recent project, showing $5.89 per title and $.41 per volume; for monographs, $1.59 per title and $.51 per volume. California State Polytechnic College Library, San Luis Obispo, wrote that the personnel cost of its current project was $1.65 per volume in 1963/64; $1.51 per volume in 1964/65. A related figure, not for true reclassification but solidly based on time records of a three-year project, is the $.61 per volume processing cost in Yale's Selective Book Retirement Program.[10]

Nothing conclusive can be proved by the per volume or per title costs from other institutions other than a general range.[11] A rough estimating value can be selected, in round figures of even dollars or dollars with halves of dollars. This value multiplied by the number of volumes or titles under consideration by the local library will show the magnitude of the project being contemplated, and whether it should be steered into total, partial, or minimal reclassification.

Thereafter, if reclassification is still being contemplated, attention would be directed toward more detailed planning: which portions of the collection really need to be reclassed or which should be reclassed first; analysis of the processing steps; and estimates based on them which can be used for determining the respective number of hours needed for professional versus clerical help. Invaluable reading at this stage are the articles by Reichmann[12] and by Fraser[13] on the genesis and initial years of the reclassification projects, still going on, at Cornell University and the University of Toronto.

Estimates by Processing Steps

A layman's impression of the reclassification process seems to be in terms of the finished product. The book has a new call number on it and is shelved in a different place. The catalog cards have new call numbers and are still in the same places. Changing a call number on a book and changing call numbers on a few cards cannot take so very much time. Trouble comes if the layman is a budgeting official. It is advisable to be able to describe the nine tenths of the iceberg submerged below the surface.

How Much Time Does It Take To Change a Number on a Book?

Changing the call number on a book might be called a 1-minute operation. It literally can be done in a minute, under some conditions. But it should not be estimated with that little time, particularly if the call number is to be, or has been, in more than one place.

Four libraries currently reclassing[14] have reported these figures for changing call numbers on the spine of the book: 1 minute; 1½ minutes; 2 minutes; and, depending on position of old label, 2–4 minutes. The indication is for an estimate of 2 minutes, more or less. The figures were for techniques using labels for the spine, and included the necessity at times for obliterating traces of the old number which might not be covered by the new label.

A penciled call number on the verso of a title page can be erased and remarked in less than a minute. The marking of a call number in this position normally is part of the cataloging process. In a reclassification project the changing may be done simultaneously with the card work, or it may be done as part of end processing. Similarly there needs to be considered erasing, lining out, or changing call numbers inside the book: on front or back covers, book plates, book pockets, or book cards. It is not unreasonable to add another 2 minutes for these changes and for a slight amount of directly related overhead: revision and supervision;

daily handling of supplies of paint, glue, shellac, labels; idling time. There is thus an estimate of 4 minutes to change the call number on a book.

For somewhat similar work in the processing of new materials, the University of Denver Graduate School of Librarianship's *Cost Analysis Study* found the time to be 4.0 minutes. The "mechanical preparations" covered in that study were: typing card and pocket, marking call number on spine, pasting card pocket and date-due slip inside back cover, property stamping, shellacking, and routing to main or divisional libraries.[15]

At 4 minutes per book, or 15 books per hour, an estimate for 15,000 volumes would be 1000 hours. For clerical help, at a rate of $1.25 an hour, the cost of remarking 15,000 volumes would be $1250.

How Much Time Does It Take To Change Numbers on Catalog Cards?

Fundamentally there are three methods for changing call numbers on cards in the catalog: (1) The cards can be removed, the call numbers changed, and the cards refiled. (2) The original cards can be left in the catalog, and new cards made with the new call numbers. The new cards will then "bump out" the original cards when the new cards are filed. (3) The original cards can be left in the catalog, and new call numbers typed on pressure-sensitive labels. The labels then will be affixed to the old cards at the catalog.

The first method probably is the most familiar. It can be used as a point of departure in estimation. Essentially it involves time figures for withdrawing the cards, for erasing the old numbers and typing the new numbers, and for refiling the cards. These are more or less normal routines, irrespective of any reclassification project, and the figures are fairly solid within any one library.

Withdrawing a set of 5 cards may be estimated at 5 minutes.[16] This is not 1 minute per card. It is .8 of 1 minute per card, plus 1 minute, more or less, for making a temporary card for the main entry.

Erasing and retyping call numbers can be estimated at 8 minutes. Erasing takes longer than typing: .9 of 1 minute per card for erasing (which is one reason some libraries just line out the call number); .5 for typing. This rounds out to 8 minutes per set of 5 cards with the inclusion of a small fraction of time for revision of the typing.[17]

Refiling at the rate of 100 cards per hour, or .6 of 1 minute per card, is 3 minutes for 5 cards.[18]

There is thus a total of 16 minutes per set for the first method.

The advantage of the second method, making new cards to "bump out" the original ones, is that new cards arranged for filing alphabetically en masse bump out the old cards in one alphabetical sequence. This is more expeditious than withdrawing old cards from the tracings on the main card for each set, which involves a certain amount of nonalphabetic footsteps, plus the refiling of the old cards after the numbers have been changed. However, in general, it is a more expensive method, because of the cost of buying or making new cards and typing headings on them. When new cards are desirable to replace unsatisfactory old ones, or extra cards are needed for some new purpose, it is a good method, but the estimating cost would be higher. This method is being used by the University of Colorado, the University of Houston, Pennsylvania State University, University of Puget Sound, and Stanford University.

The third method, using call number labels on the old cards, is relatively new.[19] The cost was investigated by the staff of the library at California State College at Los Angeles, for a study made there by the System Development Corporation on the possibility of using electronic data processing equipment.[20] The cost difference between filing new cards and affixing labels on old cards in the catalog was estimated as 12 cents more per title for the label routine, plus 4 cents per title for preparing the labels (by typewriter-punch)—a total of 16 cents. But the cost of preparing new cards (with electronic data processing methods) was figured to be twice as much as the 16 cents savings on the routines performed at the catalog. Los Angeles currently is using labels for its project reclassification, but withdraws and changes numbers on cards for reclassification in connection with added copy work.

Other libraries using the label method in reclassification work are California State Polytechnic College, University of Delaware, and Sacramento State College. The rate of affixing labels on cards in the catalog was estimated by one of these libraries as 20 sets per hour, or 3 minutes per set. If this method were used, the estimate would be lower than for the first method.

However, for this paper, the estimate is carried forward on the basis of the first method, at a rounded 4 titles per hour. For 10,000 titles this would mean 2500 hours. At a rate of $1.25 per hour for clerical help, the cost would be $3125.

The ratio of titles to volumes varies considerably from library to library. If one assumes, for use in this paper, a ratio of 2 titles to 3 volumes (10,000 titles to 15,000 volumes), the 2500 hours just derived can be added to the 1000 hours derived previously for changing the call numbers on 15,000 volumes. The total hours for these readily apparent physical processes is 3500 hours. The cost for the two processes, at $1.25 per hour, would be $4375; $.44 cents per title.

How Much Time Does It Take To Assign LC Call Numbers?

Cost estimates for the classification process with the LC schedules are doubly useful. They are needed for time figures in planning reclassification. They are significant in the policy-decision stage, especially so if they happen to show considerable savings from the local library's previous scheme. Yet they are more difficult to find, compile, or interpret than cost data in other areas.

A first requirement is some data on the proportion of the local library's material for which LC cataloging is available. It can be assumed there will be a difference in rate between LC card classification work and original classification, so a percentage will be needed for each kind of work. If this proportion is not already in hand, a test run should be made. This is relatively simple to do.

Then the desiderata are figures for classification times: (1) with the local library's present scheme; (2) with the LC scheme for original classification; and (3) with the LC scheme for work with LC card copy. Such figures are elusive and need rather strict evaluation to be meaningful. Cataloging statistics ordinarily do not isolate time figures for the classification process, nor is it easily possible to do so. Indeed, it is virtually impossible to separate subject analysis for classification from subject cataloging as a whole. Also, the derivation of a figure in the local library for the time in assigning LC call numbers by its staff, when the LC scheme is not yet in use, poses a problem.

Classification Times

For cataloging with the local library's classification scheme, there would be a figure in mind for the average time per title. This may be a half hour, an entire hour, 15 minutes, 45 minutes, or some other number of minutes. The figure varies from one library to another. A portion of the time was for classification. The rest was for subject-heading work and descriptive cataloging, together with general processing routines. One may simply call the classification time one third of the total. It would be less rather than more.

If the average time is a half hour per title, one third would be 10 minutes for classification; if an hour, it would be 20 minutes; if 15 minutes, 5; if 45, 15. The average cataloging time per title and the portion of this time allocated to classification are a matter of data and judgment within the local library.

For original classification under the LC scheme, help is needed from the outside, unless there are catalogers on the staff who have had experience with using the LC classification and could make an estimate. Four libraries which have been using the LC scheme for many years have contributed for this Institute some time figures or educated guesses on original classification time. It would seem that 10 minutes might be used as an average figure; sometimes it is less and sometimes more, and it varies according to subject area. But it would be wiser to estimate 15 minutes per title, especially for the first year's work, if not for succeeding years also. The lower limits of the ranges given by these four libraries were 4, 5, 7, and 10 minutes. Ten minutes was the upper limit in the educated guesses of three of the libraries. The fourth library, on the basis of approximate timing for two days, gave ranges for individual catalogers by subject area. These varied in lower limits from 4 to 20 minutes and in upper limits from 12 to 60 minutes for the individual books being handled on those days. The ranges for the majority of the individual catalogers were between 10 and 20 minutes.

For work with LC card copy, a time figure for classification in the future with the LC scheme can be arbitrarily selected by the local library—5 minutes or less. The figure selected would depend on the local library's policy: whether or not to accept the complete number as found; with or without comparison with the schedules; with or without checking the shelflist for possible duplication of book numbers from original classification. Unless a library has a very high proportion of LC card work, it would be expedient to estimate in terms of 5 minutes per title, thus allowing for shelflisting and some comparison with the schedules. This latter can save time in original cataloging because of familiarity gained by following the class numbers assigned by the Library of Congress, with the book in hand for judgment of its contents with relation to the display of classification headings in the schedules.

During the policy-decision stage, attention should be given to any necessary or justified exceptions to the use of LC call numbers as given on LC card copy. The local library thus will be in a position to judge whether the number of instances open to exception is negligible or should be considered in estimating time (as when not following PZ3 and PZ4). For help in thinking through a policy on literal acceptance of LC numbers, the article by O'Bryant in the Summer, 1965, issue of *Library Resources & Technical Services* has some interesting comments.[21] The higher the proportion of material with LC card copy available, and the less the variations in schedules or book numbers, the greater is the possibility of whittling down the 5 minutes to the point of elimination of the classification process by mere transcription of the LC number at some step in general processing routines.

Estimate of Savings

With time figures developed in somewhat the manner as just indicated, it is possible to make an estimate of potential savings. If classification with the library's previous scheme has been taking 15 minutes, and for LC card work would now take 5 minutes, there is a saving of 10 minutes per title for books for which LC copy is available. If the estimate were 15 minutes previously and still is 15 minutes for original cataloging with the LC scheme, there is no saving here at all. With a 50 percent proportion of original cataloging, the average saving would be 5 minutes per book.

Since the number of minutes per title for the classification process is not many, significant savings are not in prospect unless the acquisition rate is high enough to multiply a few minutes into a substantial block of hours. Of course, if classification time under the previous scheme amounted to considerably more than a few minutes per title, there would be a saving.

The University of Oregon and the University of Puget Sound each did test studies to estimate savings. Oregon estimated a savings of $1.06 per title.[22] The calculations of the University of Puget Sound showed it took $7\frac{1}{2}$ minutes (or $42\frac{1}{2}$ cents) for Dewey; 1–1½ minutes (6–9 cents) for LC.[23] At the University of Wisconsin, it was estimated that in using the classification number on the LC card there would be a saving of 42 cents per title in cataloging costs.[24]

The Morrisons, in reporting on a study in California on the use made of classification information furnished on LC cards, and the extent to which it was modified to fit local needs (in four academic libraries), noted that the most conservative estimates of savings were a three to two ratio ("three books can be classified in LC in the same time it takes to do two in the Dewey-Cutter system").[25] The librarians interviewed attributed the savings as much to the shelf-number scheme as to the classification itself. Coincidentally, a three to two ratio was found expressed on the East Coast, during this author's interviews prior to this Institute.

Downey, in reporting data from 27 college libraries in the 5000–6000 student enrollment range, wrote that "three of the five libraries where LC is in use expressed the opinion that LC cost less than Dewey overall, mainly because as much as seventy per cent of all cataloging is accepted as it appears on the LC cards. The other two libraries felt there was no appreciable difference in the cost of the two systems."[26]

In estimating savings, more particularly in libraries with homemade schedules or extreme modifications of either Dewey or Library of Congress, a significant item is the maintenance expense of the local library's scheme. This can be estimated in thousands of dollars if there are many catalogers on the staff—requiring multiple copies of schedules which have to be duplicated locally—or if there is a high turnover on the staff, or expansion of the staff, which requires a considerable amount of indoctrination.

Another factor in computing savings is the salary differential that can be applied to the amount of work which may be reallocated from professional catalogers to nonprofessional staff. In libraries where cataloging procedures are not already organized with nonprofessionals handling LC card work, plans to reorganize would make it possible to extend the estimate of savings to standardized routines in descriptive and subject cataloging also. To show a saving, there must be a sufficient volume of delegated work to exceed professional time in supervision and training. The nonprofessional staff must be competent and relatively permanent; otherwise a disproportionate amount of supervisory time will offset the estimate of savings.

The Oregon estimate of savings included this factor and was projected for the period 1964–75 in terms of the contrast in allocation of work. The computation figured that the continuation of Dewey (as modified in the past at Oregon) would require 154 man-years of librarians and 233 man-years of clerical help; a change to LC and reclassification, 99 man-years of librarians and 338 man-years of clerical help—$1,883,640 against $1,834,140. The reclassification allowed for in this estimate would include 735,000 volumes of the total 850,000.[27]

Estimate of Reclassification Time

To revert to the cost of reclassification and the generalized estimates of times for assigning LC call numbers, the figures presented were 15 minutes for original classification and 5 minutes for work with LC cards; with 50 percent original classification, an average of 10 minutes per title, or 6 titles per hour. For 10,000 titles this would mean approximately 1700 hours of professional time.

In reclassification, an estimate is also needed for the time to search LC catalogs, which in new work is part of general cataloging routines. Searching can be estimated at 3 minutes per title. The searching time would be less if cards in the catalog for previously LC-cataloged items show the LC classification numbers, so that the items do not need to be researched. The rate per title averages less when there is a high percentage of LC entries found. At 3 minutes per title, or 20 titles per hour, the clerical time for 10,000 titles would be 500 hours.

How Much Time Should Be Allowed for Other Processes and Overhead?

Other processes in a reclassification routine are less amenable to discussion in terms of unit cost per title or volume. Some of them meld with the work of other departments, and the cost quite possibly will be allowed to be absorbed by the other departments and not need to be estimated for a separate budget. The same is true within the catalog department itself for fringe areas in reclassification which involve recataloging or catalog maintenance.

The books have to be collected, charged out, matched with the catalog cards, reshelved, and discharged, in addition to the processes discussed in the previous sections. On an individual basis, these processes might add 5 or more minutes per book. On a project basis, the work can be organized more efficiently, e.g., the books can be gathered from a subject area by the truckload, a blanket charge or notice suffice for circulation control, and the books reshelved at approximately the same time. Details of records for missing books and "holds" for books in circulation can be quite burdensome, especially in added copy and added volume work. In total reclassification, arrangements can be made with the circulation department to send to the reclassifiers any books discharged or turning up after reclassification of a certain section has been completed. This procedure eliminates the necessity of maintaining individual records for books "not found," if the library is willing to forego maintaining the equivalent of a cancellation file.

During the process of handling books, unhappily, it will become apparent that some or many of the books are in need of rebinding or repair. Such books require the preparation of individual charge slips and also additional work in the binding department. If the project is anywhere near a total reclassification, there is almost continuous shifting of books in the stacks as the work progresses, unless the reclassification is being done in connection with a new building with ample expansion space.

Card withdrawing (or the bumping out of old cards by new ones, or the affixing of labels on cards in the catalog) runs into trouble with missing cards or cards "out" to catalogers. Nonreclassifying catalogers become involved in the work. The searching operation for LC call number information produces also an unexpected amount of information on changes in headings, both author entries and subject headings. Some recataloging inevitably proves necessary.[28]

Personnel has to be recruited, trained, and supervised. The various phases and processes of the work have to be coordinated, not only for the reclassification crew, but also for the public service departments and patrons. Appropriate bulletins and information signs need to be prepared. Statistical records should also be compiled, at least for a record of output if not for a cost analysis.[29]

The cost of these various activities, when not absorbed by other departments or regular cataloging, can be lumped as overhead. In the generalized figures developed thus far, for 10,000 titles with 15,000 volumes, these time estimates for clerical help have been posed: changing numbers on the books, 1000 hours; changing numbers on catalog cards, 2500 hours; searching LC call numbers, 500 hours—a sum of 4000 hours. For overhead in clerical time, a commercial 15 percent (600 hours) can be added, or some other conjectural number of hours. The clerical time thus would be estimated at 4600 hours, or about two and a half assistants for a period of one year.[30]

The professional time for assigning LC call numbers, with 50 percent original classification, was set at 1700 hours. For supervision and general problem-solving, another conjectural figure would need to be added, possibly 500 hours. This would make 2200 hours, somewhat more than the equivalent of one full-time person, although considerably less if there is a high percentage of LC card work which is assigned to nonprofessionals.

A pilot study, or a limited reclassification program during the first year after adoption of the LC scheme, would help in making a realistic estimate of overhead, and in refining estimates of the more tangible processes. Otherwise, one relies on the seventh sense, which, after all, is more valid and reliable than poor statistics. Or, one relies on the advice of a consultant or the experience of other libraries. The principal expense will be personnel, and the basic need in estimating this is the proportion of hours for clerical work versus the proportion of hours for professional work, and a general estimate of the total time required for a certain number of thousands of books.

Estimates for Staff and Span of Project

However sound an estimate may be, it seems sounder if it holds up in comparison with the estimates of other institutions or, better yet, with the actual experience of other libraries. From three of the libraries contributing information on processing steps for this Institute came supplementary material pertinent to the estimation of staff required and its allocation between professional and nonprofessional, with rate of output. This material provides some background from recent reclassification work.

Reclassification at California State Polytechnic College, San Luis Obispo, is being done with 1 cataloger and 2 clerks. In the first year (1963–64), this staff handled 8870 volumes; in the second year, 12,136 volumes.

The University of California at Santa Barbara, for its seven-year project (December, 1950–March, 1958), had a staff of 1 professional cataloger, 1 senior library assistant, and 1 half-time clerk. This project included recataloging. Volumes handled were 25,095; titles, 18,613.

Cornell's reclassification program has been accelerated this past year by provision for a special staff again. From a beginning with 2 professional catalogers, 2 library assistants, and 2 typists under a project leader, the special staff was enlarged gradually to four teams with a total personnel of 16. During the first ten months 16,431 titles and 18,698 volumes were reclassified (including recataloging). And from a high of $3.40 per title ($3.02 per volume) in the first month of new staff and also of difficult material (classics, with a high proportion of original classification), the direct labor costs went down to $2.70 per title and $2.43 per volume. Reclassification data from the Tauber questionnaire, as described by Dr. Tauber earlier in this Institute, when analyzed in greater depth will supply a wider background of general costs of recent projects.

The Jacobs and Spencer article on the University of Rochester project contains a model summary table with analysis of time and cost in terms of level of personnel. This shows that professional time was 32.5 percent; clerical time, 22.5 percent; and the time of students, 45 percent. In dollars, the professional costs were 54 percent; the clerical costs, 21 percent; and the student help, 25 percent.[31] These proportions have held up through the years better than has the value of the dollar.

Data such as these can be helpful in the estimates of a local library, but the burden of proof remains with the local library as do the policy decisions and development of procedures. The general framework pictured is a ratio of 1 professional to 2 assistants per year for each 10,000 titles reclassified.

Library of Congress Schedules and Supplementary Classification Tools

Of interest equally to all libraries about to adopt the LC classification, whether they will reclassify or not, should be the cost of acquiring and maintaining the schedules and the attendant complexities. There are 31 schedules, ranging in price from $.30 to $5.75, the sum total being approximately $67. However, this cost is equaled, or even exceeded, by the cost of binding the schedules after they have been received.

Unfortunately, in recent past years, many of the schedules have been out-of-print at various times, in some cases for extended periods of months. Thus it has been difficult for libraries to begin operations after deciding to change to the LC scheme. Copies can be begged or borrowed, or photocopies obtained. Since November, 1965, the sale and distribution of the schedules have been under the Library of Congress Card Division, and the situation is improving.

The quarterly *Additions and Changes* are $6 per year. The maintenance of schedules with these *Additions and Changes* can be done in various ways. The schedules can be annotated by hand—by the catalogers or by an assistant. The *Additions and Changes* can be clipped and pasted: in the appropriate schedule, on individual cards for a cumulative file, or on sheets (in blocks by class letters) in a loose-leaf folder. They can be ordered in multiple copies, so that each cataloger can have his own file. Schedules can be asterisked with number of the list, instead of the annotation's being copied in full. Meticulous annotation of all schedules can occupy 50 or more hours annually. Ingenuity and discretion reduce the time to negligible proportions. It is more difficult to get started with updated schedules than to maintain them.

Xerox copies, which can be ordered through the Library of Congress Photoduplication Service, are made from annotated official schedules in the Subject Cataloging Division and thus come automatically updated, but in a format more difficult to bind. The prices of the 31 schedules range from $6 to $76. The use of this service can be considered for cases where there has been no revised edition for many years, to save going through many back issues of the *Additions and Changes*.

A supplementary tool in using the LC classification is the printed LC subject catalog. This is unquestionably useful in original classification, in lieu of a general index, and also in the choice of related class numbers. The only decisions are whether to buy a set for the catalog department itself, and, if so, whether to buy just the current year, or the annual sets and the 1960–1964 cumulation with the two previous quinquennial cumulations in addition. The prices quite likely will be the determining factor. The 1960–1964 cumulation is $275; the two previous ones, $247.50 each. The evaluation of usefulness interrelates with subject-heading work.

In former years, two publications have been found very helpful in understanding the techniques of the LC schedules: the short manual on LC book numbers by Laws[32] and Grout's Columbia M.S. thesis study on the tables used in LC schedules.[33] Both of these publications have been out-of-print for some time but are well worth photocopying costs. The papers presented at this Institute by the Library of Congress staff may supplant the use of Laws and Grout.

Supplies and Equipment

Libraries deciding to reclassify should have a budget item for supplies and equipment. This is something the local library can estimate without much help from outside. Standard office supplies, from rubber bands and paper clips to desks and typewriters, would be estimated on much the same basis as for normal cataloging needs; the necessity, perhaps, for a card catalog cabinet to start the new shelflist should not be overlooked.

The additional volume of work in a reclassification project may make it advisable or imperative to change the method of card reproduction or book marking, in which instances new equipment would be taken into consideration. In this area, colleagues and printed literature would be helpful. Extra staff would require more floor space, shelving, and book trucks. The availability of adequate working space, in proximity to the regular catalog department, may somewhat dictate the size of the reclassification project and thus the estimated span of years.

Some thought should be given to the printing of special forms: charge slips for the books, with RECLASSIFICATION designated and spaces for both old and new numbers; searching or record forms for missing books; forms for recall of books, and cards, from departmental libraries; directives to typists for special situations, such as added copies which are missing or have been withdrawn; distinctive "card out" slips for main entry records in the catalog. Special forms are not necessarily needed, and they can be devised in the early stages of implementation, but some allowance should be made for printed forms or for extra quantities of normal call slips, blank 3 x 5 pads, and the like. It would be well also to provide somewhere for an increased amount of binding and repair work.

Time Schedules

In the timing of "D-day"—the beginning date of new cataloging with the new classification scheme—there is little reason for delaying implementation once the decision to change has been made. The policy-decision stage should proceed with due deliberation and caution. Implementation should be fast; and it can be fast if the policy decisions were indeed duly deliberate. The necessary steps in implementation are natural complements to the pro and con arguments considered during the policy discussions.

The catalogers do need schedules in order to assign class numbers, but a beginning date does not have to wait until multiple copies have been ordered, bound, and updated. A beginning can be made with a single set. If the library did not have a set for general usefulness previously, then a set should have been ordered during the policy-decision stage for use in the discussions thereof.

The catalogers could benefit from a certain amount of indoctrination, as has been made evident during this Institute. It would take a little time to arrange for indoctrination lectures, or a month-in-residence as consultant, by a classifier from another institution; but it is possible to be self-indoctrinated by starting with work involving only material for which there is card copy available with LC classification numbers.

Book shelved by the former scheme need to be compacted and quite likely shifted somewhat to allow for a good display and expansion of the new books in the new scheme—in the stacks and also in special rooms and branches. The general concept of operation would already be in mind from discussion of whether reclassification should be total, partial, or minimal. With enthusiasm and concentration, the details can be worked out and new shelf directory signs made in fairly short order.

The shelvers will need instructions for arranging books in LC call number order. Directives can be provided by the catalogers as needs arise, if not an overall statement at the beginning. Markers need instructions on the division points in LC call numbers for spine marking and labeling. Interdepartmental agreement for these directives will require at least one conference of the heads of cataloging, processing, and circulation departments. For official announcements of the change, the substance of the reasons will have been formulated in the statement of recommendation for the change prepared for the final decision.

The papers presented earlier have provided many salient points relative to the adoption of the LC scheme which make it easier to visualize the implementation steps. Although there are many details to encompass and coordinate—and possibly some boomerangs, such as letter conflicts when "B" has been used for biography, "L" for locked stack, or "S" for Shakespeare, for which special arrangements have to be made—a fast and zestful approach to D-day will take the hurdles easily. A month is long enough, but if the enthusiasm and capability of the staff can handle the details in a shorter period of time, so much the better.

In the timing of D-day for the beginning date of a reclassification project, however, there is good reason for delaying implementation; actually there are several good reasons. The catalogers should have a year or so in which to gain wisdom in the application of the LC scheme, or in the future they will be reclassing what they have reclassed from the former scheme. The book collection should be weeded for discards before any total reclassification; or some books should be sent to storage or isolated from the need of reclassification. There should be time for inventory or shelf reading if the reclassification is to proceed smoothly. The prospective procedure should be scrutinized, criticized by colleagues in other libraries which are reclassing, and tested on a small scale before any project with a large staff is started. And because of the rather formidable cost, it might be well to wait a year and reassess the situation with the possibility of deciding that reclassification is not necessary after all.

Timing for the project, after it has started, has been implicit throughout the discussion of cost estimates. A framework has been provided for estimating both the gross span of the project and the times of the various processes. With the sequencing of the processing steps and extent of staff known, weekly, monthly, or annual time schedules could be prepared.

Once the project has started, the staff will find it a challenge to develop more efficient techniques and routines. They will save minutes here and pennies there, but they cannot save the big dollars that a policy for reclassification requires. The time for saving dollars is when making the decision whether to reclass or not. It is a matter of relative cost versus relative worth. A cost can be estimated in dollars, although far from exactly. The worth of reclassification cannot be estimated in dollars, nor can the frustration or inconvenience of not reclassifying. The decision will be based largely on intangibles. A cost estimate of savings by changing schemes may strengthen the reasons. A cost estimate for reclassification will launch a project under the most advantageous conditions for making it a success. A cost estimate is worth its trouble in either case and whichever way the decisions ultimately are made.

Discussion

Question: If labels are put on catalog cards, how is the capacity of the catalog tray affected, and the utility of the catalog? Will not the files be lopsided?

Miss Hitchcock: They are lopsided in the beginning but even themselves out when new unlabeled cards are interfiled.

Question: When computing hours, what do you do about allowing for sick and annual leave and for coffee breaks? These might amount to 25 percent of the working hours per year.

Miss Hitchcock: When I compute hours, I subtract a considerable number of hours before I come out with an hourly wage. I subtract vacation; I subtract practically the full maximum of sick leave and full half hour of coffee break per day; and then I come to the total hours even though the salary might be low.

Notes

[1] Dale M. Bentz and Thera P. Cavender, "Reclassification and Recataloging." *Library Trends,* 2:249–63 (Oct. 1953).

[2] Conveniently at hand in the administrative offices of many libraries would be the work of Maurice F. Tauber and associates, *Technical Services in Libraries* (New York: Columbia Univ. Press, 1954), Chapter XIII (p.261–83) of which is on reclassification and recataloging. As mentioned during this Institute, preparation of a second edition of this work is under way. References citing the classic Tauber doctoral dissertation of 1941 and journal articles stemming from it in the early 1940's are in Bentz and Cavender, above, and McGaw, below.

[3] Howard F. McGaw, "Reclassification: A Bibliography," *Library Resources & Technical Services,* 9, no.4:483–88 (Fall, 1965).

[4] Felix Reichmann, "The Costs of Cataloging," *Library Trends,* 2:290–317 (Oct. 1953).

[5] Elizabeth P. Jacobs and Robinson Spencer, "What Price Reclassification?" *Catalogers' and Classifiers' Yearbook,* 3:64–78 (1932).

[6] Jessie Gilchrist Ham, "Reclassification of the University of South Carolina Library Collection," *Journal of Cataloging & Classification,* 11, no.4:221–32 (Oct. 1955).

[7] Norman L. Kilpatrick and Anna M. O'Donnel, "Reclassification at the State University of Iowa," *Journal of Cataloging & Classification,* 8, no.1:12–17 (Mar. 1952).

[8] Updated, without claim of economic expertise, by ratios derived from salaries of public school teachers given in U.S. Bureau of the Census, *Historical Statistics of the United States, Colonial Times to 1957* (Washington, 1960) and its *Continuation to 1962* (Washington, 1965), Series D728–734, "Earnings in Selected Professional Occupations."

[9] The source of data, when identified by the phrase "for this Institute," is material obtained from personal interviews, letters, or questionnaires for use in this paper. The sources are not always cited individually.

[10] Lee Ash, *Yale's Selective Book Retirement Program* (Hamden, Conn.: Archon Books, 1963), p.51.

[11] In the recent survey of library resources in the Mid-Hudson Valley, a range of $1.50 to $3 per title was given for the cost of reclassification at present. Letter from Felix Reichmann, June 3, 1966.

[12] Felix Reichmann, "Cornell's Reclassification Program," *College & Research Libraries,* 23, no.5:369–74, 440–50 (Sept. 1962).

[13] Lorna D. Fraser, "Cataloguing and Reclassification in the University of Toronto Library, 1959/60," *Library Resources & Technical Services,* 5, no.4:270–80 (Fall, 1961).

[14] California State College at Los Angeles, Cornell University, University of Delaware, University of Oregon—alphabetically.

[15] University of Denver, Graduate School of Librarianship, *Cost Analysis Study* ("Studies in Librarianship," no.4; Denver, 1965), p.68.

[16] Figures contributed for this Institute from 11 libraries, adapted to a base of 5 cards per set and including temporary entry, show a range from 2.95 to 10 minutes. Seven were more than 5 minutes. The one figure based on actual timing was 4.35 minutes.

[17] Primarily based on a test run in one library on 275 cards. The average time for erasing in the Iowa project was .85 minutes per card (Norman L. Kilpatrick and Anna M. O'Donnel, *op. cit.,* p.14).

[18] Filing times from 9 libraries ranged from 75 to 175 cards per hour (size of catalogs from 350,000 to 6,000,000 cards).

[19] Great interest in this procedure was shown during the question period after presentation of the paper at the Institute: How well do labels wear? Do they add bulk and affect the capacity of the tray? Will the file be lopsided? Will they really stick and not come off? One attendee commented the bulk was increased by one third. As far as the author knows, the method thus far has been considered satisfactory by the libraries reporting its use.

[20] System Development Corporation, *EDP for Reclassification and Technical Services in the Los Angeles State College Library* ("TM–1731/000/00"; Santa Monica, Calif., 1964). 71p.

[21] Mathilda Brugh O'Bryant, "Some Random Thoughts on the Cost of Classification," *Library Resources & Technical Services*, 9, no.3:367–70 (Summer, 1965).

[22] University of Oregon Library, Ad Hoc Committee To Study Advisability and Feasibility of Adopting Additional Cooperative Cataloging and of Reclassification, *Report* (Eugene, Ore., 1964). A brief summary of this report is given in *PNLA Quarterly*, 29, no.4:249–50 (July, 1965).

[23] Desmond Taylor, "Reclassification: A Case for LC in the Academic Library," *PNLA Quarterly*, 29, no.4:244–45 (July, 1965).

[24] Irene M. Doyle, "Library of Congress Classification for the Academic Library," *The Role of Classification in the Modern American Library; Papers Presented at an Institute Conducted by the University of Illinois Graduate School of Library Science, November 1–4, 1959* ("Allerton Park Institute, no.6"; Champaign, Ill.: Illini Union Bookstore, 1959), p.84. The change in scheme was from Cutter Expansive to LC.

[25] Perry D. Morrison and Catherine J. Morrison, "Use of Library of Congress Classification Decisions in Academic Libraries: An Empirical Study," *Library Resources & Technical Services*, 9, no.2:238 (Spring, 1965).

[26] Howard R. Downey, "Dewey or LC?" *Library Journal*, 89:2293 (June 1, 1964).

[27] University of Oregon Library, Ad Hoc Committee, *loc. cit.*

[28] Answers from 10 libraries on this question showed a range from 1 percent to 20 percent.

[29] Lee Ash, *op. cit.*, contains illustrations of time and statistical record forms.

[30] As was brought out in the question period after the paper was presented, working time is to be differentiated from salary time; vacation, sick leave, and coffee breaks are not included in these estimates of hours.

[31] Elizabeth P. Jacobs and Robinson Spencer, *op. cit.*, p.78.

[32] Anna Cantrell Laws, *Author Notation in the Library of Congress* (Washington: Govt. Print. Off., 1917). 18p.

[33] Catherine W. Grout, *An Explanation of the Tables Used in the Schedules of the Library of Congress Classification* (New York: Columbia University, School of Library Service, 1940). 108p.

Chapter # 13

General Advantages and Disadvantages of Using the Library of Congress Classification

Phyllis A. Richmond

No other general classification system has been able to respond to the tremendous volume of literature in all subject fields as well as the Library of Congress classification.[1] Though parts of it could stand improvement, and none of it, in fact, is perfection, it does, nevertheless, stand up extremely well under the stress induced by the various literature explosions. It appears, then, that the first advantage of using the LC classification is that it covers a constantly expanding universe of knowledge without signs of cracking at the seams.

The first disadvantage to the LC system has been that there are no instruction manuals for its application. At present it takes several years to teach a practicing cataloger the fine points without written instructions. One learns empirically. Users are very much dependent upon keeping a sharp eye on precedent. One learns what goes where by looking at previously classified material. The schedules give clues and offer alternatives. The shelflist or the approach through the catalog arranged by subject headings tells in which of these alternative classifications books similar to the one in hand have been placed. Now, with these Proceedings, we have the beginning step in the construction of manuals to go with the classes covered. Whether the workable arrangement based on precedent is better than formalized instructions remains to be seen. One cannot, after all, design a set of instructions based on logic for a system that is not founded on logic.

Design

This lack of logic points up the second great advantage of using the LC classification—it was not designed to be logical. Therefore, it does not have to have classes built in logical patterns. This does not mean that the classification lacks structure. It has structure, but it is not logical structure. It is a practical, functional classification designed for change. It has a tremendous potential for keeping up with the growth of knowledge, no matter how uneven or sprawling that growth may be. It makes no attempt to predict that growth. It accepts it, operating by literary warrant, expanding as growth takes place, and accommodating new knowledge as it comes along. Since it is used primarily for books, it does not have to be overly involved in new, uncertain terminology in new subjects. By the time a book is written in a new area, the terminology has pretty well settled down, at least enough for classification and indexing purposes.

The design of the classification, then, is pragmatic. However, both making and, to a lesser degree, assigning classification, as with any subject approach to knowledge, can be a highly subjective matter. Here, perhaps, more than in any other area of intellectual endeavor, one man's meat is another's poison. Librarians probably all agree that like materials should be shelved together, but they do not agree on what is like because they approach the subject with different backgrounds and viewpoints. For libraries, the important thing is less that the fields of knowledge should be distinguished precisely in some glorious, universally accepted, ideal, logical classification than that the material put into storage should be found again quickly.

In large libraries, this is much easier said than done. Using the LC classification offers the advantage of an ordinal arrangement so that one does not have to look for a subject where it *ought* to be. One only has to find it where it is. Looking for it where it *is* is considerably different from looking for it where it ought to be, and the value of this difference should not be underrated. One may achieve a great degree of consistency in classification if one does not have to fit new material into a logical pattern but only into a precedence pattern or into loopholes in an ordinal system. Changes in the classification schedules sometimes remove part of the content of a class to a new location. In such cases, the precedence pattern for that aspect of the subject becomes negative in the old class, and one searches a new precedence pattern. The connection between the two lies in the index, where old index terms are broken down to reflect the new pattern. For example, "Radio receiving apparatus" was expanded to include a class, "Special," broken down A–Z. The index term "Radio receivers" then included various kinds, which were also added to the index in their own names: "Portable radios," "Transistor radios," and so on. Changes do not alter the basic design of the system.

Is LC a Classification?

The design of the LC classification is not one that can be described easily. If one thinks of classification strictly in terms of hierarchy and logical division, the LC system is not a classification. If one thinks of classification in terms of enumerative schedules with some structural arrangement not necessarily dependent upon the internal content of the subject matter being classified, then the system is a classification. If one stipulates that the relationships between classes in any case must be clearly defined and/or delineated, LC is not a classification. It would, for example, be extremely difficult to explain a goodly proportion of the placements in the system (e.g., the HT group of "Rural Sociology," "Urban

Sociology," "Classes," and "Races"). On the other hand, there is order in the system. It simply is not *logical* order, at least not logical to specialists in the fields it covers.

If one tries to define "classification" by any definition less broad than the one adopted at the Elsinore Conference in 1964, the LC system is not a classification. For this reason it is extremely annoying, in current documentation literature,[2] to see the LC classification lumped with others as "traditional." There is nothing traditional about it. It, like the Cutter system on which it was patterned, is something relatively unique, and that uniqueness has not been fully appreciated.

Browsing

The disadvantage to LC's illogical sprawl is that it is very difficult to walk along the shelves and figure out what the classes are by reading the titles on the backs of books. This is a disadvantage if one is browsing for a purpose, for instance, to see what is available on cohomology. One is better off using subject headings as indicators to classification areas covering the subject, and browsing purposefully in those specified areas. However, for browsing of the serendipity type—just going along and, as pure curiosity suggests, picking off titles to examine—the LC classification is particularly good. It is possible to find titles *and subjects* that chance to be related to the problem whose apparent intractability led to browsing in the first place. Undoubtedly there is enough relatedness among LC class descriptions for the human mind to make connections, and since these connections are not *pre*formed with any kind of logical pattern, the LC classification allows for fairly free associative linkage to be made by the individual browser.

The system, in other words, is based on the assumption that not all users will approach a subject by any one path, not even by the path of consensus of specialists in that subject. It is assumed that there are any number of users with undefined and undefinable approaches whom the system can best serve by letting them make their own patterns of relationships. This assumption is a great advantage of the LC classification. Whether such treatment of the browser has been intentional, accidental, or subconsciously arrived at is not important. The effect has been beneficial for the serendipity type of browsing. There is no stepwise, silent logic in the arrangement of the books on the shelves to mar the pure chance possibilities of making a totally unexpected association.

Diffuseness

There is another advantage to the LC classification which does not appear on the surface and will not appear until a unified index to the whole is produced. This is the factor of diffuseness. A subject may be split up according to different aspects so that one meets it at several places in the schedules. In extreme cases, this is a disadvantage, as, for example, with optics, which is fractioned among QA, QC, QP, RE, and parts of T. Such diffusion also splits up area studies and interdisciplinary fields. On the other hand, in language and literature and many branches of the social sciences, it is a distinct advantage to be able to approach the same subject from different angles. A unified index would go a long way toward remedying the disadvantages of diffuseness and accenting the advantages.

After all, in classification one has two choices: one may emphasize differences between categories and break up or divide them, making the *differences,* according to the divisor, a factor of relationship; or one may emphasize likeness between categories and gather them together according to similarity, making the *similarity,* according to common denominators, a factor of relationship. The LC classification actually operates both ways. The differences are emphasized in the little hierarchies scattered throughout the schedules and the likenesses in the A–Z subdivisions. Where the differences are emphasized to such an extent that the subject gets split up among totally different main classes, as with optics, it is extremely difficult to get users to realize that the overlap between the content of these classes is as great as it is. Scientists, in particular, tend to develop a proprietary air toward some special subfield in one location rather than another because the classification gives the illusion that here, and here alone, is where the subject centers. A unified index might help to dispel this illusion.

The generally disadvantageous splitting of some fields has one advantage—one can buy multiple copies of the same item, such as a general treatise on optics, and place one copy in each class applicable. This possibility has the advantage of forestalling some of the endless arguments that can take place when one place is regarded as *right* for a work and all others wrong. All but the most obnoxious patrons will accept the judgment of Solomon, when it can be justified. Of course, this diffusion can be carried too far. If budgets do not permit multiple placement for badly split subjects, libraries are well advised arbitrarily to accept as final the choices of the Library of Congress in settling arguments of this type.

Another disadvantage of the diffuseness is the possibility in a small library of having a different class number for practically every book; this does not happen in a small *special* library, such as a physics library, but it could conceivably occur in a small *general* library. One would not recommend the LC classification for a school library. On the other hand, if the classification is used only as a shelving device, the diffuseness really does not make much difference. The double letters for main classes will bring most common subjects together in groups, and the distinctive numerals for subclasses are a definite advantage in shelving.

The schedules themselves give the appearance of being separate and independent, although there is uniformity in structure and format throughout (with the possible exception of the P schedules, which are more hierarchical than the others). Even without the notation it is easy to distinguish the LC classification from all but its forebear, the Cutter classification.

Notation

An added advantage to the LC classification is that its growth is not hindered by its notation, which is purely ordinal. The notation is also full of gaps—a factor which has been brought out by Dr. Bead in Chapter 2. There are five single-letter classes not yet used and dozens of double-letter combinations available for expansion. With numerals, although four places have been used before the decimal, rarely have as many as four been used after it. There is also a double A–Z breakdown for subclasses. The classification can and does go in all directions. The notation can and does go right along with it. The fortunate subdivision by A–Z instead of by logic has proved most workable. All in all, the whole notation is not only open-ended but, to a considerable extent, open in the middle, too. The potential for almost unlimited hospitality to new subjects is there; it remains to make good use of it.

Besides allowing for growth, the LC notation, which in most American libraries doubles as the shelf location symbol, has the advantage of being divisible. If written in a neat block, the notation fits well both in the margin of a card and on the spine of a book:

BL
2017.4
.A32

In spite of appearances, the notation has little relation to hierarchy because it does not reflect structure. The following example illustrates the notation for two hierarchies and one nonhierarchy in a scattered subject in the PT schedule:

PT   History of German literature
        Special forms
            Epic poetry
                Special
                    Hero legends
    207   Dietrich von Bern

PT   Middle High German
        Collections
            By form
                Poetry
                    Special forms
                        Epic
                          Special
                            Popular epics
    1413.D5   Dietrich cycle

PT   Individual author or works
        Middle High German, ca. 1050–1450/1500
    1515   D–Dz
        .D4–6 Dietrich von Bern. Legends
                Dietrichs Flucht *see* Heinrich der Vogler
        .H25   Heinrich der Vogler, ca. 1282
                Supposed author of "Dietrichs
                Flucht" and "Rabenschlacht."

The class number may also be written in linear fashion, BL 2017.4.A32, as seen at the bottom of an LC printed card. Here the levels are separated by decimals and/or by switching from numerals to letters. If shortness of expression is of less significance in the future, as, for example, could be the case with a major trend toward classified catalogs, then the linear style would probably be used more widely than is now the case.

Operational Features

Another advantage of the Library of Congress classification is that class numbers are printed on almost all LC cards. Provided one is not cataloging a set as separates in a series and provided the class numbers on older cards are checked for later changes, one may use the numbers given. In general, one gains top-level professional work in classification in return for the few cents it costs to buy or copy a card. In other words, there is little excuse for slip-shod classification when the quality of the Library of Congress is so readily available. With mechanization in the offing, standardization to LC levels is imperative. Any deviation sooner or later leads to major trouble, as all librarians know who have worked with local variations from the LC schedules.

Unified Index

The quarterly corrections (*Additions and Changes*) which bring the LC classification up to date are another great advantage. Here is a relatively painless way of changing a few books at a time to bring them into line with the expansions of knowledge. Any library which does not bring its holdings up to date as the tables are altered well deserves the criticism it undoubtedly gets from its users. There is no excuse, with all the assistance provided from the Library of Congress, for a library to become badly outdated as to either classification or subject headings. The costs of constant change should be regarded as an expenditure for improved public relations.

The quarterly corrections also correct the indexes to the various classes. These indexes are satisfactory to use because they have so many synonymous terms. A unified index to the whole probably would add to this feature. Also, when made, a unified index could be matched with the LC list of subject headings, strengthening what is now a loose connection between the two. One of the advantages of using the subject-headings list is that LC class numbers are given with a great many subject headings, offering a lead into the classification for the perplexed. It is not so good a lead as through the subject catalog for seeking precedents, but sometimes all one needs is a hint, not a thorough survey. With the seventh edition of the subject headings in machine-readable form, putting the index to the classification in similar form and matching the two might make each a better tool than it is at present.

One possibility in connection with unified indexing is obvious. So much is dependent upon alphabetical arrangement that it would be most convenient to have a "computer" whose main function would be to alphabetize, list, match, and compare at the speed of light. Such a machine is needed for processing all kinds of library records. One should not have to use the present lengthy computer-alphabetization methods of the iterative procedure that is the mainstay of library searching.

Little Hierarchies

It has been seen that the LC classification has structure, order, hospitality to new additions, updating procedures, and adequate individual indexes to most main classes, but very little logic. What logic there is appears very much as it does in modern thesauri. It is used to make little hierarchies of a few levels where these seem advantageous. Thus, by using hierarchy only on a very limited scale, as in modern thesauri, one avoids the horror of having to fit a constantly changing body of the sum total of human knowledge and belief to date into a relatively fixed, inverted tree layout based on logic. The structural advantages of a displayed order or pseudohierarchy, however, are retained in a classification schedule in a manner not possible in a thesaurus, where the basic order, of necessity, must be alphabetical. It is conceivable that such little hierarchies as are made in the LC classification could be used to make a new tool—an LC thesaurus, especially if they were combined with the terminology of the indexes and perhaps of the subject headings.[3] Even more interesting, however, are the possibilities inherent in automatic classification.

Automatic Classification

It may well turn out that the LC classification is much more amenable to use with some of the experimental systems now being developed from word frequency or proximity analysis, syntactical structure, and semantic interpretation than are hierarchical classifications based on logical division. With LC's ordinal notation, there is considerable latitude for expansion between the lines, so to speak, so that it ought to be possible to incorporate the aggregates or groupings turned out by automatic classification methods if these are developed to the point of producing meaningful classes.[4] The LC classification has features of adaptability which make it quite attractive for experimentation along these lines. In other words, the system appears to be compatible with the type of research now being undertaken with nonhierarchical types of classification.

It would certainly be possible to use LC for automatic classification of the type devised by M. E. Maron of the Rand Corporation and J. H. Williams of IBM.[5] The interesting feature of this kind of automatic classification is that any existing system can be used as base. The automatic part comes with fitting terminology in a new text to established classes, using probabilistic means. The initial analysis and weighting procedures to establish the relationships between terms and classes are quite extensive. Probably the classification's index terms and perhaps even subject headings should be used in addition to class designations. Automatic classification would make it possible to update the class schedules with new terminology, since new terms would be discovered in the process of operation. With this kind of classification, initially one would assign LC class numbers automatically to text in the form of abstracts, titles, tables of contents, chapter and section headings, a book's own index, and to every paper in a symposium, conference, or other collected work. It would be a powerful instrument for dealing more fully with books for which content notes or analytics should be made.

Augmented Classes

Augmented class descriptions are an imperative need for either thesauri or automatic classification. Considerable effort would have to be made to bring the class schedules fully up to date, particularly the scientific and technical parts which are still not in rapport with current developments. At the same time, as much as possible should be salvaged from present schedules. One way of doing this without too much relocation might be to incorporate present outdated terms within new terms which are more accurately descriptive or more inclusive, the original notation being retained in so far as possible. Since the classification is largely by enumeration within certain large groups, this procedure should not require major changes in schedules, but would include related old and new material under new class designations and with a minimum number of relocations.

As a sample, the "Analysis" section of the QA (Mathematics) schedule was redone in collaboration with Andrew T. Kitchen of the Mathematics Department, University of Rochester. It should be emphasized that the result is an approximation, not a dogmatic assertion of what the "Analysis" schedule should be like. The arrangement suggests a possible line of departure for other subjects in order to add currency without making it necessary to redo whole sections completely or rework major classes. Some of the relocations in the sample (Fig. 1) could have been avoided by the use of decimal places in the ordinal notation. It is an advantage to the LC classification that interpolation is possible at practically any point by adding decimals, though for long-term usage relocation is perhaps preferable.

Library Automation

Finally, since the "in" word in the library now is "automation," one should consider the LC classification in this respect. No overpowering problems would be presented. Automatic classification has already been mentioned, as well as the possibility of thesaurus-making, which is currently done with the assistance of a computer. For library *circulation* purposes, the chief problems involving classification is LC's alphanumeric notation.

The notational representation of the LC classification is made in five positional blocks (Fig. 2). All of these are left-justified, except number 2 which is right-justified. The diagram was made up from actual LC numbers taken from the schedules.

ANALYSIS

[Classes 300–311 unchanged]

312 Measure and generalized integrals, incl. Lebesque's integrals, etc.

[Classes 315–316 unchanged]

320 Functional analysis.*
.2   Banach spaces.
.4   Hilbert space.
322 Banach algebras.

THEORY OF FUNCTIONS.

330   Functions of a real variable.
331   Functions of a complex variable. General works.*
.3   Rudiments. Elementary works.*
332   Functions of several complex variables.
333   Riemann surfaces, incl. multiform, uniform functions.
355   Miscellaneous special topics.*
360   Geometric principles of analysis. Mapping of regions.*
     Conformal representation, Cf. QA646.*

[Classes 371–381 unchanged]

385 LIE GROUPS [Continuous groups of transformations] Infinitesimal transformations.

ANALYTICAL METHODS CONNECTED WITH PHYSICAL PROBLEMS.

393   General works.
     Special functions.
394   Logarithmic, circular, and exponential functions.
395   Elliptic functions. Elliptic integrals. Modular functions.
396   Abelian functions (including hyperelliptic). Theta functions.
397   Laplace's and Legendre's functions (Spherical harmonics).
398   Bessel's functions (Cylindrical harmonics).
399   Lamé's functions (Ellipsoidal harmonics).
400   Miscellaneous special functions.
       Gamma, hypergeometric, automorphic, etc.
403   Harmonic analysis (General).*
404   Fourier's series.*
.5   Orthogonal series. Orthogonal functions. Orthogonal polynomials.*
405   Harmonic functions.*
406   System analysis.
.3   Control theory.
.5   Mathematical optimization.

[Classes 411–433 unchanged]

* Indicates class number and designation unchanged.

Fig. 1. Example of augmented classes

THE LIBRARY OF CONGRESS CLASSIFICATION: NOTATION

All characters left-justified within positional blocks except second block, which is right-justified.

There are 5 positional blocks, as follows:

1. Letter block   Cols. 1–3
2. Number block before first decimal   Cols. 4–7
3. Number block after first decimal   Cols. 8–11
4. A–Z block after second decimal   Cols. 12–16
5. Second A–Z block   Cols. 17–19

1	2	3	4	5
X	1	1	A1	A1
XX	11	11	A11	A11
XXX	111	111	A111	
	1111	1111	A1111	

Worst possible case requires 19 positions:

XXXOOOOOOOOOAOOOOAOO

Decimals always between cols. 7–8, 11–12

Fig. 2. Mechanization of the LC class number

In Figure 3, the third column is spread out, and the decimals omitted. The first decimal is in the column between the 9 and 7 of the first number. The second decimal is much easier to see in front of the A–Z notational breakdown. It is possible to make a computer program that would take the actual number written in linear form, as in the second column, spread it out, sort it, or whatever, and then put it back together in the original linear form.

The class number itself would take a few *microseconds* longer in a computer's central processing unit for most operations than a purely numerical notation would. (A microsecond is one millionth of a second. It takes 60 million microseconds to make a minute.) Somehow one cannot get very excited about sacrificing the advantages of the LC classification for less than a minute's time in a day's transactions.[6] Also, if a book number is used with the class numbers, all call numbers in any system become alphanumeric. For library procedures other than automated circulation, the material to be manipulated is alphanumeric to begin with, so the form of the class number is of little moment.

The Noncirculating Library

Another aspect of automation is the noncirculating library. In these days, when a research library is required to serve a vastly increasing number of patrons, the library of the future is beginning to be thought of as a library whose holdings are always *in* and available for immediate use. When the library's catalog is in machine-readable form, it will be possible at last to give out printed bibliogra-

EXAMPLES

Code	Actual numbers	Fixed field for mechanical sorting			
XX11.1	HC59.7	HC	597		
XX111.111	TL521.312	TL	521312		
XX1111.111	BL2017.422	BL	2017422		
X111.1111	D769.3055	D	7693055		
XX1.A1	TK1.A1	TK	1	A1	
XX1111.A11	BL1245.V32	BL	1245	V32	
XX1111.A111	BX6510.B758	BX	6510	B758	
XX1111.A1111	TH9505.A1065	TH	9505	A1065	
XX111.1.A1	TP873.5.D5	TP	8735	D5	
XX1111.1.A11	BL2017.4.A32	BL	20174	A32	
XX1111.11.A1	BL1478.45.A2	BL	147845	A2	
XX1111.A1A1	HE5668.Z6G7	HE	5668	Z6	G7
XX1111.A11A1	HE8901.A35A2	HE	8901	A35	A2
XX1111.A1A11	BX2037.A3G32	BX	2037	A3	G32
XX111.1.A1A1	TL789.8.U6R3	TL	7898	U6	R3
XXX111.1.A1	ZTP873.5.D5	ZTP	8735	D5	

Fig. 3. Examples of LC class numbers blocked for machine sorting

phies tailored to the needs of the individual patron. The initial searching for suitable entries may be done via console-computer combination, using (1) the normal dictionary catalog approach; (2) a classification approach, either ordinary or à la Maron/Williams; or (3) the thesaurus made from the classification schedules, indexes, and subject headings as suggested earlier. When the time comes that the content of books and journals is also in machine-readable form and searchable by various types and combinations of entry procedures, then the noncirculating library may be able to give out parts of the text directly in some photoduplication form after man-machine dialogue directs the selection.

The idea of a noncirculating library raises many interesting points with regard to classification. For example, would the classification system be used for shelf location, as now, or could some form of compact storage be used and the dictionary catalog replaced or augmented with a classified catalog? In American libraries, the use of the classification system as a shelf location device makes browsing through a classification on foot a necessity. With a machine-readable catalog in classified form, could one not browse in a more sedentary manner at a console? The loss here would be in the inability to handle the physical book as one browsed. The gain would be in not having to go upstairs, downstairs, or around corners to distant locations or different buildings while browsing. With the LC classification, browsing by machine could pull together subjects like Optics, which have been split physically by the operation of the system. Needless to say, for browsing by console a unified index to the classification is a minimal condition. Some way of producing something more than a catalog entry to look at is equally important. The advantages and disadvantages should be weighed carefully before one seriously considers giving up classification as a shelving device.

In conclusion, the old cliché, "What's past is prologue," certainly applies to the Library of Congress classification. It has a tremendous potential for adaptation, growth, expansion, and change. It is wide open in an age of logical dead ends and leaping cross fertilization. The limits of its future extension are bounded only by human imagination.

Notes

[1] Richard S. Angell, "On the Future of the Library of Congress Classification," *Classification Research: Proceedings of the Second International Study Conference held at . . . Elsinore, Denmark, 14th to 18th September, 1964*, ed. by Pauline Atherton (Copenhagen: Munksgaard, 1965), p.101–12.

[2] See, for example, Lauren B. Doyle, "Semantic Road Maps for Literature Searchers," *Journal of the Association for Computing Machinery*, 8, no.4:555 (Oct. 1961); Gerald Salton, "Manipulation of Trees in Information Retrieval," *Communications of the Association for Computing Machinery*, 5, no.2:104 (Feb. 1962); David Lefkovitz, "The Application of the Digital Computer to the Problem of a Document Classification System," *Colloquium on Technical Preconditions for Retrieval Center Operations*, ed. by Benjamin F. Cheydeleur (Washington: Spartan Books, 1965), p.133.

[3] A much more comprehensive thesaurus than this is being made for a section of the Universal Decimal Classification. See Gertrude London, "A Classed Thesaurus as an Intermediary between Textual, Indexing and Searching Languages," *Revue de la Documentation*, 32, no.4:145–49 (1965).

[4] Harold Borko and Myra Bernick, "Automatic Document Classification," *Journal of the ACM*, 10, no.2:151–62 (Apr. 1963); H. Borko, "Research in Computer Based Classification Systems," *Classification Research: Proceedings* . . . (Elsinore Conference), p.220–57; R. M. Needham and K. Sparck Jones, "Keywords and Clumps: Recent Work on Information Retrieval at the Cambridge Language Research Unit," *Journal of Documentation*, 20, no.1:5–15 (Mar. 1964); A. G. Dale and N. Dale, "Some Clumping Experiments for Associative Document Retrieval," *American Documentation*, 16, no.1:5–9 (Jan. 1965); Frank B. Baker, "Information Retrieval Based on Latent Class Analysis," *Journal of the ACM*, 9, no.4:512–21 (Oct. 1962); Lauren B. Doyle, "Is Automatic Classification a Reasonable Application of Statistical Analysis of Text?" *Journal of the ACM*, 12, no.4:437–89 (Oct. 1965); Gerard Salton, "Data Manipulation and Programming Problems in Automatic Information Retrieval," *Communications of the ACM*, 9, no.3:204–10 (Mar. 1966).

[5] M. E. Maron, "Automatic Indexing: An Experimental Inquiry," *Journal of the ACM*, 8, no.3:404–17 (Apr. 1961); J. H. Williams, *Results of Classifying Documents with Multiple Discriminant Functions* ("IBM Research Progress Report"; Rockville, Md.: Federal Systems Division, International Business Machines Corporation, 15 Mar. 1965). 28 l.

[6] It would take 60,000 transactions per day to make one minute's difference in time between alphanumeric and pure numeric notation, if we assume a 100 μ sec. difference per computer operation and allow 10 operations per transaction. Input-Output time *with present equipment* is considerably longer than central processing unit time.

A List of Libraries Using the Library of Congress Classification Wholly or in Part

Maurice F. Tauber

The following list of libraries in the United States using the LC classification has been developed from various sources. It is as full as could be made by the time of the preparation of this volume. The compiler would be interested in having omissions called to his attention. The arrangement by states seems to be satisfactory for quick location of institutions.

Alabama

Birmingham-Southern College

Alaska

Alaska Methodist University
University of Alaska

Arizona

University of Arizona Library

Arkansas

University of Arkansas

California

Alameda County Medical Library, Oakland
California Lutheran College
California State College, Hayward
California State College, San Luis Obispo
California State Library
California State Polytechnic Institute, Kello-Vohrs
California Western University
Chabot College
Claremont College
College of Notre Dame

College of the Holy Cross
College of the Pacific
Contra Costa College
Diablo Valley College
Fresno City College
Fresno State College
Lassen College
Long Beach State College
Los Angeles State College of Applied Arts and Sciences
Mount St. Mary's College
Orange State College
Pacific Lutheran Theological Seminary
Pacific School of Religion
Pomona College
San Diego Scientific Library, Newport Beach
San Diego State College
San Fernando Valley State College
San Francisco College for Women
Scripps College
Sonoma State College
Stanislaus State College
University of California, Berkeley
University of California, Davis
University of California, Los Angeles

University of California, Riverside
University of California, San Diego
University of California, San Francisco
University of California, Santa Barbara
Whittier College

Colorado

Colorado State University
St. Thomas Seminary
Southern Colorado State College
U.S. Air Force Academy
University of Colorado
University of Denver

Connecticut

Fairfield University
Holy Apostles Seminary
U.S. Coast Guard Academy
University of Connecticut
Yale University

Delaware

University of Delaware

District of Columbia

American University
Association of American Railroads
Bureau of Railway Economics
Capitol Radio Engineers Institute
Carnegie Institution Geophysical Laboratory
Catholic University of America
George Washington University
Georgetown University
Oblate College
Strayer Junior College of Finance
U.S. Army. Industrial College
U.S. Army. Walter Reed General Hospital
U.S. Bureau of Public Roads
U.S. Dept. of Health, Education, and Welfare
U.S. Dept. of Justice
U.S. Dept. of State
U.S. Federal Communications Commission
U.S. Federal Power Commission

U.S. Federal Reserve System. Board of Governors
U.S. Geological Survey
U.S. Interstate Commerce Commission
U.S. Navy Dept. Hydrographic Office
U.S. Tariff Commission
U.S. Treasury Dept.
U.S. Veterans Administration

Florida

Barry College
Embry-Riddle Aeronautical Institute
Hampton Junior College
University of Miami
University of South Florida
Volusia Community College

Georgia

Atlanta University
Augusta College
Emory University
Georgia Institute of Technology
Georgia State College
Morehouse College
Spelman College
University of Georgia

Illinois

Abbott Laboratories, Chicago
American Conservatory of Music
Barat College of the Sacred Heart
Chicago College of Osteopathy
Chicago Historical Society
Chicago Teachers College North
Concordia Theological Seminary
Lake Forest College
Lutheran Theological School, Rock Island
McCormick Theological Seminary
McKendree College
Maryknoll College
Mundelein College
National Association of Real Estate Boards, Chicago
Northern Illinois University
Rosary College
St. Bede College

Southern Illinois University,
  Edwardsville
Swift and Co.
Trinity Christian College
University of Chicago

Indiana

Concordia Senior College
Earlham College
Indiana University
Marian College, Indianapolis
St. Mary's College
St. Meinrad Seminary
University of Notre Dame

Iowa

Dordt College
Iowa State College
Iowa State University
Luther College
Marycrest College
University of Iowa
Wartburg Theological Seminary

Kansas

St. Benedict's College

Kentucky

Our Lady of Gethsemane Trappist-Cistercian Abbey

Louisiana

Louisiana State University
Loyola University

Maine

Bliss College
Bowdoin College
Colby College
Fort Kent State Teachers College

Maryland

Anne Arundel Community College
Catonsville Community College
Enoch Pratt Free Library,
  Baltimore

Johns Hopkins University
Mount St. Mary's College
St. John's College
U.S. Chemical Warfare School, Edgewater Arsenal
U.S. National Institutes of Health
University of Baltimore
University of Maryland
Washington College

Massachusetts

American International College
Boston College
Boston Public Library
Boston University
Brandeis University
Cardinal Cushing College
College of the Holy Cross
Fletcher School of Law and Diplomacy
Massachusetts Institute of Technology
Merrimack College
Mount Holyoke College
New Bedford Institute of Technology
St. John's Seminary, Brighton
State College, Framingham
Stonehill College
Suffolk University
Tufts University
U.S. Arsenal
University of Massachusetts
Wellesley College
Williams College

Michigan

Andrews University
Calvin College
Charles Stewart Mott Library
Cranbrook Academy of Art
Delta College
Detroit College of Law
Duns Scotus College
Kalamazoo College
Michigan College of Mining and Technology
Michigan State University
Oakland University
Sacred Heart Seminary
Siena Heights College

University of Michigan, Ann Arbor
Wayne State University

Minnesota
College of St. Catherine
College of St. Thomas
Crosier Seminary
Hamline University
James Jerome Hill Reference Library
Luther Theological Seminary
McPhail College of Music
Minneapolis School of Arts
Minnesota Historical Society
Northwestern Lutheran Theological Seminary
St. Mary's College
St. Olaf College
St. Paul Public Library

Mississippi
University of Mississippi

Missouri
Central Methodist College
Concordia Seminary
Covenant College
Kirksville College of Osteopathy
School of the Ozarks
University of Missouri
Washington University

Montana
Montana School of Mines
Montana State University
U.S. Rocky Mountain Laboratory

Nebraska
Municipal University of Omaha
University of Nebraska

New Hampshire
Dartmouth College

New Jersey
Douglass College
Glassboro State College
Institute for Advanced Study, Princeton
Newark State College

Princeton University
Rutgers University, New Brunswick
Villa Walsh College

New Mexico
New Mexico State University
University of New Mexico

New York
Academy of Aeronautics
Alfred University
American Foundation for the Blind
Boyce Thompson Institute for Plant Research, Yonkers
Brooklyn Museum
Buffalo and Erie County Library
Buffalo Society of Natural Resources
Canisius College
Chemists' Club Library
City University of New York (all units)
Columbia University
Cornell University
Corning College
D'Youville College
Elmira College
Fordham University
Grosvenor Public Library, Buffalo
Hamilton College
Hispanic Society of America
Ithaca College
Jewish Theological Seminary of America
Julliard School of Music
King's College
Le Moyne College
Manhattan Borough Community College
Manhattanville College of the Sacred Heart
Monroe Community College
Nassau Community College
New School for Social Research
New York Law School
New York University
Notre Dame of Staten Island
Pace College
Rockefeller University
St. Bernardine of Siena College
St. John Fisher College

St. John's University
St. Joseph's Seminary
Simmons-Boardman Publishing Corp.
State University of New York, Fredonia
State University of New York, Geneseo
State University of New York, Harpur College
State University of New York, Stony Brook
State University of New York, Syracuse University
State University of New York, Villa Maria College, Buffalo
Suffolk Community College
University of Rochester
Wells College
West Point Military Academy

North Carolina

Agricultural and Technical College of North Carolina, Greensboro
Asheville Biltmore College
North Carolina State College of Agriculture and Engineering
University of North Carolina, Chapel Hill
University of North Carolina, Greensboro
University of North Carolina, Raleigh

North Dakota

Assumption College

Ohio

College of Steubenville
Findlay College
Hayes Memorial Library, Fremont
Miami-Jacobs Junior Business College
Ohio State University
University of Akron
University of Cincinnati
University of Dayton
Wittenberg University

Oklahoma

East Central State College
Southeastern State College

U.S. Field Artillery School
University of Oklahoma

Oregon

Oregon State College
Oregon State University
Portland State College
Reed College
Southern Oregon College
University of Oregon
University of Portland

Pennsylvania

Beaver College
Bucknell University
Curtis Institute of Music
Drexel Institute of Technology
Franklin and Marshall College
Gettysburg College
Hahnemann Medical College and Hospital
Hamot Hospital, Erie
Haverford College
Holy Family College
Lutheran Theological Seminary, Gettysburg
Manor Junior College
Mary Immaculate Seminary
Mellon Institute of Industrial Research
Pennsylvania Military Academy
Pennsylvania State College, Lock Haven
Pennsylvania State Teachers College
Pennsylvania State University
Pittsburgh Theological Seminary
Pittsburgh-Zenia Seminary
Rosemont College
St. Joseph's College
St. Thomas College
St. Vincent College
Susquehanna University
Swarthmore College
Temple University
U.S. Bureau of Mines Experimental Station
University of Pittsburgh
University of Scranton
Villanova University

Women's Medical College of Pennsylvania

Rhode Island
Brown University
Providence Public Library
U.S. Naval War College
Warwick Public Library
West Warwick Public Library

South Carolina
Winthrop College

South Dakota
South Dakota State College of Agriculture and Mechanic Arts

Tennessee
Martin College
University of Tennessee

Texas
Abilene Christian College
Alvin Junior College
Arlington State College
Austin Presbyterian Theological Seminary
Austin State College
Celanese Corporation of America, Clarkwood
Rice University
Southwest Texas State College
Texarkana College
Texas Technological College
University of Dallas
University of Houston
University of St. Thomas

Vermont
St. Michael's College

Virgin Islands
College of the Virgin Islands

Virginia
Coast Artillery School, Fort Monroe
Emory and Henry College
Mary Baldwin College
Medical College of Virginia
Protestant Episcopal Seminary, Alexandria
Southern Seminary and Junior College
University of Virginia
University of Virginia Clinch Valley College
Virginia Historical Society
Virginia State Library

Washington
Olympia College
University of Washington
Washington State University, Pullman
Western Washington State College

West Virginia
Glenville State College
Wheeling College

Wisconsin
Barron County Teachers College
Cardinal Stritch College
Carroll College
Milwaukee-Downer College
Oshkosh Public Library
University of Wisconsin
University of Wisconsin, Milwaukee
Wisconsin State College, Oshkosh
Wisconsin State Historical Society

Bibliography
on the Library of Congress
Classification

Nathalie C. Batts and Maurice F. Tauber

The magnitude and growth of the use of and interest in the Library of Congress classification since the turn of the century is indicated by the 186 entries presented here. These citations are culled from many sources, chief of which are the following:

Cannons, H. G. T. *Bibliography of Library Economy*. Chicago, American Library Assn., 1927. 680p.

Columbia University. School of Library Service. *Outline for the Course in Problems in Cataloging and Classification* (*Library Service 278*), prepared by Bertha M. Frick. New York, 1959. 28p.

La Montagne, L. E. *American Library Classification, with Special Reference to the Library of Congress*. Hamden, Conn., Shoe String Press, 1961. 433p. (Bibliography: p.375–86)

Library Literature, 1921/32–Sept. 1966. New York, Wilson, 1934–66.

Library Science Abstracts, v.1–17, pt.2, Jan./Mar. 1950–Apr./June 1966. London, Library Assn., 1950–66.

Phinazee, A. L. Hoage. "Library of Congress Classification in the United States: A Survey of Opinions and Practices, with Attention to Problems of Structure and Application." 233 l. (D.L.S. Thesis, Columbia University, 1961)

Basically, the bibliography is divided into three sections: Section I, Tools; Section II, LC in the Literature; and Section III, Reclassification. Within this arrangement, Section I is in alphabetical order by author, and Sections II and III are in reverse chronological order by year of publication (alphabetical by author within each year). Thus current materials in both Sections II and III are given prominence.

It is hoped that this bibliography will prove useful in the location of discussions and reports on work completed and also encourage more publication of reports in the literature of work in progress. Communication and problem- and experience-sharing can result in mutual benefit for both authors and the profession.

Section I: Tools
(Arranged in alphabetical order by author)

U.S. Library of Congress. "Classification," in its *Report of the Librarian*, 1898–1965. Washington: Govt. Print. Off., 1899–1966. Various pagings.

—————— "Libraries Using the Library of Congress Classification as a Whole or in Part," in its *Report of the Librarian*, 1932. Washington, 1932. p.245–48; *ibid.* 1937. p.241–44.

—————— *Papers Concerning a Classification for Law*. Washington, 1949. 3 pts. in 1 v. Contents: Interim Report by the Library of Congress Committee on a Classification for Law; Suggestions for Structure of Class K . . . by T. S. Dabagh (with comments by W. B. Stern); Comment on Classification Submitted to F. H. Wagman by M. O. Price.

—————— Card Division. *An Account of the Catalogs, Classifications and Card Distribution Work of the Library of Congress* . . . Washington, 1904. 28p.

—————— Classification Division. *Author Notation in the Library of Congress*, by Anna C. Laws. Washington, 1930. 18p.

—————— Subject Cataloging Division. *Classification Schedules*. Washington, various dates. (Lists of schedules and prices available from the Card Division, Library of Congress, Washington, D.C. 20540)

—————— —————— *Library of Congress Classification—Additions and Changes*, no.1– . Washington, 1928– . Issued quarterly.

—————— —————— *Outline of the Library of Congress Classification*. Washington, 1942; reprinted 1965. 22p.

—————— —————— *Subject Cataloging Division*. Washington, 1950. 62p. Planographed. (U.S. Library of Congress. Departmental and Divisional Manuals, no.3)

Section II: LC in the Literature
(Arranged in reverse chronological order by year of publication; alphabetical within each year)

1966

Batts, N. C. "LC in NY: Institute on the Use of the Library of Congress Classification," *Library Journal*, 91: 3649–50 (Aug. 1966).

Bead, C. C. and Holmes, R. R. "Institute on the Use of the Library of Congress Classification," *Library of Congress Information Bulletin*, 25: 402–5 (July 14, 1966).

McGaw, H. F., comp. "Academic Libraries Using the LC Classification System," *College & Research Libraries*, 27: 31–36 (Jan. 1966).

Tauber, M. F. "Further Considerations of the Library of Congress Classification." (Unpublished paper given at the Library School, Louisiana State University, Nov. 18, 1966) 28p.

1965

Angell, R. S. "On the Future of the Library of Congress Classification," in International Study Conference on Classification Research, 2d, Elsinore, Denmark, *Classification Research: Proceedings*, ed. by Pauline Atherton. Copenhagen: Munksgaard, 1965. p.101–12.

Casellas, E. "Relative Effectiveness of the Harvard Business, Library of Congress, and the Dewey Decimal Classifications for a Marketing Collection," *Library Resources & Technical Services,* 9: 417–37 (Fall, 1965).

Clapp, V. W. "DC Numbers on LC cards," *Library Resources & Technical Services,* 9: 393–403 (Fall, 1965).

International Study Conference on Classification Research, 2d, Elsinore, Denmark. *Classification Research: Proceedings,* ed. by Pauline Atherton. Copenhagen: Munksgaard, 1965. 563p.

"LC Card Division To Distribute Classification Schedules," *Library Journal,* 90: 4312 (Oct. 15, 1965).

Lorenson, R. W. "Adapting LC Schedules to DC Notation," *Library Resources & Technical Services,* 9: 210–12 (Spring, 1965).

Morrison, P. D. and Morrison, C. "Use of Library of Congress Classification Decisions in Academic Libraries," *Library Resources & Technical Services,* 9: 235–42 (Spring, 1965).

Peterson, K. G. *Further Expansion of Library of Congress Classification Schedules for the Lutheran Church Based upon the Modification and Expansion as Compiled by Karl T. Jacobsen.* Berkeley, Calif., 1965. 10p.

Richmond, P. A. *Aspects of Recent Research in the Art and Science of Classification.* Copenhagen: Danish Centre for Documentation, 1965. (International Federation for Documentation. Committee on Classification Research. "FID/CR Report Series," no.3) 35p.

Slavens, T. B. "Classification Schemes for the Arrangement of the Literature of Protestant denominations," *Library Resources & Technical Services,* 9: 439–42 (Fall, 1965).

1964

Angell, R. S. "Development of Class K at the Library of Congress," *Law Library Journal,* 57: 353–60 (Nov. 1964).

Charpentier, A. A. "Library of Congress Classification Schedule for Anglo-American Law," *Law Library Journal,* 57: 352–76 (Nov. 1964).

Garrett Theological Seminary, Evanston, Ill. Library. *A Methodist Book Classification,* by Lucy W. Markley. 2d ed., rev. by D. E. Hollenberg. Evanston, 1964. 68p.

1963

Datta, D. C. "The Classification of Maps and Geographical Publications," *IASLIC Bulletin,* 8: 78–86 (June 1963).

1962

McDougall, B. "The Reduction of Cataloguing Costs," in Seminar on Technical Services, University of Melbourne, 1961. *Seminar on Technical Services . . . Working Papers.* Canberra: Australian Advisory Council on Bibliographic Services, 1962. p.70–88. (Directed by M. F. Tauber)

Metcalfe, J. W. "The Use of Overseas Central Cataloguing in Australia with Special Reference to Library of Congress Cataloguing," in Seminar on Technical Services, University of Melbourne, 1961. *Seminar on Technical Services . . . Working Papers.* Canberra: Australian Advisory Council on Bibliographic Services, 1962. p.59–69. (Directed by M. F. Tauber)

Phinazee, A. L. H. "Librarians Rate LC Classification," *Special Libraries*, 53: 484–85 (Oct. 1962).

—— "Patron Use of the LC Classification," *Library Resources & Technical Services*, 6: 247–49 (Summer, 1962).

Samore, T. "Form Division in L.C. and D.C. Classification Schemes," *Library Resources & Technical Services*, 6: 243–46 (Summer, 1962).

1961

Danes, D. L. "A Bibliography of Juvenile Holdings in the Library of Congress in Classification CT." 105 l. (M.S. Thesis in L.S., Catholic University of America, 1961 Microfilm)

Grout, C. W. *La Clasificación de la Biblioteca del Congreso; Explicación de la Tablas Usadas en los Esquemas . . . Traducida por la Dra. Violeta Angulo M.* Washington: Unión Panamericana, 1961. 107 l. (Pan American Union. Columbus Memorial Library. Estudios Bibliotecarios, 3)

Hagedorn, R. "Random Thoughts on LC Classification," *Special Libraries*, 52: 256–57 (May/June 1961). (Also appeared in Special Libraries Assn. Southern California Chapter. *Bulletin*, 22: 1–2 (Sept. 1960).

La Montagne, L. E. *American Library Classification, with Special Reference to the Library of Congress.* Hamden, Conn.: Shoe String Press, 1961. 433p. (Bibliography: p.375–86)

Phinazee, A. L. H. "Library of Congress Classification in the United States: A Survey of Opinions and Practices, with Attention to Problems of Structure and Application." 233 l. (D.L.S. Thesis, Columbia University, 1961)

Tauber, M. F. and Wise, E. "Classification Systems," in *The State of the Library Art*, v.1, pt.3, ed. by R. R. Shaw. New Brunswick, N.J.: Graduate School of Library Service, Rutgers University, 1961. p.140–88.

"Workshop on the Library of Congress Classification and Its New BL–BX Schedules," in American Theological Library Assn. *Summary of Proceedings . . . Annual Conference, 1961.* Washington, 1961. p.68–83.

1960

Doyle, I. M. "Library of Congress Classification for the Academic Library," in Illinois. University. Graduate School of Library Science. *Role of Classification in the Modern American Library*; ed. by T. Eaton and D. E. Strout. Champaign, Ill.: Illini Union Bookstore, 1960. p.76–92. (Bibliography)

Engel, M. L. "A Bibliography of Juvenile Holdings in the Library of Congress in Classification DC1–DC53, DR, DU, and DX." 107 l. (M.S. Thesis in L.S., Catholic University of America, 1960. Microfilm)

Kyle, B. "Merits and Demerits of Various Classification Schemes for the Social Sciences," *Unesco Bulletin for Libraries*, 14: 54–60 (Mar./Apr. 1960).

1959

Coffin, L. C. "Special Report on the Progress of the Anglo-American Law Classification under Development by the Library of Congress," *Law Library Journal*, 52: 442–44 (Nov. 1959).

Metcalfe, J. W. *Subject Classifying and Indexing of Libraries and Literature.* New York: Scarecrow Press, 1959. p.113–17.

Special Libraries Assn. *SLA Loan Collection of Classification Schemes and Subject Heading Lists on Deposit at Western Reserve University as of November 1, 1958.* Compiled by Bertha R. Barden and Barbara Denison. 4th ed. New York, 1959. ("Classification Expansions and Revisions: Dewey Decimal Classification . . . Library of Congress Expansions": p.44–47)

1957

Benyon, E. V. "Classification of Law Books," *Law Library Journal*, 50: 542–67 (Dec. 1957). (L.C.: p.550–51, 558)

Eaton, T. "The Classification of Books in Public Libraries," in her *Classification in Theory and Practice.* Champaign, Ill.: Illini Union Bookstore, 1957. p.45–58.

Metcalfe, J. W. *Information Indexing and Subject Cataloging.* New York: Scarecrow Press, 1957. 338p. (LC: various pagings) (Bibliography: p.309–18)

Ranganathan, S. R. "Common Isolates in Documentation Work (4). Space Isolate," *Review of Documentation*, 24: 18–28 (Feb. 1957).

Tauber, M. F. "Classification, Cataloging, and Indexing Systems," in Western Reserve University. School of Library Science. *Information Systems in Documentation.* Ed. by J. H. Shera, A. Kent, and J. W. Perry. New York: Interscience Publishers, 1957. p.39–65. (Advances in Documentation and Library Science, v.2)

———— "The Shelf-Listing Section of the Library of Congress." New York, 1957. (Unpublished manuscript)

1956

Canada. Parliament. Library. *Class K, Law, Based on Law Library of Congress Classification Scheme.* Ottawa, 1956. 28 l.

Dawson, J. M. "The Acquisition and Cataloging of Research Libraries." (Ph.D. Thesis, Graduate Library School, University of Chicago, 1956) p.82–157.

Sayers, W. C. B. "The Library of Congress Classification," in his *An Introduction to Library Classification.* 7th ed. London: Grafton, 1956. p.99–114.

U.S. Bureau of Public Roads. Library. *A Classification Scheme for Highway Engineering, Adapted from the Library of Congress Schemes by the Library Staff of the Bureau of Public Roads.* Washington, 1956. 147p. (COMM-DC-10174)

1955

Butz, H. S. "Princeton Theological Seminary Library and the Library of Congress Classification for Church History." 114 l. (M.S. Thesis in L.S., Drexel Institute of Technology, 1955)

Ellinger, W. B. "Progress of Class K," *Law Library Journal*, 48: 384–88 (Nov. 1955).

Mills, J. "Chain Indexing and Classified Catalogue," *Library Association Record*, 57: 141–48 (Apr. 1955).

Phelps, R. H. and Soroka, J. "Filing, Classification and Indexing Systems for Engineering Offices and Libraries," *Special Libraries*, 56: 109–12 (Mar. 1955).

Sayers, W. C. B. "Library of Congress Classification," in his *A Manual of Classification for Librarians and Bibliographers.* 3d ed., rev. London: Grafton, 1955. p.151–74.

Stouffer, M. I. "Round Table on Library of Congress Classification," in American Theological Library Assn. *Proceedings . . . Annual Conference, 9th, 1955, New York.* 1955. p.46–47.

1954

Haykin, D. J. "The Classification of Medical Literature in the Library of Congress,"
    Libri, 3: 104–8 (1954).

1953

Columbia University Libraries. Avery Architectural Library. "Classification System
    (Revised)." (Unpublished expansion of LC's Class N. Prepared, 1926–30, by
    Winifred Fehrenkamp; revised by E. M. Abbott and A. K. Placzek, 1953)
Davis, N. E. "Modification and Expansions of the Library of Congress Classification
    Schedule at the University of Chicago," in American Theological Library Assn.
    Proceedings . . . Annual Conference, 7th, 1953, Evanston. 1953. p.23–24.
De Grolier, E. "L'étude des problèmes de classification documentaire sur le plan
    international (The Study of Problems of Documentary Classification according to
    an International Plan)," *Review of Documentation*, 20: 105–17 (Sept. 1953).
Hallam, B. B. and Goodman, O. "Library of Congress Classification with Emphasis on
    Edition 3, 1952, of Class R: Medicine," *Medical Library Association Bulletin*, 41:
    353–56 (Oct. 1953).
Herrick, M. D. "The Development of a Classified Catalog for a University Library,"
    College & Research Libraries, 14: 418–24 (Oct. 1953).
Institute on the Subject Analysis of Library Materials, Columbia University. *The
    Subject Analysis of Library Materials.* Ed. by M. F. Tauber. New York: School of
    Library Service, Columbia University, 1953. 235p.
Jacobsen, K. T. *Library of Congress Classification Schedules for the Lutheran Church,
    Modified and Expanded* . . . Minneapolis: Board of Christian Education, Evangeli-
    cal Lutheran Church, 1953. 38p. (Evangelical Lutheran Church. Board of Christian
    Education. Monograph series, v.2, no.4)
Stouffer, M. I. "Princeton and the Library of Congress Schedule," in American
    Theological Library Assn. *Proceedings . . . Annual Conference, 7th, 1953, Evans-
    ton.* 1953. p.21–23.
Swann, A. W. "Comparison of Dewey and L.C. Classifications," in American Theologi-
    cal Library Assn. *Proceedings . . . Annual Conference, 7th, 1953, Evanston.* 1953.
    p.19–21.
"Symposium on Use of Main (Medical) Classification Schemes," Medical Library
    Assn. *Bulletin*, 41: 333–60 (Oct. 1953).
Uhrich, H. B. "Abridgment of the LC Schedule in Religion," in American Theological
    Library Assn. *Proceedings . . . Annual Conference, 7th, 1953, Evanston.* 1953.
    p.24–27.

1952

Bogardus, J. "Classification Schemes for Business and Financial Libraries," *Special
    Libraries*, 43: 409–12 (Dec. 1952).
Cressaty, M. "Integration of Chinese Publications," *College & Research Libraries*, 13:
    38–40 (Jan. 1952).
Line, M. B. "A Classified Catalogue of Musical Scores; Some Problems," *Library
    Association Record*, 54: 362–64 (Nov. 1952).
McCloy, T. R. "A Classification Schedule for Canadian Literature," *Ontario Library
    Review*, 36: 91–92 (May 1952).

Tauber, M. F. "Book Classification in University Libraries," in Tennessee. University. *University of Tennessee Library Lectures no.1.* Knoxville: Division of University Extension, Univ. of Tennessee, 1952. p.1–15.

Wohl, S. "The Place of the History of Mathematics in the Dewey Decimal and Library of Congress Classifications." (Unpublished paper, School of Library Service, Columbia University, 1952)

1951

Gray, G. "Five Years' Cataloguing in Retrospect," *Library World*, 53: 346–48 (Oct. 1951).

La Montagne, L. E. "Revision of the Classification Schedule for Medicine," *Library of Congress Information Bulletin*, 10: 11–12 (Jan. 22, 1951).

1950

Dewton, J. L. "Subject Index According to Library of Congress Classification," *Library of Congress Information Bulletin*, 8: 12–13 (Dec. 27, 1949/Jan. 2, 1950).

Kaczanowska, J. "Katalog Rzeczowy Jako Wyraz Spolecznej Ideologii Srodowiska (The Subject Catalogue as Expression of a Social Ideology of a Community)," *Bibliotekarz*, no.9/10 142–46 (1950).

Lacy, D. "The Library of Congress: A Sesquicentenary Review: II. The Organization of the Collections," *Library Quarterly*, 20: 235–58 (Oct. 1950).

La Montagne, L. E. "Adaptation of Library of Congress Classification," *Library of Congress Information Bulletin*, 9: 28 (Dec. 18, 1950).

——— "The Library of Congress and Classification." (Unpublished manuscript, 195?)

1949

Edinburgh. Public Libraries Committee. *Subject and Name Index of Books Contained in the Libraries.* 3d ed. Edinburgh, 1949. 615p. (May be used as a general relative index to the Library of Congress classification)

Savage, E. A. *Manual of Book Classification and Display for Public Libraries.* London: Allen & Unwin, 1949. p.69–70.

Turner, D. "Report of Round Table on Library of Congress Classification," in American Theological Library Assn. *Proceedings . . . Annual Conference, 3d, 1949, Chicago.* 1949. p.47.

Wagman, F. H. "Class K, Law," *Library of Congress Information Bulletin*, May 24–30, 1949, p.4–5.

1948

Ambartsumian, Z. N. "Russian View of Library of Congress Classification. Bibliotechnaia Klassifikatsiia v.1, 1947," *Library of Congress Information Bulletin*, 7: 12–13 (Sept. 7–13, 1948).

Benyon, E. V. *Classification. Class K. Law.* Washington: Library of Congress, 1948. 172p. ("This law classification . . . makes use of the notation reserved by the Library of Congress for law")

1947

Mearns, D. C. *The Story Up to Now: The Library of Congress, 1800–1946.* Washington: Govt. Print. Off., 1947. 226p. ("Reprinted from the *Annual Report of the Librarian of Congress for the Fiscal Year Ending June 30, 1946,* with the addition of illustrations and a slight revision of text")

1945

Trager, G. L. "A Bibliographical Classification System for Linguistics and Languages," *Studies in Linguistics,* 3: 54–108 (Dec. 1945). ("Originally planned to fit into the Library of Congress classification by replacing LC's Classes P, PA–PM."—p.55)

Pincherle, A. "La literatura y la historia italiana a traves de la clasificaciones Dewey y del Congreso," *Fenix,* no.3: 459–84 (1945).

Sahaya, S. "Library of Congress and Its Classification," *Modern Librarian,* 15: 82–86 (July/Sept. 1945).

1943

Mann, M. "Cutter Expansive and the Library of Congress Classification Systems," in her *Introduction to Cataloging and the Classification of Books.* 2d ed. Chicago: American Library Assn., 1943. p.68–85.

1942

Columbia University. Fine Arts Library. "Classification." (Unpublished adaptation of LC's Class N, Fine Arts, as used at Columbia University, 1942)

Tauber, M. F. "Classification of Books in College and University Libraries: Historical Aspects," *Library Quarterly,* 12: 706–24 (July 1942).

1940

Miller, H. G. "Why Library of Congress?" *New Zealand Libraries,* n.s., 3: 137–38 (July 1940).

Wilson, M. "Library of Congress Classification," in Library Assn. of Australia. *Proceedings, 2d, 1939.* Melbourne: Brown, Prior, Anderson, 1940. p.113–17.

1938

Grout, C. W. "Explanation of the Tables as Used in the Schedules of the Library of Congress Classification; Accompanied by an Historical and Explanatory Introduction." 143p. (M.S. Thesis, Columbia University, 1938)

1937

Kelley, G. O. *The Classification of Books: An Inquiry into Its Usefulness to the Reader.* New York: Wilson, 1937. p.31–33. (Bibliography: p.131–37)

Lund, J. J. and Taube, M. "A Non-expansive Classification: An Introduction to Period Classification," *Library Quarterly,* 7: 373–94 (July 1937).

Mogk, H. "Das System der Kongressbibliothek in Washington," in Runge, O. S., ed. *Beiträge zur Sachkatalogisierung.* Leipzig: O. Harrassowitz, 1937. p.51–62.

Satory, M. "Class B—Philosophy and Religion of the Library of Congress Classification Schedules," *Library Journal,* 62: 450–53 (June 1, 1937).

1936

Perry, F. C. "Library of Congress Classification Adapted for School Libraries," *School Library Review,* I: 68–73 (Christmas Term, 1936).

Tiffy, E. "Library of Congress Classification Simplified for Use in the Smaller College Library: Schedules for History and the Auxiliary Sciences; C. D. E–F," in American Library Assn. Division of Cataloging and Classification. *Catalogers and Classifiers Yearbook, no.5, 1936.* Chicago, 1936. p.95. (Abstract of a thesis presented to the School of Library Service, Columbia University, in 1935)

1935

Tiffy, E. "Library of Congress Classification Simplified for Use in the Smaller College Library." p.13–14, 164–74. (M.S. Thesis, School of Library Service, Columbia University, 1935)

1933

Allen, F. P. "Anthropology: Its Library Classification Problems," *Special Libraries,* 24: 90–93 (May 1933).
————— "Pure Science: L.C. vs. D.C.," *Library Journal,* 58: 124–27 (Feb. 1, 1933).
Bliss, H. E. "The Library of Congress Classification," in his *The Organization of Knowledge in Libraries and the Subject Approach to Books.* New York: Wilson, 1933. p.242–78. (1939 ed.: p.250–78)
Bushnell, G. H. "Notes by a British Librarian on the Library of Congress Classification Scheme," *Special Libraries,* 24: 41–43 (Mar. 1933).

1932

MacPherson, H. D. "Libraries Using the L.C. Classification Scheme in Part or in Whole," Library Journal, 57: 421–22 (May 1, 1932).

1930

Clemons, H. "D.C. vs. L.C.," *Libraries,* 35: 1–4 (Jan. 1930).

1929

Hanson, J. C. M. "The Library of Congress and Its New Catalogue," in *Essays Offered to Herbert Putnam.* New Haven: Yale Univ. Press, 1929. p.178–94.
Jefferd, D. "The Library of Congress Classification in a University Library," Pacific Northwest Library Assn. *Proceedings,* 20: 25–26 (1929).
Martel, C. "The Library of Congress Classification," in *Essays Offered to Herbert Putnam.* New Haven: Yale Univ. Press, 1929. p.327–32.
Perley, C. W. "Recent Developments in the Library of Congress Classification," *ALA Bulletin,* 23: 300–301 (June 1929). (Also appeared in *Catalogers and Classifiers Yearbook, no.1, 1929,* p.64–65)
Robertson, D. A. "The L.C. Classification as an Aid to Research," in American Library Assn. Division of Cataloging and Classification. *Catalogers and Classifiers Yearbook, no.1, 1929.* Chicago, 1929. p.66–69.

Prior to 1929

Mann, M. *Use of the Library of Congress Classification.* Chicago: American Library Assn., 1927. 28p.
Dorkas, F. "Library of Congress Classification vs. Decimal Classification," *Library Journal,* 50:291–95 (Apr. 1, 1925).

Hanson, J. C. M. "Library of Congress Classification for College Libraries," *Library Journal*, 46: 151–54 (Feb. 15, 1921).

American Library Assn. Committee on D.C.–L.C. Equivalent Tables. "Report," *ALA Bulletin*, 11: 38 (Jan. 1917). (Also appeared in *Library Journal*, 42: 199 [Mar. 1917])

Sharp, H. A. "Library of Congress Classification" (review), *Library World*, 18: 355–59 (June 1916).

Sayers, W. C. B. *Canons of Classification Applied to "The Subject," "The Expansive," "The Decimal" and "The Library of Congress" Classifications*. London: Grafton, 1915. p.135.

Hawkes, A. J. "Library of Congress Classification," *Library Association Record*, 16: 188–89 (Apr. 15, 1914).

Smither, R. E. "Library of Congress Classification," *Library World*, 16 (n.s. 89): 130–36 (Nov. 1913).

Hulme, E. W. "Principles of Book Classification, Chapter 4," *Library Association Record*, 14: 39–46 (Jan. 15, 1912). (LC: p.43–44)

"Library of Congress Classification of the Social Sciences" (review), *American Journal of Sociology*, 17: 418 (Nov. 1911).

Martel, C. "Classification: A Brief Conspectus of Present Day Library Practice," *Library Journal*, 36: 410–16 (Aug. 1911).

——— "Library of Congress Classification," *ALA Bulletin*, 5: 230–32 (July 1911).

Noé, A. C. von. "The New Classification of Languages and Literature by the Library of Congress," in Bibliographical Society of America. *Papers*, v.6, 1911. Chicago, 1912. p.59–65.

Headicar, B. M. "Library of Congress Classification—Classes B, N, R, Z," *Library Association Record*, 12: 515–16 (Nov. 15, 1910).

"United States Library of Congress Classification Scheme," *Library Association Record*, 8: 663–64 (Dec. 15, 1906).

Johnston, W. D. "Classification of the Library," in his *History of the Library of Congress, 1800–1864*. Washington: Govt. Print. Off., 1905. Appendix VI, p.521.

Section III: Reclassification

(Arranged in reverse chronological order by year of publication; alphabetical within each year)

1966

Gore, D. "Mismanagement of College Libraries," American Assn. of University Professors. *Bulletin*, 52: 46–51 (Apr. 1966).

Holley, E. G. "The Trend to L.C.: Thoughts on Changing Academic Library Classification Schemes." 34 l. (Unpublished paper given at Louisiana State University, Spring, 1966)

"Revolution at Enoch Pratt," *Wilson Library Bulletin*, 40: 494 (Feb. 1966).

Wolfert, R. J. "Reference and Loan Library Converts to LC," *Wisconsin Library Bulletin*, 62: 106–7 (Mar. 1966).

1965

Gattinger, F. E. "Reclassification—Are You Converted Yet?" *APLA Bulletin*, 29: 16–22 (Feb. 1965).

Gore, D. "In Praise of Error: With Some Animadversions on the Cost of Descriptive Cataloging," *Library Journal,* 90: 582–85 (Feb. 1, 1965).

"L.C. Classification at the University of Oregon Library," *PNLA Quarterly,* 29: 249–50 (July 1965).

McGaw, H. F. "Reclassification: A Bibliography," *Library Resources & Technical Services,* 9: 483–88 (Fall, 1965).

"Statement on Types of Classification Available to New Academic Libraries," *Library Resources & Technical Services,* 9: 104–11 (Winter, 1965). (American Library Assn. Resources and Technical Services Division. Classification Committee. *Report, May 15, 1964*). (Bibliography).

—— Correction by B. A. Custer. *Library Resources & Technical Services,* 9: 212 (Spring, 1965).

Taylor, D. "Reclassification: A Case for LC in the Academic Library: That . . . Dewey was a Rat-fink," *PNLA Quarterly,* 29: 243–49 (July 1965).

Thiessen, A. "Pacific Lutheran University Library in Process of Reclassifying," *PNLA Quarterly,* 30: 87 (Oct. 1965).

Williams, M. "Reclassification Program at Memorial University of Newfoundland," *APLA Bulletin,* 29: 99–104 (Oct. 1965).

1964

Downey, H. R. "Dewey or LC?," *Library Journal,* 89: 2292–93 (June 1, 1964).

Gore, D. "A Neglected Topic: The COST of Classification," *Library Journal,* 89: 2287–91 (June 1, 1964).

—— "Subject Cataloging: Some Considerations of Costs," *Library Journal,* 89: 3699–3703 (Oct. 1, 1964).

1963

"Bowdoin College To Recatalog and Reclassify Book Collections," *Library Journal,* 88: 1501 (Apr. 1, 1963).

Cox, C. R. "Reclassification Planning at the University of Maryland." 1963. 11p. (Mimeographed)

Tauber, M. F. "Report on the Cataloging and Classification Operations in the Dartmouth College Library." 1963. 5p.

"University of Houston Changes to LC Classification," *Library Journal,* 88: 1640 (Apr. 15, 1963).

1962

Reichmann, F. "Cornell's Reclassification Program," *College & Research Libraries,* 23: 369–74, 440–50 (Sept. 1962).

Tauber, M. F. "A Report on the Cataloging, Catalogs, and Classification of the Bowdoin College Library." 1962. 16p.

1961

Collins, W. S., Jr. "A Change of Horses: Some Aspects of Reclassification," *Library Journal,* 86: 757–59 (Feb. 15, 1961).

Fraser, L. D. "Cataloging and Reclassification in the University of Toronto Library, 1959/60," *Library Resources & Technical Services,* 5: 270–80 (Fall, 1961).

1960

Eaton, T. "What Price Revision?" *Illinois Libraries*, 42: 297–305 (May 1960).

Tauber, M. F. "Reclassification and Recataloging," in *The State of the Library Art,
v.1, pt.1*, ed. by R. R. Shaw. New Brunswick: Graduate School of Library Service,
Rutgers University, 1960. p.149–66.

1957

"Adoption of L.C. Classification," Alabama Polytechnic Institute Library. *Staff Bulletin*, 6: 56 (Apr. 1957).

1956

Moriarty, J. H. "Plea for Management Study of Partial Reclassification Problems,"
Journal of Cataloging and Classification, 13: 34 (Jan. 1956).

Tauber, M. F. "Partial Reclassification," *Journal of Cataloging and Classification*, 12:
221–23 (Oct. 1956).

1955

Eaton, T. "Classification in College and University libraries," *College & Research
Libraries*, 16: 168–76 (Apr. 1955).

1954

Tauber, M. F. "Reclassification and Recataloging," in his *Technical Services in
Libraries*. New York: Columbia Univ. Press, 1954. p.261–83. (References: p.447–
48) (Columbia University Studies in Library Service, no.7)

1953

Bentz, D. M. and Cavender, T. "Reclassification and Recataloging," *Library Trends*,
2: 249–63 (Oct. 1953). (References: p.262–63)

"Reclassification at the University of Mississippi Library," *Library Journal*, 78: 199
(Feb. 1, 1953).

1952

Kilpatrick, N. L. and O'Donnel, A. "Reclassification at the State University of Iowa,"
Journal of Cataloging and Classification, 8: 12–17 (Mar. 1952).

1951

Gerould, A. C. and Noyes, R. "Shortcuts in Reclassifying Literature," *Journal of
Cataloging and Classification*, 7: 41–42 (Spring, 1951).

1945

Tauber, M. F. "Reorganizing a Library Book Collection, Part I," *College & Research
Libraries*, 6: 127–32 (Mar. 1945).

────── "Reorganizing a Library Book Collection, Part II," *College & Research
Libraries*, 6: 341–45 (Sept. 1945).

1944

Boisen, H. L. "Venture in Reclassification," *College & Research Libraries*, 6: 67–72
(Dec. 1944).

Danielson, R. H. "Reclassification, Recataloging, and Revision of Stock," *Library Journal*, 69: 1033–35 (Dec. 1, 1944).

Tauber, M. F. "Reclassification of Special Collections in College and University Libraries Using the Library of Congress Classification," *Special Libraries*, 35: 111–15+ (Apr. 1944).

1942

Tauber, M. F. "Reclassification and Recataloging in College and University Libraries: Reasons and Evaluation," *Library Quarterly*, 12: 827–45 (Oct. 1942).

——— "Special Problems in Reclassification and Recataloging," *College & Research Libraries*, 4: 49–56 (Dec. 1942).

——— "Subject Cataloging and Classification Approaching the Crossroad," *College & Research Libraries*, 3: 149–56 (Mar. 1942).

1941

Tauber, M. F. "Reclassification and Recataloging in College and University Libraries." 356 l. (Unpublished Ph.D. dissertation, Graduate Library School, University of Chicago, 1941)

1940

MacPherson, H. D. "Reclassification of College and University Libraries," *College & Research Libraries*, 1: 159–64, 175 (Mar. 1940).

Tauber, M. F. "Reclassification and Recataloging of Materials in College and University Libraries," in Randall, W. M., ed. *The Acquisition and Cataloging of Books: Papers Presented before the Library Institute at the University of Chicago.* Chicago: Univ. of Chicago Press, 1940. p.187–219. (References: p.387)

1939

Tauber, M. F. "Checklist on Reclassification and Recataloging in College and University Libraries, From Libraries Adopting the Library of Congress Classification Scheme." 1939. 11p.

1937

Lynn, J. M., comp. *An Alternative Classification for Catholic Books: A Scheme for Catholic Theology, Canon Law and Church History, To Be Used with the Dewey Decimal, Classification Decimal, or Library of Congress Classifications . . .* Milwaukee: Bruce Pub. Co.; Chicago: American Library Assn., 1937. lxv, 400p.

1934

Bishop, W. W. "Recataloging and Reclassifying in Large Libraries," *ALA Bulletin*, 28: 14–20 (Jan. 1934).

Jacobsen, K. T. "The Reorganization of the Library of a Small College," *Library Quarterly*, 4: 234–43 (Apr. 1934).

1928

Gjelsness, R. H. "Reclassification: Its Problems and Technique," *Library Journal*, 53: 597–600 (July 1928).

1924

Gulledge, J. R. "L.C. vs. D.C. for College Library," *Library Journal*, 49: 1026–27 (Dec. 1924).

Kafafi, M. "Hoover Institute and Library Classification." n.d. 17p. (A modification of the Library of Congress classification for Arabic books)

Index

Prepared by Katherine M. Hartley

A Schedule (General works and polygraphy), 20
AC Schedule (Collections. Series. Collected works), 77
Abbreviations, 160
Academic libraries, 2, 3, 162-75, 183-91
Aeronautics *see* TL Schedule
Agricultural economics *see* HD Schedule
Agriculture *see* S Schedule
Alloys, 105, 106
Alternative class numbers, 24, 25, 29, 30, 79
America (General) and the United States (General) *see* E Schedule
American Library Association, 11, 193
American literature, 119; *see also* PS Schedule
Anatomy—Human *see* QM Schedule
Angell, Richard S., 29, 30, 31, 32, 60, 78, 79
Anthologies, 123
Arabic literature, 19
Arick, Mary Catherine, 135-61
Arrearages, 6, 184
Astronautics *see* TL Schedule
Astronomy *see* QB Schedule
Audio-visual materials, 31
Author numbers, 5, 7, 8, 10, 11, 26, 66, 67, 69, 72, 74, 77, 78, 107-20, 121-34, 166, 167, 174
Author numbers sheet, 108, 109, 111, 114, 133
Author tables *see* PN-PZ Schedules
Autobiography, 128, 187
Automation, 11, 31, 164, 214, 215, 216, 217, 218, 219, 220

Automotive engineering *see* TJ-TL Schedules
Aviation materials, 189

B Schedule (Philosophy), 27, 190
BF Schedule (Psychology), 80, 86, 88, 104
BL Schedule (Religions), 19
BP Schedule (Mohammedanism. Bahaism. Theosophy), 19
Bead, Charles C., 18-32, 58, 60, 212
Bengali language and literature: Table, 64
Bibliography, 23, 29, 30, 31, 165, 166; *see also* Z Schedule
Biography, 22, 23, 120, 127, 128, 165, 166, 187; *see also* CT Schedule; Cutter numbers: Biography
Biology *see* QH Schedule
Biscoe time numbers, 191
Block classification, 12, 15, 176
Blume, Edward J., 80-106
Book numbers *see* Cutter numbers
Boston University, 189, 191
Botany *see* QK Schedule
Browsing, 8, 9, 10, 24, 122, 164, 175, 183, 211, 219
Building *see* TH Schedule

CT Schedule (Biography), 7, 14, 23, 187
Captions, 80, 83, 86
Cards *see* Library of Congress cards
Cards—Temporary, 114, 173, 179, 180
Chemical engineering *see* TN-TR Schedules
Chemistry *see* QD Schedule
Chinese, Japanese, and Korean literature *see* PL Schedule

Civil engineering *see* TA–TH Schedules
Classical antiquity *see* DE Schedule
Classical languages and literature *see* PA Schedule
Closed-stack policy, 8, 9, 164, 171, 183
Collected works, 105, 123
Collections—Nonserial, 85
Colonial literature, 74, 77
Commerce *see* HF Schedule
Computers, 11, 169, 214, 215
Congresses and conference materials, 85; *see also* Cutter numbers: Congresses and conferences
Connors, William, 162
Conservation, 105
Consultants, 177, 186, 190, 191, 202
Correction fluid, 13, 170
Cox, Carl R., 162–75
Criticisms, 127, 128, 133
Cross references, 27
Cutter numbers, 26, 37, 52, 55, 63, 66, 67, 70, 79, 86, 89, 90, 95, 98, 121, 125, 129, 135–61, 163, 164, 173, 174, 179, 187, 188, 189, 190, 213
  Biography, 120, 161
  Congresses and conferences, 153, 154, 156; Table, 154
  Document A, 135, 137, 143, 146, 150, 151, 156, 188
  Document monographs, 140, 141, 146
  Document serials, 147, 148
  Double, 30, 86, 116, 119, 125, 129, 133, 148, 149, 188
  General serials, 149, 156
  Societies and institutions, 154, 155, 156; Tables of subdivisions, 155
  Translations, 116, 118, 119, 120
  Triple, 116, 148
Cybernetics, 103, 104, 105

D Schedule (History), 19, 103, 190
D–F Schedules (History), 22, 23, 27
DC Schedule (French history), 119
DE Schedule (Classical antiquity), 76
DF Schedule (Greece), 76
DG Schedule (Italy), 76
Dates, 123, 140, 141, 143, 146, 150, 153, 156, 160, 161, 188
Dewey Decimal System, 2, 5, 9, 16, 163, 164, 165, 166, 167, 171, 175, 182, 186, 200
Domestic science *see* TX Schedule

E Schedule (America and the United States), 26, 103, 190
Economic geography *see* HC, HD, HF Schedules
Economics *see* HB, HC, HD Schedules
Education *see* L Schedule
Electrical engineering *see* TK Schedule
Electronic data processing equipment, 197
Electronics *see* TK Schedule
English literature, 64; *see also* PR Schedule
Enoch Pratt Free Library, 2, 176–82
Erasers and erasing, 13, 16, 195, 196
Essays, lectures, addresses, 85; *see also* AC Schedule

F Schedule (United States and America except the United States), 26
Faculty use of libraries, 164, 174, 175, 183–91
Fiction *see* PZ Schedules
Finance *see* HG Schedule
Fine arts *see* N Schedule
Flexowriters, 13
Forestry *see* SD Schedule
French history *see* DC Schedule

G Schedule (Geography), 22
GB Schedule (Physical geography), 80, 96, 102
GC Schedule (Oceanography), 80
General special, 25, 187
General works and polygraphy, 25, 84, 85; *see also* A Schedule
Geography *see* G Schedule
Geology *see* QE Schedule
Geomorphology *see* QE Schedule
Geophysics *see* QE Schedule
German literature *see* PT Schedule
Greece *see* DF Schedule

H Schedule (Social sciences), 20, 25, 26, 33–55, 59, 60, 103, 111, 187, 190; Tables of geographical divisions, 46, 49, 53, 54, 55
HA Schedule (Statistics), 23
HB Schedule (Economic theory), 23, 25, 27, 33, 34, 35, 36
HC Schedule (Economic history and conditions), 22, 27, 41, 42, 43, 44, 45, 139, 140
HD Schedule (Agricultural economics and industry), 21, 22, 23, 47, 48, 50, 51, 111,

HD Schedule—*continued*
112, 113, 114, 115, 138, 139, 140, 141,
142, 143, 149, 151, 152; Tables, 50, 148,
150, 151; Tables of subdivisions, 56, 57,
58
HE Schedule (Transportation and
communication), 22, 25, 38, 39,
40, 98, 189
HF Schedule (Commerce), 22, 25
HG Schedule (Finance), 22, 61
HX Schedule (Utopias), 160
Hebrew literature, 19
Hedlesky, Nicholas, 33–61
Herrick, Mary Darrah, 183–91
Hines, Patricia S., 62–79, 119, 121–34
Historical libraries, 2
History *see* D, D–F, DC Schedules
Hitchcock, Jennette E., 192–208
Holmes, Robert R., 107–20, 121
Hunting *see* SK Schedule
Hydraulic engineering *see* TC Schedule
Hydrodynamics, 98, 100

IBM 1401, 169
International law *see* JX Schedule
Italy *see* DG Schedule

J Schedule (Political science), 20, 22,
55–58, 190; Table, 55
JK Schedule (Constitutional history,
United States): Table, 58
JL–JQ Schedules (Constitutional history
in countries other than United States),
58
JS Schedule (Local government), 58
JX Schedule (International law), 27
Jeffersonian classification, 18
Juvenile literature, 7, 70, 73, 79, 82, 83, 84

K Schedule (Law), 5, 10, 20, 21, 22, 23,
26, 58, 167, 185

L Schedule (Education), 23
Labels, 13, 16, 114, 169, 170, 196, 197,
206, 207
Language and literature *see* P Schedule
Latin American materials, 189
Law *see* K Schedule
Law materials, 21, 167, 185
Library of Congress
Cards, 28, 29, 172, 175, 189

Classification, 1–17, 18–32, 104, 162–75,
183–91, 197, 198, 209–20
Advantages and disadvantages, 209–20
History, 18
Index to schedules, 4, 11, 20, 21, 189, 211,
212, 214
New class numbers, 27, 28, 29, 120, 172,
187, 188
Old class numbers, 28, 29, 172, 175, 189
Photoduplication service, 204
Library of Congress classification: Additions and changes, 20, 21, 28, 29, 32, 104,
172, 189, 203, 204, 214
Literature, 62–79, 121–34; *see also* American
literature; Arabic literature; Bengali
literature; Colonial literature; English
literature; Hebrew literature; Juvenile
literature; Theological literature
Lockwood, Elizabeth, 121–34

ML Schedule (Literature of music), 23
Magazines, 105
Manufactures *see* TS Schedule
Mathematics *see* QA Schedule
Mechanical engineering *see* TJ–TL
Schedules
Medicine *see* R, RA, RC Schedules
Military science *see* U, UA Schedules
Mohammedanism. Bahaism. Theosophy
see BP Schedule
Monographic series, 105, 168
Motor vehicles *see* TL Schedule
Multiple classification, 12, 16, 163
Music *see* ML Schedule
Music materials *see* Audio-visual materials

N Schedule (Fine arts), 72
National Library of Medicine, 12, 16
National Union Catalog, 31, 170, 180
Natural history *see* QH Schedule
Naval maintenance *see* VC Schedule
Naval science *see* V Schedule
Newspapers, 105
Numeral 1, 114, 118, 119, 125, 155, 160, 187
Numeral 2, 134
Numeral 3, 134

Oceanography *see* GC Schedule
Official publications, 135–61
Open-stack policy *see* Browsing

P Schedule (Language and literature), 14,
20, 62–79

PA Schedule (Classical languages and
   literature), 27, 63, 72, 73, 75
PC Schedule (Romance languages), 78
PK Schedule (Indo-Iranian. Indo-Aryan.
   Iranian), 72; Table XXIII, 65;
   Table G, 66
PL Schedule (Chinese, Japanese, and
   Korean literature), 19
PN–PZ Schedules (Literature), 116,
   121–34; 190
   Table II, 121
   Table VIII, 121, 122
   Table VIIIa, 122, 124, 127, 128
   Table VIIIb, 122, 124
   Table IX, 121, 122, 123
   Table IXa, 122, 124, 127, 128
   Table IXb, 122, 124
   Table X, 127, 128
   Table Xa, 127, 128
   Table XI, 129
PQ Schedule (Romance literatures), 68, 71,
   74, 77, 128, 130, 131, 132, 133
PR Schedule (English literature), 72, 126,
   127
PS Schedule (American literature), 74,
   117, 118, 119, 125, 126
PT Schedule (Teutonic literatures), 69,
   123, 213
PZ1 Schedule (Fiction), 67, 68, 69
PZ3, PZ4 Schedules (Fiction), 4, 5, 7, 9,
   11, 14, 24, 69, 70, 71, 78, 133, 134, 165,
   166, 167, 174, 175
PZ5–PZ90 Schedule (Juvenile literature)
   see Juvenile literature
Peabody Institute Library, 182
Periodicals, 14, 85, 105, 149, 150, 187
Personnel, 8, 165, 168, 180, 181, 201, 202,
   203
   Morale, 190, 191, 206
   Quarters, 13, 16, 168, 204
   Staff orientation, 183–91
   Training programs, 5, 8, 173, 205
Philosophy see B Schedule
Phonorecords see Audio-visual materials
Physical geography see GB Schedule
Physics see QC Schedule
Physiology see QP Schedule
Picture books, 86
Plant culture see SB Schedule
Political science see J Schedule
Popular works, 84
Pratt Library see Enoch Pratt Free Library
Precedence, 103, 187, 209

Psychiatry see RC Schedule
Psychology see BF Schedule
Public health see RA Schedule
Public libraries, 2, 3, 176–82, 183

Q Schedule (Science), 80–86, 103, 104, 109,
   175
Q–V Schedules (Science and technology),
   80–106
QA Schedule (Mathematics), 23, 86, 87, 98,
   99, 103, 216, 217
QB Schedule (Astronomy), 81, 82, 83, 84,
   85, 86, 103
QC Schedule (Physics), 86, 87, 98, 99
QD Schedule (Chemistry), 100, 156
QE Schedule (Geology), 80, 102, 103
QH Schedule (Natural history), 100
QK Schedule (Botany), 22, 100
QL Schedule (Zoology), 103, 109, 110, 111
QM Schedule (Human anatomy), 104
QP Schedule (Physiology), 80, 100, 101,
   104

R Schedule (Medicine), 23, 80, 104
RA Schedule (State medicine. Hygiene),
   22, 100, 101
RC Schedule (Practice of medicine), 22,
   80, 189
Railroad engineering and operation see TF
   Schedule
Railroad law see K Schedule
Railroad organization and management see
   HE Schedule
Ranganathan's principle of osmosis, 15
Rare book collection, 70, 127, 129
Reclassification, 12, 13, 14, 15, 16, 162–75,
   176–82, 183–91, 192–208
   Budget, 13, 16, 168, 180, 181, 204
   Cost estimate, 192–208
   Partial, 12, 164, 168, 173
   Savings estimate, 199, 200
   Supplies and equipment, 13, 16, 169, 204,
   205
   Time estimate, 14, 168, 192–208
   Total, 12, 164, 165, 166, 167, 168, 169,
   170, 185
Religions see BL Schedule
Richmond, Phyllis A., 209–20
Romance languages see PC Schedule
Romance literatures see PQ Schedule
Rudiments, 83

S Schedule (Agriculture), 21, 80, 86–91,
   157, 158, 159; Table, 156

SB Schedule (Plant culture), 22
SD Schedule (Forestry), 90, 91; Table, 89
SF Schedule (Veterinary medicine), 136, 137; Geographical distribution table, 89
SK Schedule (Hunting), 103
Sacred works, 72
Sanitary engineering see TD Schedule
Sanner, Marian, 176–82
Sanskrit, 72
Science and technology, 80–106; see also Q–V Schedules
See references, 24, 27, 30
See also references, 27, 33
Sel-In labelers, 13
Selections see Anthologies
Separate works, 125, 168
Series, 7, 85, 105, 165, 167, 168; see also Monographic series
Social sciences see H Schedule
Societies, 105
Space sciences, 102, 103
Special libraries, 2, 183, 212
State libraries, 2, 3
State University of New York, 164, 169
Statistics, 23; see also HA Schedule
Storage, 173, 206
Student use of libraries, 164, 174, 183
Subclassification, 121–34, 135–61
Superintendent of Documents classification system, 12, 14, 16

T Schedule (Technology), 28, 80, 91–104, 175; Table, 92
TA–TH Schedules (Civil engineering), 80, 98, 99, 100, 102
TC Schedule (Hydraulic engineering), 91, 94, 95, 100; Table, 93
TD Schedule (Sanitary and municipal engineering), 96, 98; Table, 93
TF Schedule (Railroad engineering and operation), 22, 97, 98; Table, 93
TH Schedule (Building), 100, 102

TJ–TL Schedules (Mechanical engineering), 80, 102
TK Schedule (Electrical engineering and industries), 30, 31, 103
TL Schedule, (Motor vehicles. Cycles. Aeronautics), 21, 102, 103
TN–TR Schedules (Chemical engineering), 80
TS Schedule (Manufactures), 103
TX Schedule (Domestic science), 100, 101
Tauber, Maurice F., 1–17, 177, 203
Technology see Science and technology
Textbooks, 14, 83, 84
Theological literature, 7
3M 107 dry photocopier, 170
Translations, 24, 69, 72, 78, 116, 118, 119, 120, 122, 125, 187
Transportation and communication see HE Schedule
Treatises, 25, 86, 111
Typewriters, 13, 16, 171
Typing, 13, 170, 171, 196

U Schedule (Military science), 80, 103
UA Schedule (Armies), 22
United Nations publications, 7, 16
United States and America except the United States see F Schedule
United States constitutional history see JK Schedule
University of Maryland, 162–75

V Schedule (Naval science), 80, 103
VC Schedule (Naval maintenance), 143, 144, 145, 146; Table, 146
Veterinary medicine see SF Schedule

Weeding of books, 165, 206

Xerox 914 models, 13, 16, 170

Z Schedule (Bibliography), 7, 14, 23, 26, 29, 30, 31, 166, 185, 186
Zoology see QL Schedule